Lynda Weinman's | Hands-On Training

CSS
Web Site Design

Includes Exercise Files and Demo Movies

lynda.com

By Eric A. Meyer

CSS Web Site Design Hands-On Training

By Eric A. Meyer

lynda.com/books | Peachpit Press
1249 Eighth Street • Berkeley, CA • 94710
800.283.9444 • 510.524.2178 • 510.524.2221(fax)
http://www.lynda.com/books
http://www.peachpit.com

lynda.com/books is published
in association with Peachpit Press,
a division of Pearson Education
Copyright ©2007 by lynda.com

ISBN: 0-321-29391-6

0 9 8 7 6 5 4 3 2

Printed and bound in the
United States of America

H•O•T Credits

Director of Product Development and Video Production: Tanya Staples

Operations Manager: Lauren Harmon

Project Editor: Karyn Johnson

Production Coordinator: Tracey Croom

Compositors: David Van Ness, Myrna Vladic

Copyeditor: Kim Wimpsett

Proofreader: Haig MacGregor

Interior Design: Hot Studio, San Francisco

Cover Design: Don Barnett

Cover Illustration: Bruce Heavin (bruce@stink.com)

Indexer: Emily Glossbrenner

Video Editors and Testers: Scott Cullen, Alex Marino, and Eric Geoffroy

H•O•T Colophon

The text in *CSS Web Site Design H·O·T* was set in Avenir from Adobe Systems Incorporated. The cover illustration was painted in Adobe Photoshop and Adobe Illustrator.

This book was created using QuarkXPress and Microsoft Office on an Apple Macintosh using Mac OS X. It was printed on 60 lb. Influence Matte at Courier.

Table of Contents

Introduction

A Note from Lynda Weinman

Most people buy computer books to learn, yet it's amazing how few books are written by teachers. I take pride that our HOT (**H**ands-**O**n **T**raining) books are written by experienced teachers, who are familiar with training students in specialized subject matter. In this book, you'll find carefully developed exercises to help you learn CSS (**C**ascading **S**tyle **S**heets)—one of the most compelling and versatile Web design languages used today.

This book is targeted to beginning-level and intermediate-level Web authors, programmers, and Web designers who want to learn about Web styling and the basic properties of CSS quickly and easily. The premise of the hands-on approach is to get you up to speed quickly with CSS while actively working through the lessons in this book. It's one thing to read about document styling, markup, and principles, and it's another experience entirely to write it yourself and achieve measurable results. Our motto is, "Read the book, follow the exercises, and you'll learn the subject." I have received countless testimonials, and it is my goal to make sure this motto remains true for all our HOT books.

This book doesn't set out to cover every single aspect of CSS, but it will build a strong foundation that will enable you to learn the more difficult techniques much more easily. What Eric and I saw missing from the bookshelves was a process-oriented tutorial teaching readers core principles, techniques, and tips in a hands-on format.

I welcome your comments at **csshot@lynda.com**. If you run into any trouble while you're working through this book, check out the technical support link at **www.lynda.com/books/HOT/css**.

Eric and I hope this book will enhance your skills in CSS and Web design in general. If it does, we have accomplished the job we set out to do!

—Lynda Weinman

About lynda.com

lynda.com was founded in 1996 by Lynda Weinman and Bruce Heavin in conjunction with the first publication of Lynda's revolutionary book, *Designing Web Graphics*. Since then, lynda.com has become a leader in software training for graphics and Web professionals and is recognized worldwide as a trusted educational resource.

lynda.com offers a wide range of HOT books, which guide users through a progressive learning process using real-world projects. lynda.com also offers a wide range of video-based tutorials, which are available on CD and DVD and through the lynda.com Online Training Library. In addition, lynda.com owns the Flashforward Conference and Film Festival.

For more information about lynda.com, check out **www.lynda.com**. For more information about the Flashforward Conference and Film Festival, visit **www.flashforwardconference.com**.

Product Registration

Register your copy of *CSS Web Site Design HOT* today, and receive the following benefits:

- A *free* 24-hour pass to the lynda.com Online Training Library with more than 13,000 professionally produced video tutorials covering more than 200 topics by leading industry experts and teachers

- News, events, and special offers from lynda.com

- The lynda.com monthly newsletter

To register, visit **www.lynda.com/register/HOT/css**.

Additional Training Resources from lynda.com

To help you further develop your skills with CSS, register to use the free 24-hour pass to the lynda.com Online Training Library, and check out the following video-based training resources:

CSS for Designers
with Andy Clarke and Molly E. Holzschlag

Learning CSS 2
with Chris Deutsch

XHTML Essential Training
with William E. Weinman

Interaction Design: Process and Inspiration
with Brendan Dawes

About Eric A. Meyer

Eric A. Meyer has been working with the Web since late 1993 and is one of the world's foremost experts on the subjects of HTML, CSS, and Web standards. A widely read author, he is also the founder of Complex Spiral Consulting (www.complexspiral .com), which focuses on helping clients save money and increase efficiency through the use of standards-oriented Web design techniques: It counts Apple Computer, Macromedia, and Wells Fargo Bank among its clients.

Author of *Eric Meyer on CSS* (New Riders) and *Cascading Style Sheets: The Definitive Guide* (O'Reilly & Associates), as well as numerous articles for A List Apart, Vitamin, the O'Reilly Network, Web Techniques, and Web Review, Eric was a member of the CSS Working Group for seven years and coordinated the authoring and creation of the W3C's official CSS Test Suite. He has lectured for a wide variety of organizations including Los Alamos National Laboratory, the New York Public Library, Cornell University, and the University of Northern Iowa. Eric has also delivered addresses and technical presentations at numerous conferences, among them An Event Apart (which he cofounded), the IW3C2 WWW series, Web Design World, the CMP Web conference series, SXSW, the User Interface conference series, and The Other Dreamweaver Conference.

Eric lives in Cleveland, Ohio, which is a much nicer city than you've been lead to believe. For nine years, he was the host of "Your Father's Oldsmobile," a weekly Big Band-era radio show heard on WRUW 91.1-FM in Cleveland, and he hopes to get back to it one day. When not otherwise busy, Eric is usually playing with his wife and daughter.

Acknowledgments from Eric A. Meyer

I'd like to thank the whole gang at lynda.com for sticking with me through all the twists and turns of this particular project. That includes, but is very likely not limited to, Garo Green, Tanya Staples, Max Smith, Lauren Harmon, Garrick Chow, Scott Cullen, Alex Marino, and of course Lynda Weinman herself.

Perhaps paradoxically—though my fellow authors will understand instantly—writing an introductory book is one of the most challenging tasks a writer can undertake. Everyone at lynda.com supported, encouraged, and shepherded me through the long effort to get things just right, and never once stepped away from the commitment to do what was best for the project. Thank you one and all.

Thanks also to Dan Short, who agreed to help me out during a rough patch; and to Molly Holzschlag, for lending her support early on.

And my deepest thanks, as always, to my wife and daughter.

How to Use This Book

The following sections outline important information to help you make the most of this book.

The Formatting in This Book

This book has several components, including step-by-step exercises, commentary, notes, tips, sidebars, and video tutorials. Step-by-step exercises are numbered. File names, folder names, commands, keyboard shortcuts, and URLs (**U**niform **R**esource **L**ocators) are in bold so they pop out easily, such as **filename.htm**, the **images** folder, **File > New**, **Ctrl+click**, **www.lynda.com**.

Captions and commentary are in dark gray text:

This is commentary text.

Interface Screen Captures

Most of the screen shots in the book were taken on an Apple Power Mac G5 computer, because I do most of my designing, developing, and writing on the Mac platform. I also own and use a Windows-based computer, and I note important differences between the two platforms when they occur.

What's on the CSS Web Site Design HOT CD-ROM?

You'll find a number of useful resources on the **CSS HOT CD-ROM**, including the following: exercise files, video tutorials, and information about product registration. Before you begin the hands-on exercises, read the following sections so you know how to set up the exercise files and video tutorials.

Exercise Files

The files required to complete the exercises are on the **CSS HOT CD-ROM** in a folder called **exercise_files**. These files are divided into chapter folders, and you should copy each chapter folder onto your desktop before you begin the exercise for that chapter. For example, if you're about to start Chapter 5, copy the **05_color** folder from the **exercise_files** folder on the **CSS HOT CD-ROM** to your desktop.

On Windows, when files originate from a CD, they automatically become write protected, which means you cannot alter them. Fortunately, you can easily change this attribute. For complete instructions, read the "Making Exercise Files Editable on Windows Computers" section on the next page.

Video Tutorials

Throughout the book, you'll find references to video tutorials. In some cases, these video tutorials reinforce concepts explained in the book. In other cases, they show bonus material you'll find interesting and useful. To view the video tutorials, you must have Apple QuickTime Player installed on your computer. If you do not have QuickTime Player, you can download it for free from Apple's Web site at **www.apple.com/quicktime**.

To view the video tutorials, copy the videos from the **CSS HOT CD-ROM** to your hard drive. Double-click the video you want to watch, and it will automatically open in QuickTime Player. Make sure the volume on your computer is turned up so you can hear the audio content.

If you like the video tutorials, refer to the "Product Registration" section earlier in this introduction, and register to receive a free pass to the lynda.com Online Training Library, which is filled with more than 13,000 video clips from more than 200 tutorials.

Making Exercise Files Editable on Windows Computers

By default, when you copy files from a DVD to a Windows computer, the files are set to read-only (write protected). This causes a problem with the exercise files because you will need to edit and save many of them. You can remove the read-only property by following these steps:

1 Open the **exercise_files** folder on the **CSS HOT CD-ROM**, and copy one of the subfolders, such as **05_color**, to your desktop.

2 Open the **05_color** folder you copied to your desktop, and choose **Edit > Select All**.

3 Right-click one of the selected files, and choose **Properties** from the contextual menu.

4 In the **Properties** dialog box, click the **General** tab. Deselect the **Read-Only** option to disable the read-only properties for the selected files in the **05_color** folder.

Making File Extensions Visible on Windows Computers

By default, you cannot see file extensions, such as **.htm**, **.fla**, **.swf**, **.jpg**, **.gif**, or **.psd**, on Windows computers. Fortunately, you can change this setting easily. Here's how:

1 On your desktop, double-click the **My Computer** icon.

Note: If you (or someone else) has changed the name, it will not say My Computer.

2 Choose **Tools > Folder Options** to open the **Folder Options** dialog box. Select the **View** tab.

3 Turn off the **Hide extensions for known file types** check box to make all file extensions visible.

CSS System Requirements

Windows/Macintosh

- A Web browser that recognizes CSS (Internet Explorer, Firefox, Safari, Opera, Mozilla)

- Text-editing software

- Internet connection

Getting Demo Versions of the Software

If you'd like to try demo versions of the software used in this book, you can download them at the following locations:

Firefox: **www.getfirefox.com**

BBEdit from Bare Bones Software: **www.barebones.com/products/bbedit/index.shtml**

1

Getting Started

CSS (**C**ascading **S**tyle **S**heets) have been part of Web design for many years now, but it has been only within the past few years that the use of CSS has really exploded. More and more, Web designers are realizing the power and capabilities of CSS, and if you're reading this book, you most likely have at least a fundamental idea of what CSS can do for you and how it can make your life easier. This chapter discusses the purpose and effects of using CSS as well as which software applications you can use to create it.

⟨CSS is a markup language⟩

Understanding Why You Need This Book

Before you start reading, it's probably fair to wonder what to expect. In this chapter, you'll learn all about this book.

Intended Audience

If you've been working with CSS for a while and are looking to boost your skills to expert status, this book isn't for you. But if you know how to write basic XHTML and you're just getting started with CSS, or have dabbled and would like to establish a solid grounding in CSS, this book is absolutely for you.

In general, the audience we envisioned while writing this book was a beginners' class—a "CSS 101" sort of crowd. If we were teachers at a night school or a local college and we needed our Web design class to learn CSS in order to make them better designers, this is the kind of book we'd want them to read. It doesn't spend pages and pages on every nuance of the technology. It isn't heavy on theory. It's a practical text, designed to instill a working knowledge of CSS, with just enough of the theory woven in to let you advance on your own if you so choose.

This CSS 101 class does have a prerequisite: You need to have at least a basic working knowledge of XHTML. A lot of working with CSS deals with redefining existing XHTML tags, so you'll need to know one tag from another in order to write CSS.

Scope of Coverage

As you might have guessed from the previous section, the level of this book is from beginner to intermediate. For example, the text doesn't get into the details and complexity of positioning, and it doesn't take time to talk about features you can't use in the browsers most commonly used now.

I'll present the basic concepts of CSS in a direct manner to show how they relate to creating Web pages.

Among the topics covered in this book are the following:

- Understanding the structure of CSS rules
- Learning how CSS and XHTML work together
- Understanding selectors and using them efficiently
- Understanding inheritance and specificity
- Setting fonts, colors, and backgrounds
- Creating whitespace in a layout
- Using basic floats for page layout
- Dealing with form elements
- Styling tables
- Creating a style sheet for print

Objectives

The overriding objective of this book is to establish your core competency with CSS. To that end, this book will discuss basic techniques, teach you some fundamentals of CSS, and concentrate on applying the concepts in the real world. As mentioned, this book does not attempt to turn you into a world-class expert in CSS; doing so would require five times the pages and several years of hands-on practice.

No introductory text can make you an expert. Instead, the goal of any good introduction is to lay the groundwork for you to move in that direction after finishing the work. That's exactly what I've tried to do in this book.

So let's get to it, shall we?

NOTE:

Learning HTML

If you're looking to learn the essentials of HTML (**H**yper**T**ext **M**arkup **L**anguage), register for the free 24-hour pass to the lynda.com Online Training Library provided in the introduction of this book, and check out the following video-based training resource:

HTML Essential Training with William E. Weinman

What is CSS?

Before you invest the time needed to read this book, you should know how you can put CSS to use.

Like the Clothes on Your Back

To describe it in terms of a simple analogy, CSS is the clothes you put on a Web page, and the XHTML document is the body. When you want a new look, you just change your clothes, right? In an ideal world, a new look for a Web page would require nothing more than a new style sheet.

Back in the "old days," when the look of a page was driven by tables, spacer GIFs, sliced-up images, and background colors in table cells, it was as though your clothes were actually a surgical implant rather than a thin covering of cloth. Back then, altering the appearance of a Web page was akin to changing your look by going for reconstructive surgery!

So, the XHTML document is like your body (or, if you prefer, your **<body>**), and the various elements making up its structure are like your skeleton. Rather than demanding a change to the skeleton just to make a page look different, CSS lets you drape a set of clothes over that skeleton.

The CSS-as-clothes analogy holds up in another fashion: In the same way your clothes depend on your body's skeleton to take their intended shape, CSS depends on a Web page's structure in order to work properly. This doesn't mean it requires a change of structure for a change of appearance, but it does need the structure to function properly.

Simple Yet Powerful

A more geeky way of describing CSS is that it's a simple declarative language for suggesting the presentation of a Web page. This means CSS comprises straightforward declarations, such as **h1 {color: red;}**. Even if you've never seen a lick of CSS, as long as you know what an **h1** is, you can probably make a good guess as to the intended result of that statement: Any **h1** should be colored red.

As for "suggesting the presentation," it's important to establish that CSS does not guarantee that a page will look a certain way. This might sound scary, but in all honesty, nothing has ever guaranteed the layout of a page. What's that, you say? Table layouts looked the same in all browsers? Not so! Netscape 1.0, for example, didn't support tables. It couldn't have: Netscape 1.1 was the first widely available browser to implement tables. It was also the browser to give us the **font** element, image alignment, and a whole host of other features. So, the first table-and-spacer designers created layouts knowing their pages would fall apart for some people.

To return to CSS, the general idea is that a style sheet offers a strong suggestion for a page's presentation, and the browser will generally go along with those suggestions unless it can't or unless it has been set to ignore some or all of them. In practice, however, hardly anyone ever tells their browser to ignore CSS.

Here's another simple example of CSS:

```
h1 {color: red; background: #CCCCCC;
letter-spacing: 5px;}
```

Again, even if you've never seen CSS before, you can probably make some intelligent guesses about the intended effect here. The color of **h1**s should be red; their backgrounds should be a light gray (OK, I admit you had to be able to recognize hexadecimal color notation there); and the spacing between letters should be 5 pixels.

about tea: history

The result of the simple CSS example

In each case, a simple declaration was made: the color should be red, the background should be **#CCCCCC**, and so on. Each one of these is simple to understand and limited in scope—but put them together, and you can arrive at some pretty sophisticated effects. (Granted, red text on a light gray background isn't exactly sophisticated, but bear with us. The book is still young.)

It's this combined complexity that makes CSS something like one of those abstract strategy board games advertised so heavily in the 1970s: "minutes to learn, but a lifetime to master." Fortunately, from personal experience, I can tell you that it takes considerably less than a lifetime to master CSS.

VIDEO: | **what_is_css.mov**
You can make a single Web page look radically different just by changing its style sheet, without touching a single line of the XHTML. To learn more about what CSS is, check out **what_is_css.mov** in the **videos** folder on the **CSS HOT CD-ROM**.

Why Use CSS?

Maybe the promise of complex presentation through simple declarations isn't enough for you. In that case, I have some other reasons why using CSS is a good idea.

It Makes Markup More Maintainable

Honestly, which would you rather have to edit? This is the first snippet:

```
<table cellspacing="0" cellpadding="1">
<tr>
<td bgcolor="#332200">
<table cellspacing="0" cellpadding="2"
bgcolor="#F0E6C3">
<tr>
<td>
<font size="+2" color="#FFFFFF">Search
Site</font>
</td>
</tr>
<tr>
<form action="/scripts/search">
<td nowrap>
<input type="text" name="search-terms" />
<input type="image" src="/images/search.gif" />
</td>
</form>
</tr>
</table>
</td>
</tr>
</table>
```

And this is the second snippet:

```
<div class="portlet input-allowed">
<h3>Search Site</h3>
<form action="/scripts/search">
<input type="text" name="search-terms" />
<input type="image" src="/images/search.gif" />
</form>
</div>
```

Consider that the first snippet has invalid markup whereas the second does not, and consider that the second example can look the same as the first, if not better.

Search Site

Search Site

Which one was done with tables? Which one was done with CSS? Hey, if you can't tell, why should we?

It Makes Pages Smaller

In the previous section, it's pretty obvious which example uses less code and therefore would produce a smaller XHTML document. Now envision a similar degree of markup reduction throughout an entire page.

In fact, a number of studies over the years have determined that if you take a site and rework its markup using CSS for layout instead of tables, you can cut the size of the XHTML document in half. That's right, you'll get a 50 percent reduction in document size. On occasion, that reduction can be less than or greater than 50 percent, but in the majority of cases, a 50 percent reduction is possible.

It is true that some of what's lost in markup weight is gained back in increased CSS weight. However, usually the final style sheet is 25 to 35 percent of the original page's weight. So, you end up with an XHTML+CSS combination that's 15 to 25 percent smaller than the table-and-spacer XHTML document alone.

Furthermore, that 15 to 25 percent savings comes when a visitor loads their first page on your site. After that, assuming you've set up your site properly, the savings can jump to 50 percent. (You'll see how to set up your site properly in Chapter 2, "Understanding CSS.")

It Makes Sites Faster

CSS is a magic Web accelerator? Well, yes.

Consider this: Your visitors don't care how your pages are constructed. They care only about two issues: getting the information they want and getting it quickly. A site that takes 2 seconds for its pages to load will seem superior to one that takes 4 seconds per page. Because CSS uses less code, it makes your overall file sizes smaller, which in turn means your pages will load more quickly into your visitors' browsers.

The number-one factor in page response time is how many bytes are shipped over the wire. So if your pages are half their former size, they'll take half as long to load. That may seem like an obvious point, but it needs to be said.

It Helps with Search Engine Optimization

No, CSS is not the magic bullet that will put your site at the top of the Google rankings; we're not selling snake oil here. However, properly using CSS can help boost your site in the rankings, even if just a little bit.

The way search engines work (at least as of this writing) is that content coming at the top of a page has more weight than content appearing later in the page. In other words, the "further down" a piece of content appears in a document's source, the less relevant it's considered to be by search engines.

Thanks to CSS, you can order a document so the most important information comes sooner and the less important stuff comes later. This is true even if you visually lay out the page so the more important stuff goes on the right and the less important stuff goes on the left. (This might not be a good idea in left-to-right languages such as English, but hey, it's your design.)

NOTE:

Recognizing the Exception

The assertion here that "the number-one factor in page response time is how many bytes are shipped over the wire" does have an exception. For extremely high-traffic sites, page load times are actually shorter when the CSS is embedded in the document, even if that makes the page bigger. This is because the server resources required to handle two requests (one for the XHTML document and one for the style sheet) become significant when the servers are loaded with so much traffic.

You aren't likely to run into this situation unless you have a really high-traffic site—and when we say "really high-traffic," we mean traffic levels like those at eBay or Yahoo. So, odds are you'll never have to worry about this. Just in case, though, forewarned is forearmed.

Authoring CSS

You can create CSS in many ways. You can use anything from free text-editing applications that come with your Mac or Windows operating system to full-blown Web development programs, such as GoLive or Macromedia Dreamweaver, both from Adobe. The following sections introduce some popular applications you can use to create your style sheets.

A Plain Old Text Editor

You can write CSS in anything you can use to write XHTML. If you use Windows, you already have the free Notepad and WordPad applications that come with the operating system. If you're on a Mac, you have TextEdit. You can even use professional word-processing software such as Microsoft Word or Corel WordPerfect or even programs such as emacs, vi, joe, pico… anything you can use to write and save text files.

My personal favorite is BBEdit (**www.barebones. com**), an editor for the Mac from Bare Bones Software. I'll be using BBEdit for the majority of the examples and exercises in this book. If you're using Windows and would like to use a program similar to BBEdit, I suggest EditPlus (**www. editplus.com**) from ES-Computing. Both applications are high-powered text editors that allow for grep-style search-and-replace tasks and have features such as syntax coloring for programming languages built in. At their cores, however, they're text editors.

If text editors are a little too plain for you, some programs are specifically for CSS authoring, or at least for Web development.

Style Master

A product of Western Civilisation (**http://westciv. com**) and John Allsopp, who was one of the original CSS Samurai at the Web Standards Project, Style Master is a commercial (read: not free) CSS-authoring program available for both the Mac and Windows. Among hundreds of other features, Style Master features several design templates, a built-in tutorial, and browser compatibility information. As with many other Web design programs, Style Master has autocompletion for CSS code, a design preview mode, and the ability to work with content management systems such as blogging software.

TopStyle

TopStyle (**http://bradsoft.com/topstyle**) from NewsGator Technologies is the brainchild of Nick Bradbury, the author of HomeSite, a venerable markup editor. It's available for Windows and is promoted as a CSS/XHTML editor. Like Style Master, it offers autocompletion, compatibility checking, and a preview mode, along with hundreds of other features. Also like Style Master, TopStyle is oriented more toward hands-on authors who like to see the code as they write it instead of having it hidden behind a point-and-click interface.

Dreamweaver

Dreamweaver (**www.adobe.com**) is a complete Web development application offered by Adobe (formerly Macromedia). In many ways, Dreamweaver offers a visually oriented development space as well as the ability to dig into the code of a Web page. It offers powerful CSS-centric tools, dialog boxes that let authors fill in values, and help files to make using CSS easier.

Now that you understand what CSS is and the benefits of using it, in the next chapter, *"Understanding CSS,"* you'll learn about some of the fundamental principles of working with CSS, including understanding key terms, adding rules to a style sheet, and using selectors.

2

CSS
margins = TRBL

Understanding CSS

Every journey has to start somewhere, and on your journey to learn CSS (**C**ascading **S**tyle **S**heets), you will understandably start with the basics. In fact, in this chapter, you'll take a step back and review the basics of XHTML (e**X**tensible **HTML**) so you can understand how XHTML and CSS work together. You'll then learn basic CSS terms and practice writing some simple CSS to style a Web page. You'll also learn about the different types of style sheets, including embedded and external style sheets, and the benefits of working with each as you develop Web sites. Finally, you'll learn some important techniques for managing style sheets so you can determine which way works best for you and for the Web sites you build.

Reviewing XTHML Basics

XHTML (eXtensible HyperText Markup Language) is— like HTML—a simple document markup language. Its purpose is to give structure and meaning to what would otherwise be plain-text documents.

To that end, XHTML defines a number of elements. When you look at the source of a Web page, these elements are easy to spot. Here's a small fragment of an XHTML document that you will be working with throughout this book:

```
<h1><b>about tea:</b> history</h1>
<h2>The Legendary Origins of Tea</h2>
<p>
   The history of tea extends so far into the
past that its very origins are shrouded by
legend. It is said that Emperor Shen Nung, who
ruled China in 2700 BC, used to enjoy relaxing
in his garden with a cup of hot water. It was
during one of these respites that a tea leaf
happened to float down from a nearby bush, and
land directly in the Emperor's cup.
   <img src="images/teapot.jpg" width="96"
height="140" class="illus" alt="" />
   The new drink quickly became the Emperor's
favorite, and a taste for tea quickly spread
throughout the aristocracy, and it wasn't long
before tea was the favored drink throughout all
of China.
</p>
```

This fragment contains the following:

Elements:

Elements are the "atomic pieces" of the document. The elements in the markup fragment above are **h1**, **h2**, **b**, **p**, and **img**. Every element has a start tag and an end tag, even those that look like stand-alone elements, such as **img**. For the paragraph, the start and end tags are **<p>** and **</p>**, respectively. The slash is how you designate the end tag for certain elements. For the image, the end tag is represented with the trailing slash (**<img … />**).

Most elements in XHTML can contain content, such as the text appearing between the header tags **h1**, **h2**, and so on. Elements such as this are called **non-replaced** elements. The **<img>** tag represents an image element, which is called a **replaced** element. In other words, this element points to another resource that will appear at the element's location when the document is rendered. In the example code above, the image **teapot.jpg** will appear when the document is opened in a browser.

Attributes:

In XHTML, elements don't crop up terribly often, but when they do, they're important. Attributes describe certain aspects of elements. In the previous example, the only element in the markup fragment that has attributes is the **img** element; its attributes are **src**, **width**, **height**, **class**, and **alt**, which define the location of the image file (the **source**); the width and height of the image in pixels; the class of the element (described in Chapter 3, *"Selectors and the Cascade"*); and alternate text for the image.

Values:

Every attribute has a value, even if it is an empty value. For example, the value of `src` is `images/teapot.jpg`. A value can be empty, but it must be present. In the markup shown previously, `alt` has an empty value, which is indicated as follows: `alt=""`. The equal sign and quotation marks are required, regardless of whether the value is empty. (You can use single quotation marks instead of double quotation marks, as long as you don't try to mix them, e.g. `"lead'`.)

These are the basics of XHTML terminology. You might be wondering why you've spent time learning or reviewing XHTML in a CSS book. I'll be referring to elements quite a bit throughout the rest of the book,

because styling elements is one of the most common tasks in CSS. Attributes come into play too, particularly the `class` attribute.

Without using some sort of structure, you'd have no way to style a document. In the overwhelming majority of Web pages, XHTML or HTML provides the necessary structure. Next, you'll move on to styles!

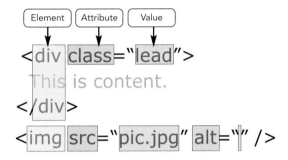

VIDEO: | **xhtml_essentials.mov**
To review XHTML terminology, check out **xhtml_essentials.mov** in the **videos** folder on the **CSS HOT CD-ROM**.

Understanding CSS Terminology

As with any language, CSS has a few terms you need to understand before you can start to learn the language.

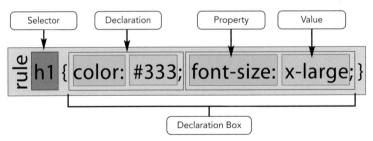

The illustration shown here presents the basic terminology you need to learn in order to start understanding the basics of CSS. From the inside working out, these terms are as follows:

Property: A property describes an aspect of an element's presentation, such as `color`, `font-size`, or `border-width`. CSS 2.1 offers 138 properties. Throughout this book, you'll work directly with many of them. However, since I can't cover them all here, see Appendix A, *"CSS 2 Properties,"* for all 138 definitions. The important point now is that a property is always followed by a value, and the two are always separated by a colon (`:`).

Value: A value is a descriptor defining a specific appearance, such as a color name, a measurement of length, a percentage value, or a number of other values. These are just a few of the possible values you can define in CSS. In the example, the values shown are **#333** and **x-large**. As you work through this book, you'll learn about many other values. When you write CSS code, always follow a value with a semicolon (;) to create a declaration.

Declaration: A declaration is a property-value pair. So, the pairing **color: #333** is a single declaration. The pairing **font-size: x-large** is another declaration. Every declaration should end with a semicolon (;). If you have more than one declaration, as in this example, you technically can omit the terminating semicolon, but it is generally regarded as best practice to include it, in case you need to add another declaration to the series later. If you were to add another declaration without the separating semicolon, CSS would read them not as two declarations but as one, and therefore the declaration would not be rendered properly in your document.

Declaration block: A declaration block is a set of declarations grouped together. A declaration block is always surrounded by curly braces ({ }), as shown in the previous illustration. The curly braces are the beginning and ending points of your declaration block, just as the semicolon is the endpoint of the declaration. Each rule has only one declaration block.

Selector: A selector defines the elements of a document that will have the declarations applied to them. In the previous example, the **h1** selector means **h1** elements will take on the color and font size properties and values defined in the declaration block.

Rule: A rule is the pairing of a selector and a declaration block. In the previous illustration, the line of code shown is a rule, because it combines both a selector and a declaration block.

Style sheet: A style sheet is a collection of rules that will be applied to a document. A single style sheet can have, in theory, an infinite number of rules. A style sheet can either be embedded in an XHTML document or live as a separate, external file that is associated with the XHTML document. You'll explore how to use embedded and external style sheets, and the pros and cons of each, later in this chapter.

With those terms tucked firmly into your tool belt, next you'll start writing some CSS.

VIDEO: | **css_essentials.mov and design_tour.mov**

To learn more about CSS terminology, check out **css_essentials.mov** in the **videos** folder on the **CSS HOT CD-ROM**.

To preview the finished site design and the specific elements that you will be styling throughout this book, check out **design_tour.mov** in the **videos** folder on the **CSS HOT CD-ROM**.

NOTE: | **Setting Up to Write CSS**

For the exercises in this book, you'll need two programs: a browser, such as Microsoft Internet Explorer, Safari (Mac), or Firefox (Windows); and a text editor, such as TextEdit or BBEdit (Mac) or Notepad (Windows). If you'd rather edit in an HTML editing environment, such as Macromedia Dreamweaver or GoLive, both from Adobe, you can do that too. Throughout this book, I'll be using BBEdit from Bare Bones Software, a popular and powerful editing program for Mac OS X, but feel free to use whichever text or HTML editor you're most comfortable with.

1 | Adding Rules to a Style Sheet

As you learned previously in this chapter, rules define which elements of a document to style and how to style them. Rules contain two key elements—a selector, which defines which element to style, and a declaration block, which defines how to style the selected element. In this exercise, you'll edit a simple style sheet to add two rules to style two different elements on a Web page.

1 Copy the **02_xhtml** folder from the **CSS HOT CD-ROM** to your desktop. Double-click the **02_xhtml** folder to open it so you see the exercise files inside, as shown in the illustration here.

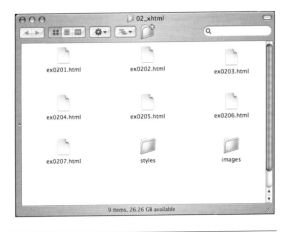

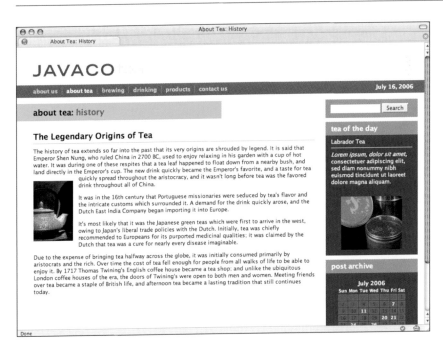

2 In a browser, open **ex0201.html** from the **02_xhtml** folder you copied to your desktop, as shown in the illustration here.

Notice the page has a plain white background. In this exercise, you'll brighten up this page by replacing the bland white background with a light green one.

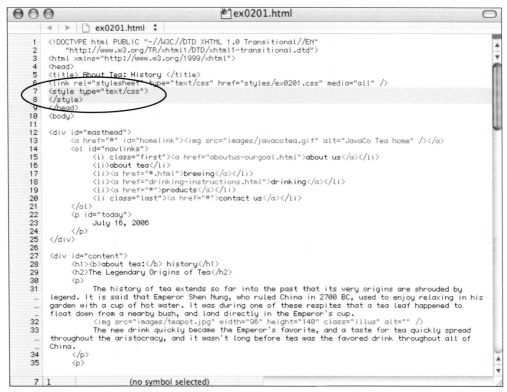

```
1    <!DOCTYPE html PUBLIC "-//W3C//DTD XHTML 1.0 Transitional//EN"
2        "http://www.w3.org/TR/xhtml1/DTD/xhtml1-transitional.dtd">
3    <html xmlns="http://www.w3.org/1999/xhtml">
4    <head>
5    <title> About Tea: History </title>
6    <link rel="stylesheet" type="text/css" href="styles/ex0201.css" media="all" />
7    <style type="text/css">
8    </style>
9    </head>
10   <body>
11
12   <div id="masthead">
13       <a href="#" id="homelink"><img src="images/javacotea.gif" alt="JavaCo Tea home" /></a>
14       <ol id="navlinks">
15           <li class="first"><a href="aboutus-ourgoal.html">about us</a></li>
16           <li>about tea</li>
17           <li><a href="#.html">brewing</a></li>
18           <li><a href="drinking-instructions.html">drinking</a></li>
19           <li><a href="#">products</a></li>
20           <li class="last"><a href="#">contact us</a></li>
21       </ol>
22       <p id="today">
23           July 16, 2006
24       </p>
25   </div>
26
27   <div id="content">
28       <h1><b>about tea:</b> history</h1>
29       <h2>The Legendary Origins of Tea</h2>
30       <p>
31           The history of tea extends so far into the past that its very origins are shrouded by
...      legend. It is said that Emperor Shen Nung, who ruled China in 2700 BC, used to enjoy relaxing in his
...      garden with a cup of hot water. It was during one of these respites that a tea leaf happened to
...      float down from a nearby bush, and land directly in the Emperor's cup.
32           <img src="images/teapot.jpg" width="96" height="140" class="illus" alt="" />
33           The new drink quickly became the Emperor's favorite, and a taste for tea quickly spread
...      throughout the aristocracy, and it wasn't long before tea was the favored drink throughout all of
...      China.
34       </p>
35       <p>
```

Handwritten note: embedded style — only affects this document

3 Open **ex0201.html** with your text or HTML editor. Near the beginning of the file, find the following block of code:

```
<style type="text/css">
</style>
```

This is a **style** element—a special container inside which you can add CSS rules.

```
 ● ● ●                    🖹 ex0201.html                            ⬭
 ◀  ▶  🖹 ex0201.html  ▾
1   <!DOCTYPE html PUBLIC "-//W3C//DTD XHTML 1.0 Transitional//EN"
2       "http://www.w3.org/TR/xhtml1/DTD/xhtml1-transitional.dtd">
3   <html xmlns="http://www.w3.org/1999/xhtml">
4   <head>
5   <title> About Tea: History </title>
6   <link rel="stylesheet" type="text/css" href="styles/ex0201.css" media="all" />
7   <style type="text/css">
8   body {background: #E3EDC2;}
9   </style>
10  </head>
11  <body>
12
13  <div id="masthead">
14      <a href="#" id="homelink"><img src="images/javacotea.gif" alt="JavaCo Tea home" /></a>
15      <ol id="navlinks">
16          <li class="first"><a href="aboutus-ourgoal.html">about us</a></li>
17          <li>about tea</li>
18          <li><a href="#.html">brewing</a></li>
19          <li><a href="drinking-instructions.html">drinking</a></li>
20          <li><a href="#">products</a></li>
21          <li class="last"><a href="#">contact us</a></li>
22      </ol>
23      <p id="today">
24          July 16, 2006
25      </p>
26  </div>
27
28  <div id="content">
29      <h1><b>about tea:</b> history</h1>
30      <h2>The Legendary Origins of Tea</h2>
31      <p>
32          The history of tea extends so far into the past that its very origins are shrouded by
    legend. It is said that Emperor Shen Nung, who ruled China in 2700 BC, used to enjoy relaxing in his
    garden with a cup of hot water. It was during one of these respites that a tea leaf happened to
    float down from a nearby bush, and land directly in the Emperor's cup.
33          <img src="images/teapot.jpg" width="96" height="140" class="illus" alt="" />
34          The new drink quickly became the Emperor's favorite, and a taste for tea quickly spread
    throughout the aristocracy, and it wasn't long before tea was the favored drink throughout all of
    China.
35      </p>
  8  28             (no symbol selected)
```

4 After the `<style type="text/css">` line, insert a new line by pressing **Return** (Mac) or **Enter** (Windows), and then type the following:

`body {background: #E3EDC2;}`

You just added a new rule to the style sheet, defining a background color for the Javaco tea page. This rule contains the necessary elements: a selector (**body**) and the declaration block (`{background: #E3EDC2;}`), which contains a single declaration defining the color of the background. Next, you'll preview the results in a browser.

5 Save **ex0201.html**, switch to your browser, and reload **ex0201.html**.

Congratulations, you've written your first CSS rule! The result is fairly straightforward—you defined the page's **body** element to have its **background** filled with the color #E3EDC2.

Note: #E3EDC2 is a hexadecimal value, which is one of five ways you can define color in CSS. For more information about the ways you can define color in CSS, refer to the tip after Exercise 3.

```
  ⊖ ⊖ ⊖                         📄 ex0201.html                              ⊂⊃
         ◀  ▶  [ ] ex0201.html  ▲
    1    <!DOCTYPE html PUBLIC "-//W3C//DTD XHTML 1.0 Transitional//EN"
    2         "http://www.w3.org/TR/xhtml1/DTD/xhtml1-transitional.dtd">
    3    <html xmlns="http://www.w3.org/1999/xhtml">
    4    <head>
    5    <title> About Tea: History </title>
    6    <link rel="stylesheet" type="text/css" href="styles/ex0201.css" media="all" />
    7    <style type="text/css">
    8    body {background: #E3EDC2;}
    9    #masthead {background: #ABD240;}
   10    </style>
   11    </head>
   12    <body>
   13
   14    <div id="masthead">
   15         <a href="#" id="homelink"><img src="images/javacotea.gif" alt="JavaCo Tea home" /></a>
   16         <ol id="navlinks">
   17             <li class="first"><a href="aboutus-ourgoal.html">about us</a></li>
   18             <li>about tea</li>
   19             <li><a href="#.html">brewing</a></li>
   20             <li><a href="drinking-instructions.html">drinking</a></li>
   21             <li><a href="#">products</a></li>
   22             <li class="last"><a href="#">contact us</a></li>
   23         </ol>
   24         <p id="today">
   25             July 16, 2006
   26         </p>
   27    </div>
   28
   29    <div id="content">
   30         <h1><b>about tea:</b> history</h1>
   31         <h2>The Legendary Origins of Tea</h2>
   32         <p>
   33             The history of tea extends so far into the past that its very origins are shrouded by
         legend. It is said that Emperor Shen Nung, who ruled China in 2700 BC, used to enjoy relaxing in his
   ...   garden with a cup of hot water. It was during one of these respites that a tea leaf happened to
   ...   float down from a nearby bush, and land directly in the Emperor's cup.
   34             <img src="images/teapot.jpg" width="96" height="140" class="illus" alt="" />
   35             The new drink quickly became the Emperor's favorite, and a taste for tea quickly spread
   ...   throughout the aristocracy, and it wasn't long before tea was the favored drink throughout all of
   ...   China.
                                                                                              ▲
                                                                                              ▼
    9 | 33              (no symbol selected)
```

6   Return to your text or HTML editor. Add the following rule to the style sheet:

`#masthead {background: #ABD240;}`

TIP:

Identifying Selectors

In Step 6, you created the selector **#masthead**, which means "select any element with an ID of **masthead**." This is what's called an **ID selector**—and this is the first time you've seen one in this book, so don't panic if it's unfamiliar! You'll explore ID selectors (along with several other types) in more detail in Chapter 3, *"Selectors and the Cascade."* For now, just remember that it's applying the styles to the top of the page.

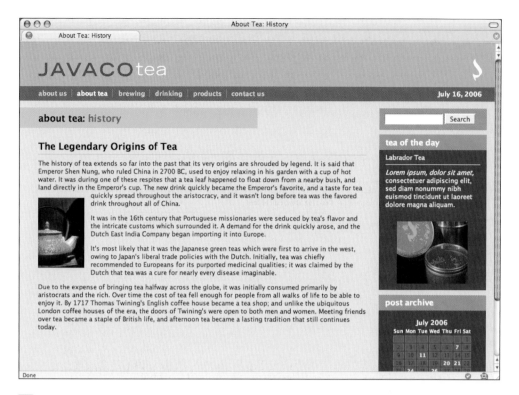

7   Save and close **ex0201.html**, switch to your browser, and reload **ex0201.html**.

The second rule you created is much like the first, except here you've set the background color for an element with a specific label (`masthead`). Don't worry about how that happened right now. The important point is that you added a second rule to the style sheet, and it changed the look of the page. Congrats!

Now that you know how to add rules to a style sheet, next you'll learn how to identify incomplete rules and learn how to add selectors to a declaration block to make them a complete rule.

2 | Adding Selectors

As you know from earlier in this chapter, just having a declaration block with values and properties is not enough information—you need to apply the declaration block to a specific element on the page. To do this, you need to add a selector to the code. In this exercise, you'll edit a simple style sheet to add some selectors so the preexisting styles will be applied to some of the content in the document.

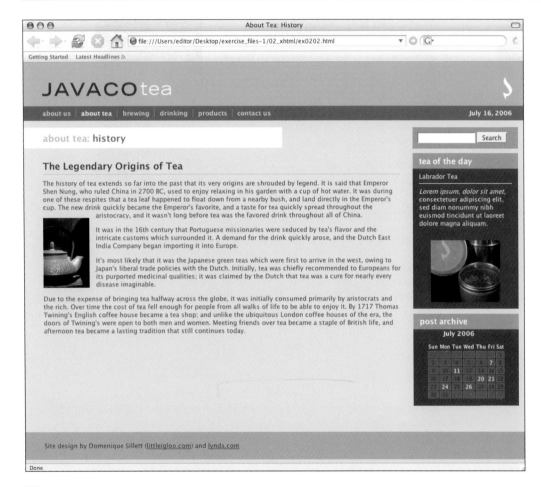

1 In a browser, open **ex0202.html** from the **02_xhtml** folder you copied to your desktop, as shown in the illustration here.

Look at the text on the page. Notice no bold text or italic text appears in the "about tea: history" heading at the top of the page or in the body text.

2 Open **ex0202.html** with your text or HTML editor. Near the beginning of the file, find the following block of code:

```
<style type="text/css">
{font-style: italic;}
{font-weight: bold;}
</style>
```

This style sheet has two unfinished rules, one on each line, for styling text as italic and bold. At the moment, they're not having any effect on the page in the browser. As you saw in the previous step, the heading or body text of the page didn't contain any italic or bold text.

Although these lines of code contain declaration blocks with properties and values, each is an incomplete rule because the selector is missing. As a result, the style sheet doesn't have any information about the element to which these properties apply. Not to worry, you'll add a selector in the next step.

---

3 Edit the first line of the style sheet (the `{font-style: italic;}` line) as follows:

```
h1 {font-style: italic;}
```

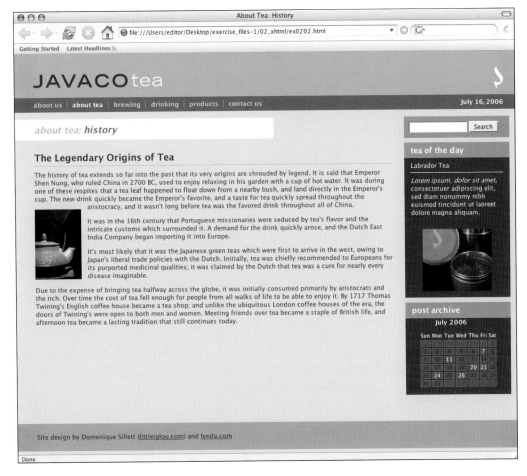

4 Save **ex0202.html**, switch to your browser, and reload **ex0202.html**.

Notice the "about tea: history" heading is now italic. Congratulations, you've made your first selection! In this case, you selected all **h1** elements in the document. In this example, the only **h1** is the "about tea: history" heading. Therefore, it now appears as italic. The selector **h1** is what made that possible.

Next, you'll add a selector to the second unfinished rule in the style sheet.

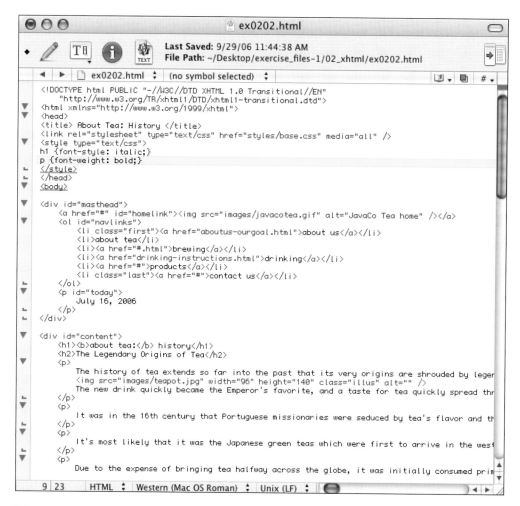

```
<!DOCTYPE html PUBLIC "-//W3C//DTD XHTML 1.0 Transitional//EN"
    "http://www.w3.org/TR/xhtml1/DTD/xhtml1-transitional.dtd">
<html xmlns="http://www.w3.org/1999/xhtml">
<head>
<title> About Tea: History </title>
<link rel="stylesheet" type="text/css" href="styles/base.css" media="all" />
<style type="text/css">
h1 {font-style: italic;}
p {font-weight: bold;}
</style>
</head>
<body>

<div id="masthead">
    <a href="#" id="homelink"><img src="images/javacotea.gif" alt="JavaCo Tea home" /></a>
    <ol id="navlinks">
        <li class="first"><a href="aboutus-ourgoal.html">about us</a></li>
        <li>about tea</li>
        <li><a href="#.html">brewing</a></li>
        <li><a href="drinking-instructions.html">drinking</a></li>
        <li><a href="#">products</a></li>
        <li class="last"><a href="#">contact us</a></li>
    </ol>
    <p id="today">
        July 16, 2006
    </p>
</div>

<div id="content">
    <h1><b>about tea:</b> history</h1>
    <h2>The Legendary Origins of Tea</h2>
    <p>
        The history of tea extends so far into the past that its very origins are shrouded by leger
        <img src="images/teapot.jpg" width="96" height="140" class="illus" alt="" />
        The new drink quickly became the Emperor's favorite, and a taste for tea quickly spread thr
    </p>
    <p>
        It was in the 16th century that Portuguese missionaries were seduced by tea's flavor and th
    </p>
    <p>
        It's most likely that it was the Japanese green teas which were first to arrive in the west
    </p>
    <p>
        Due to the expense of bringing tea halfway across the globe, it was initially consumed prim
```

5 Return to your text or HTML editor. Edit the second line of the style sheet so it reads as follows:

```
p {font-weight: bold;}
```

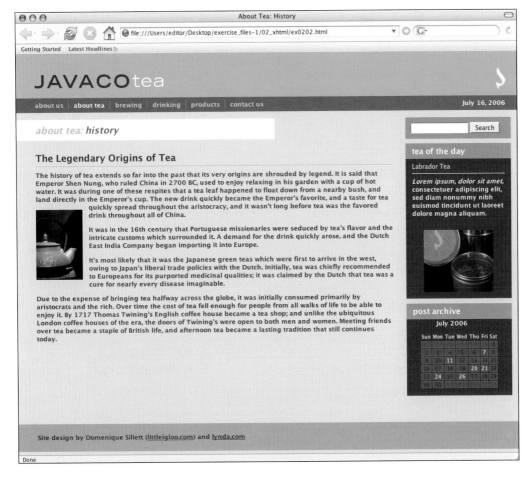

6 Save and close **ex0202.html**, switch to your browser, and reload **ex0202.html**.

Now the text in every paragraph on the page is bold. This change is happening to every **p** element, regardless of where it appears on the page, including the main body text, the date in the upper-right corner of the page, and the text in the "tea of the day" section in the right column.

As you can see from this exercise, a declaration block without a selector has no impact on the styling of a page because the style sheet doesn't contain any information about which element to style. The selector defines which element to style, and the declaration block defines how to style it. To have a complete rule, you must use both a selector and a declaration block together.

Now that you know a little bit more about how selectors work, next you'll learn how to work with declaration blocks, specifically how to change multiple styles using a single declaration block.

3 | Working with Multiple Declarations

In the previous two exercises, you worked with simple rules with only one declaration in the declaration block. One of the many benefits of working with CSS is the ability to apply multiple styles to an element at the same time. Although you could create a new rule for each style, it is easier and more efficient to create one rule with multiple declarations in a single declaration block so you can apply multiple styles at the same time. In this exercise, you'll learn to do just that.

1 In a browser, open **ex0203.html** from the **02_xhtml** folder you copied to your desktop, as shown in the illustration here.

Look at the right column (the **sidebar**) of the page. The sidebar headings, "Tea of the Day" and "Post Archive," don't stand out very well. In this exercise, you'll learn how to add multiple declarations to a single declaration block to spruce up the formatting of these sidebar headings.

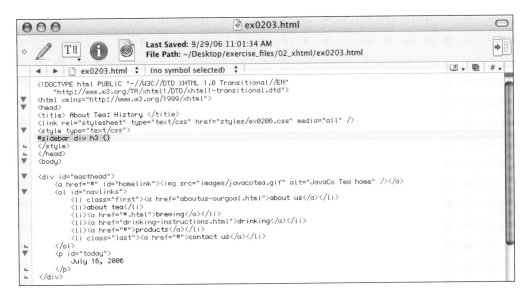

```
<!DOCTYPE html PUBLIC "-//W3C//DTD XHTML 1.0 Transitional//EN"
    "http://www.w3.org/TR/xhtml1/DTD/xhtml1-transitional.dtd">
<html xmlns="http://www.w3.org/1999/xhtml">
<head>
<title> About Tea: History </title>
<link rel="stylesheet" type="text/css" href="styles/ex0206.css" media="all" />
<style type="text/css">
#sidebar div h3 {}
</style>
</head>
<body>

<div id="masthead">
    <a href="#" id="homelink"><img src="images/javacotea.gif" alt="JavaCo Tea home" /></a>
    <ol id="navlinks">
        <li class="first"><a href="aboutus-ourgoal.html">about us</a></li>
        <li>about tea</li>
        <li><a href="#.html">brewing</a></li>
        <li><a href="drinking-instructions.html">drinking</a></li>
        <li><a href="#">products</a></li>
        <li class="last"><a href="#">contact us</a></li>
    </ol>
    <p id="today">
        July 16, 2006
    </p>
</div>
```

2   Open **ex0203.html** with your text or HTML editor. Near the beginning of the file, find the following block of code:

```
<style type="text/css">
#sidebar div h3 {}
</style>
```

This rule has the opposite problem of the rules you worked with in Exercise 2—it has a selector but no declarations. The curly braces mark the beginning and end of an empty declaration block. In the next few steps, you'll add multiple declarations to the empty declaration block.

TIP:

Working with Descendant Selectors

In Step 2, you were introduced to the selector `#sidebar div h3`. Briefly, what this means is "select any **h3** element inside a **div** when that **div** is inside an element with an ID of **sidebar**." This is what's called a **descendant selector**. Confused? Don't worry. You'll learn all about descendant selectors (along with several other types of selectors) in Chapter 3, *"Selectors and the Cascade."* For now, just recognize the selector you're working with in this exercise is a descendant selector.

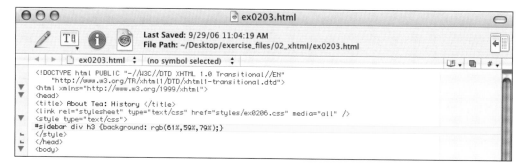

```
<!DOCTYPE html PUBLIC "-//W3C//DTD XHTML 1.0 Transitional//EN"
    "http://www.w3.org/TR/xhtml1/DTD/xhtml1-transitional.dtd">
<html xmlns="http://www.w3.org/1999/xhtml">
<head>
<title> About Tea: History </title>
<link rel="stylesheet" type="text/css" href="styles/ex0206.css" media="all" />
<style type="text/css">
#sidebar div h3 {background: rgb(61%,59%,79%);}
</style>
</head>
<body>
```

3 In your text or HTML editor, edit the rule as follows:

`#sidebar div h3 {background: rgb(61%,59%,79%);}`

With this change, all the **h3** elements in the sidebar will gain a dusky, light purple background.

In this step, you specified color using RGB (**R**ed, **G**reen, **B**lue) percentage. In Exercise 1, you specified color using a long hexadecimal value. For more information about the different ways to specify color when working with CSS, refer to the tip after this exercise.

4 Save **ex0203.html**, switch to your browser, and reload **ex0203.html**.

Notice the headings in the right sidebar now have a dusky, light purple background.

Although the headings stand out a bit more than they did before, the font size is a bit small, and it looks a little strange for the light purple not to expand to the full width of the sidebar. In the next step, you'll add two more declarations to address both these issues.

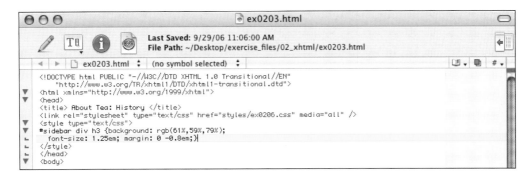

5 Return to your text or HTML editor. Edit the same rule as follows:

```
#sidebar div h3 {background: rgb(61%,59%,79%);
  font-size: 1.25em; margin: 0 -0.8em;}
```

You just added two more declarations to the rule. The first will adjust the font size of the sidebar headings, and the second will adjust the width of the light purple background you created in this exercise. So far, you have added three declarations to the rule—the background color for the sidebar headings, the font size for the sidebar headings, and the margins of the sidebar headings.

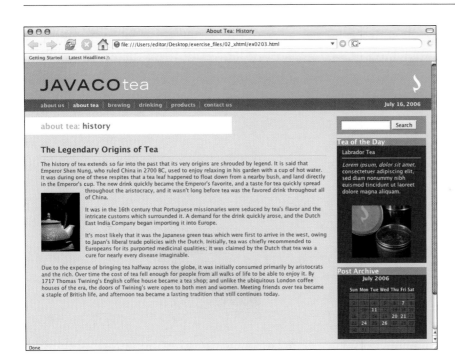

6 Save **ex0203.html,** switch to your browser, and reload **ex0203.html**.

As a result of the declarations you added in the previous step, the text in the sidebar headings is a little bit bigger, and the light purple background has expanded to fill the width of the sidebar. The latter effect is because of the negative margins you added to its sides. You'll learn more about working with margins in Chapter 7, *"Using Margins and Borders to Create Whitespace and Separation."*

Although the sidebar is looking better than when you started, the text looks a bit cramped because the width of the light purple background is pretty narrow—it would look nicer if a bit more light purple space appeared above and below the text. Also, many of the headings on the page use exclusively lowercase letters. Although you could retype the text, you don't have to when you're working with CSS. You'll learn how in the next steps.

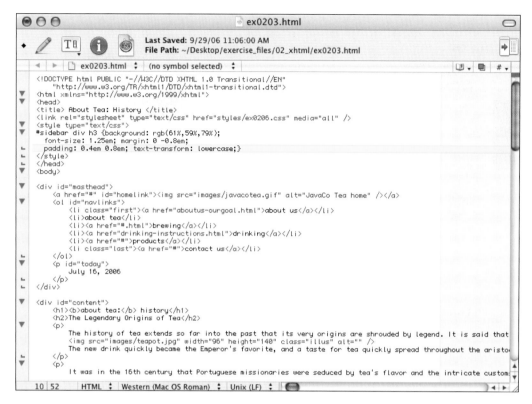

7 Return to your text or HTML editor. Edit the rule as follows:

```
#sidebar div h3 {background: rgb(61%,59%,79%);
    font-size: 1.25em; margin: 0 -0.8em;
    padding: 0.4em 0.8em; text-transform: lowercase;}
```

8 Save **ex0203.html**, switch to your browser, and reload **ex0203.html**.

Thanks to the latest additions, the sidebar headings now have some space around the actual text. This is a result of padding, which is the first of the two declarations you added in Step 7. You'll learn more about padding in Chapter 7, *"Using Margins and Borders to Create Whitespace and Separation."*

Notice the letters in the sidebar headings are now lowercase, changing "Tea of the Day" to "tea of the day." This is entirely a CSS effect—if you look at the XHTML document, you'll see the uppercase letters are still there! The **lowercase** value for the **text-transform** property you specified in Step 7 causes the browser to convert all the letters in these headings to lowercase, without ever touching the XHTML. Very cool!

Although these changes may seem small when you're working with just one page, imagine a client asks you to change all the headings on a Web site with several hundreds of pages so it doesn't contain any capital letters. Changing this manually would take days. With CSS, you can easily change all the headings on an entire site with a few simple changes to the style sheet. Again, the value of CSS is separating the presentation or style from the content.

Another cool thing about CSS is the flexibility it offers you when you're writing multiple declarations. In the next step, you'll try formatting the **h3** rule a little differently and see how that affects how the browser renders the page.

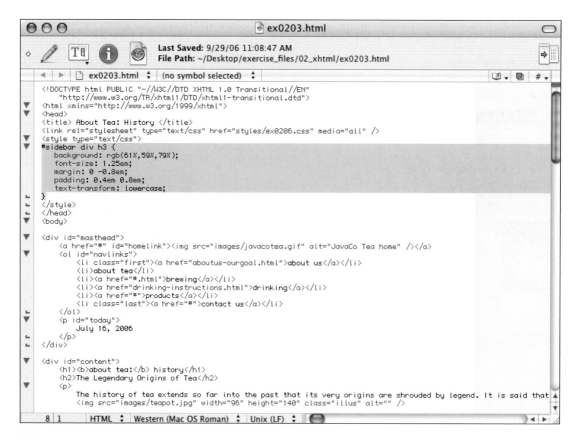

```
<!DOCTYPE html PUBLIC "-//W3C//DTD XHTML 1.0 Transitional//EN"
    "http://www.w3.org/TR/xhtml1/DTD/xhtml1-transitional.dtd">
<html xmlns="http://www.w3.org/1999/xhtml">
<head>
<title> About Tea: History </title>
<link rel="stylesheet" type="text/css" href="styles/ex0206.css" media="all" />
<style type="text/css">
#sidebar div h3 {
    background: rgb(61%,59%,79%);
    font-size: 1.25em;
    margin: 0 -0.8em;
    padding: 0.4em 0.8em;
    text-transform: lowercase;
}
</style>
</head>
<body>

<div id="masthead">
    <a href="#" id="homelink"><img src="images/javacotea.gif" alt="JavaCo Tea home" /></a>
    <ol id="navlinks">
        <li class="first"><a href="aboutus-ourgoal.html">about us</a></li>
        <li>about tea</li>
        <li><a href="#.html">brewing</a></li>
        <li><a href="drinking-instructions.html">drinking</a></li>
        <li><a href="#">products</a></li>
        <li class="last"><a href="#">contact us</a></li>
    </ol>
    <p id="today">
        July 16, 2006
    </p>
</div>

<div id="content">
    <h1><b>about tea:</b> history</h1>
    <h2>The Legendary Origins of Tea</h2>
    <p>
        The history of tea extends so far into the past that its very origins are shrouded by legend. It is said that
        <img src="images/teapot.jpg" width="96" height="140" class="illus" alt="" />
```

9 Return to your text or HMTL editor. Edit the rule as follows:

```
#sidebar div h3 {
    background: rgb(61%,59%,79%);
    font-size:   1.25em;
    margin:      0 -0.8em;
    padding:     0.4em 0.8em;
    text-transform: lowercase;
}
```

10 Save and close **ex0203.html**. Switch to your browser, and reload **ex0203.html**.

No matter how closely you look when you reload the page, it shouldn't change one iota. Changing the way the CSS is formatted doesn't change its effect in the browser. You can write your CSS in many ways. For example, instead of having all the declarations on single lines, you could put them all on the same line, or you could have one line with three declarations, one line with one declaration, and one line with two declarations. In the end, you will see the same results in the browser.

Of these options, what's the best way to write a rule with multiple declarations? Well, no right way exists. Just pick the one you think works best for you, provided you observe the following rules: First, declaration blocks must begin and end with curly braces. Second, each selector can have only one associated declaration block. (However, as you've seen in this exercise, you can have multiple declarations in a single declaration block.) Third, each declaration must end with a semicolon. Finally, each declaration requires a colon between the property and the value.

That's it! Other than these rules, you can put spaces before or after the colons, put every declaration on its own line, run them all together on a single line…whatever works best for you.

Now that you have a solid understanding of how to write rules, including selectors, declarations, and declaration blocks, next you'll learn about different types of style sheets and the pros and cons of each.

Understanding Color Values

So far in this chapter, you've seen two kinds of color values: long hexadecimal, such as **#ABD240**, and RGB percentage, such as **rgb(61%,59%,79%)**. These are two of the five ways you can specify color when you're working with CSS. Here is an overview of the five types, which you will explore in more detail in Chapter 5, *"Setting Foreground and Background Properties"*:

RGB percentage: This defines red, green, and blue on a scale of 0 to 100 percent. When using RGB percentage, separate the values with a comma, and surround them with an **rgb()** container as follows:

rgb(61%,59%,79%)

In RGB percentage, black is **rgb(0%,0%,0%)**, and white is **rgb(100%,100%,100%)**. You can also use decimal numbers, such as 66.667%, though a few browsers may ignore the decimal value and round down (in this example to 66%).

RGB integer: This defines red, green, and blue on a scale of 0 to 255, much like common graphics programs, such as Adobe Photoshop. Like RGB percentage, separate values with a comma, and surround them with an **rgb()** container as follows:

rgb (171,210,64)

For example, in RGB integer, black is **rgb(0,0,0)**, and white is **rgb(255,255,255)**.

Long hexadecimal: This defines red, green, and blue on a scale of 00 to FF, which is the hexadecimal equivalent of 255 in decimal counting. When using long hexadecimal, each color level is represented by a two-digit pair, and the whole set of digits is preceded by a number sign (#—also sometimes called an octothorpe), as follows:

#ABD240

For example, in long hexadecimal, black is **#000000**, and white is **#FFFFFF**. This type is mathematically the same as the RGB integer type.

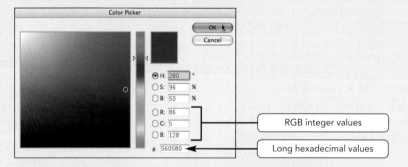

Note: Most common graphics programs, such as Photoshop and Adobe Illustrator, automatically display a long hexadecimal value with an RGB integer value when you're choosing colors. The illustration shown here presents the Color Picker dialog box in Photoshop. You can see it displays the RGB integer values as well as the associated long hexadecimal value. (It doesn't matter whether you use lowercase or uppercase letters when defining hexadecimal colors in CSS.)

continues on next page

TIP:

Understanding Color Values *continued*

Short hexadecimal: This is a specialized variation of long hexadecimal that uses only three digits, each of which is duplicated. In short hexadecimal, black is shortened from **#000000** to **#000**, and white is shortened from **#FFFFFF** to **#FFF**. Other equivalents are **#FF9900** and **#F90**, **#008800** and **#080**, and **#CC7722** and **#C72**.

Named colors: This is a set of words corresponding to specific colors. Commonly used names include **black, white, blue, purple**, and **red**. It doesn't get much simpler than **h1 {color: red;}**, for example. The CSS 2.1 specification defines specific color values for each of 17 basic names. Most browsers recognize a much longer list of about 140 keywords, but these will not necessarily be identical from browser to browser.

Working with Style Sheets

So, you've edited a few style sheets and seen the impact that rules, selectors, declarations, and declaration blocks have on the styling of XHTML content. The real question is, how do style sheets get associated with the XHTML in the first place?

Styles are linked to the XHTML document through the selectors, but how do the documents know that the style sheets are meant to be applied to them? And how many ways are there to associate style sheets with a document?

CSS offers three types of style sheets to style your documents, some more efficient than others. Knowing the difference between them is important so you can decide which one is best for your projects. The following sections outline the different types of style sheets.

Using embedded style sheets

Embedded style sheets are an internal part of the XHTML document. All the styles are written in a **style** element that's placed inside the **head** element of the document, and those styles affect only the XHTML page in which they have been embedded. Embedded style sheets are useful if you want to apply a style sheet to a single page because you just put the style sheet in that page. The style sheets you saw previously in this chapter were all embedded style sheets.

Using external style sheets

External style sheets, also referred to as **linked** style sheets, are the most powerful type of style sheet because you can use a single style sheet to format hundreds, thousands, even millions of pages. If you make a change to the external style sheet, all the pages that link to the style sheet are instantly updated to reflect the new styles. The contents of an external style sheet are not part of the HTML page. Instead, they are stored in a separate CSS file. The CSS file simply lists styles with no other XHTML code. Instead of embedding the code in the XHTML document, you create a link to the external CSS file. You can also import the contents of a style sheet, to much the same effect. The advantages of importing versus linking are discussed in Exercises 5 & 6 in this chapter.

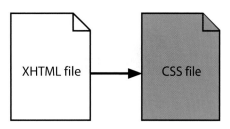

Using inline styles

Inline styles are vaguely similar to embedded style sheets, in the sense that they are part of the XHTML document, which is why I'm mentioning them here. However, they are written as an attribute of the element you want to style. Here's an example:

```
<p style="background: red;">
This paragraph has a red background that results from an inline style. No other paragraphs (or any
other elements) will be affected by the inline style.
</p>
```

Inline styles are much less powerful than embedded and external style sheets, because if you ever want to change the style, you have to do it in every place the inline style appears in your document. That rather soundly defeats the purpose of using CSS in the first place—you may as well be using **font** tags!

4 | Embedding a Style Sheet

Embedded style sheets live inside XHTML documents. In this exercise, you will add an embedded style sheet to an XHTML document.

1 In a browser, open **ex0204.html** from the **02_xhtml** folder you copied to your desktop, as shown in the illustration here.

When you open the file in a browser, you'll see no formatting—just plain text, the Javaco tea logo, and a small photo. Right now, this XHTML file doesn't have a style sheet associated with it, so it looks plain and not at all designed. By the end of the exercise, you'll have corrected this.

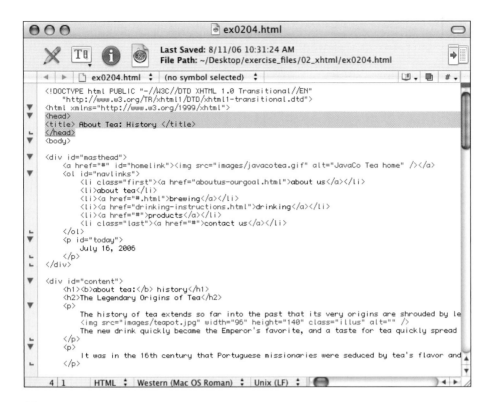

2 Open **ex0204.html** with your text or HTML editor. Near the beginning of the file, find the following block of code:

```
<head>
<title> About Tea: History </title>
</head>
```

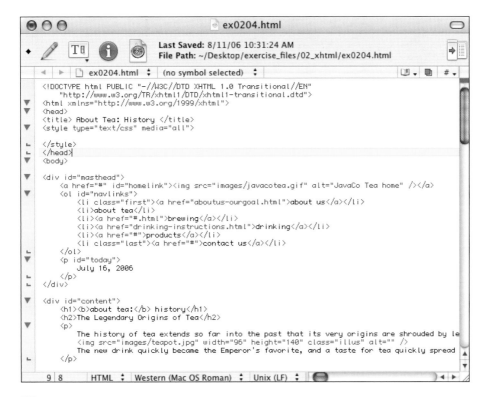

```
<!DOCTYPE html PUBLIC "-//W3C//DTD XHTML 1.0 Transitional//EN"
    "http://www.w3.org/TR/xhtml1/DTD/xhtml1-transitional.dtd">
<html xmlns="http://www.w3.org/1999/xhtml">
<head>
<title> About Tea: History </title>
<style type="text/css" media="all">

</style>
</head>
<body>

<div id="masthead">
    <a href="#" id="homelink"><img src="images/javacotea.gif" alt="JavaCo Tea home" /></a>
    <ol id="navlinks">
        <li class="first"><a href="aboutus-ourgoal.html">about us</a></li>
        <li>about tea</li>
        <li><a href="#.html">brewing</a></li>
        <li><a href="drinking-instructions.html">drinking</a></li>
        <li><a href="#">products</a></li>
        <li class="last"><a href="#">contact us</a></li>
    </ol>
    <p id="today">
        July 16, 2006
    </p>
</div>

<div id="content">
    <h1><b>about tea:</b> history</h1>
    <h2>The Legendary Origins of Tea</h2>
    <p>
        The history of tea extends so far into the past that its very origins are shrouded by le
        <img src="images/teapot.jpg" width="96" height="140" class="illus" alt="" />
        The new drink quickly became the Emperor's favorite, and a taste for tea quickly spread
    </p>
```

3 Edit the block as follows:

```
<head>
<title> About Tea: History </title>
<style type="text/css" media="all">
</style>
</head>
```

Don't get excited just yet. You haven't actually embedded the style sheet. What you've done is create a container for the style sheet.

Here is an overview of the code you added: First, the **style** element creates the container where the style sheet lives. Second, the **type** attribute defines *what* you're putting in the **style** element. When you're putting a CSS style sheet in a **style** element, you must define the **type** attribute as **text/css**. Finally, the **media** attribute determines when to apply the style sheet based on what media, such as a browser, printer, mobile device, and so on, is being used to view the page. For example, **screen** applies the style sheet only when the page is viewed in a browser (but not when printed). **print** applies the style sheet when the page is printed (but not when it is displayed in a browser). **all**, which you specified in this step, uses the same style sheet regardless of the media used to view the page.

Note: You'll learn more about media-specific styling in Chapter 9, "Styling for Print."

You should always place **style** elements in the **head** element as you've done in this step. Some browsers allow you to put them anywhere in the document, but I strongly discourage you from doing so because you don't know whether future browsers will start to ignore embedded style sheets found outside the **head** element (or, worse still, display them as if they were ordinary text).

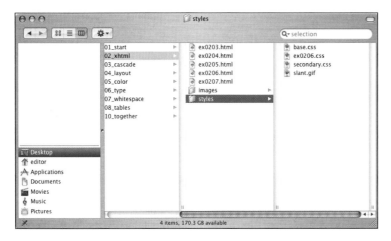

4 Open the **styles** folder from the **02_xhtml** folder you copied to your desktop, as shown in the illustration here.

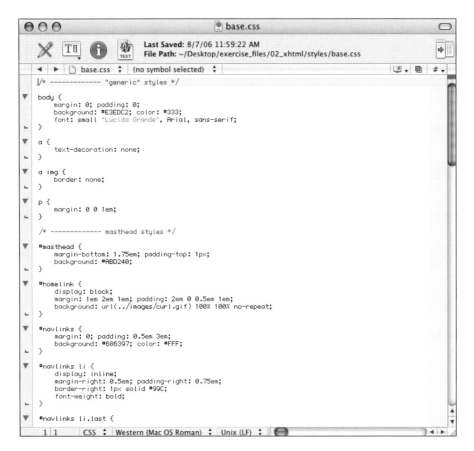

5 Open **base.css** with your text or HTML editor.

6 Select all the contents of **base.css**, and choose **Edit > Copy**.

You should now have a copy of the entire contents of base.css on your computer's Clipboard.

Tip: To select the contents of the file, you can click and drag over the contents of the document. Or (in most editors), you can use a Select All command, which is usually accomplished by pressing Cmd+A (Mac) or Ctrl+A (Windows); alternatively, you should be able to find it in the Edit menu of your text or HTML editor. If it isn't there and you can't find it anywhere, it's time to think about finding a better text or HTML editor!

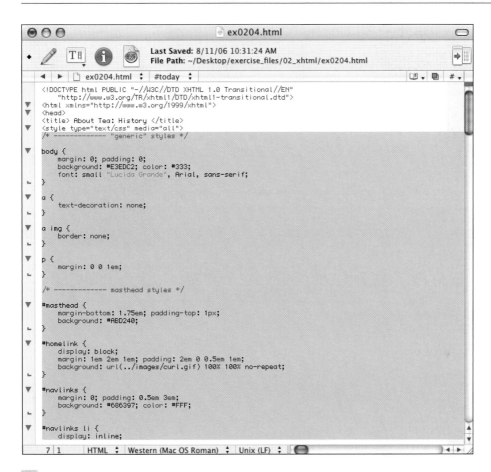

7 Return to **ex0204.html**. Place your cursor on the blank line between `<style type="text/css" media="all">` and `</style>`, and choose **Edit > Paste** to paste the copied style sheet.

Now an entire style sheet—everything you copied in Step 7—should be residing in ex0204.html. One might even say it's been "embedded" within the document. This is exactly how embedded style sheets get their name—they reside in the HTML document.

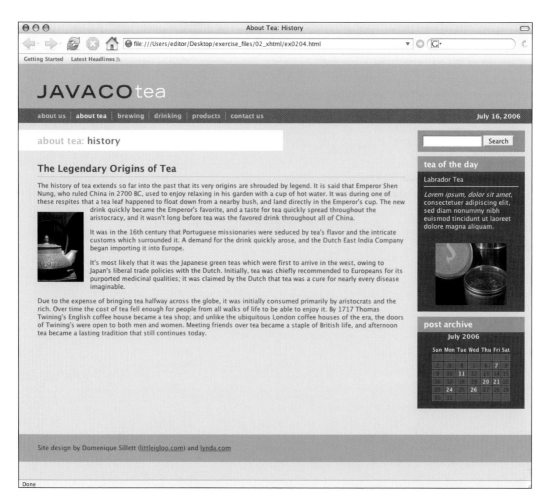

8 Save and close **ex0204.html**, switch to your browser, and reload **ex0204.html**.

The unstyled page is now magically styled. Congratulations, you've just created your first embedded style sheet!

Now, what if you have multiple pages in your Web site, not just one? (The chances are pretty good you'll have multiple pages!) Well, you'd have to repeat this process for every page. This is the limitation of embedded style sheets and the reason developers rarely use them in the real world. As a result, you should shy away from them. What's the alternative? External style sheets are the answer. You'll learn all about them in the next few exercises.

NOTE:

Embedding Multiple Style Sheets

In case you were wondering, it is possible to embed multiple style sheets in a single document. Why would you ever want to do this? The usual example is that one would be for screens and another would be for print. In that case, you create a **head** structure as follows:

```
<style type="text/css" media="screen">
  [...style sheet here...]
</style>
<style type="text/css" media="print">
  [...style sheet here...]
</style>
```

As the previous exercise illustrated, it's possible to embed an entire style sheet in an XHTML document. Even better, though, is the ability to have a style sheet live in a separate file and be associated with the XHTML document. This is what's known as an **external style sheet**, because it's completely external to the XHTML document.

There are two ways to associate an external style sheet with an XHTML document—importing and linking. You'll learn both techniques in the next few exercises.

5 | Importing an External Style Sheet

In this exercise, you will import an external style sheet by means of an embedded style sheet. The result will be a fully styled page.

1 In a browser, open **ex0205.html** from the **02_xhtml** folder you copied to your desktop, as shown in the illustration here.

Just as in the previous exercise, when you open the file in a browser, you'll see no formatting—just plain text, the Javaco tea logo, and a small photo. This XHTML file doesn't have a style sheet associated with it. You'll fix that in this exercise by importing an external style sheet.

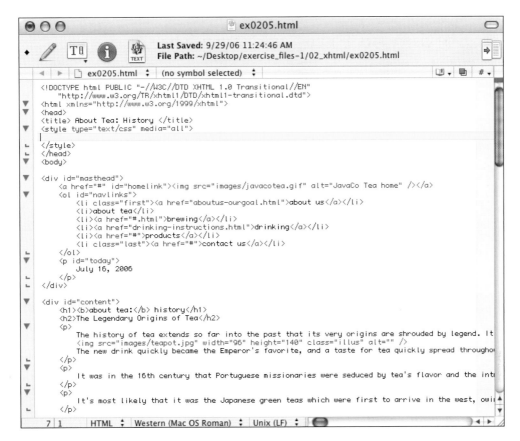

2 Open **ex0205.html** with your text or HTML editor. Near the beginning of the file, find the following block of code:

```
<head>
<title> About Tea: History </title>
<style type="text/css" media="all">
</style>
</head>
```

So far, it's just an ordinary **style** element, but this is where you will import the style sheet.

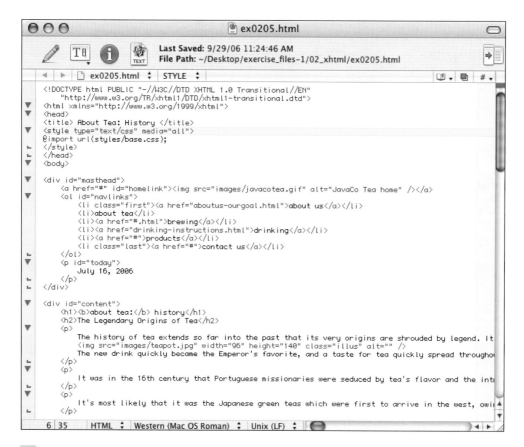

3 Edit the block as follows:

```
<head>
<title> About Tea: History </title>
<style type="text/css" media="all">
@import url(styles/base.css);
</style>
</head>
```

Now your embedded style sheet has only one line of content, but this causes an entire external style sheet to be loaded and applied to the document.

In this step, you set the `@import` directive to reference an external file, base.css. This is not a selector-value pair but, instead, a way to say "import this external file and apply it to the XHTML document in which this style sheet is embedded." In a way, it's very similar to what you did in Exercise 4, when you copied base.css and pasted it into the embedded style sheet. Certainly the result is the same. The difference here is that instead of having to manually copy and paste, you make the browser do it for you. The other benefit of importing over embedding is that if you have multiple pages referencing base.css, changing base.css will instantly change all those pages. With embedding, you would have to open and manually update each page.

The **url (…)** format indicates the value inside the parentheses is a URL (**U**niform **R**esource **L**ocator) reference, just like the value of an image's **src** attribute. In this case, the reference is to a file called base.css, which is in a directory called styles, where that directory is in the same directory as the XHTML document. This is what's called a **relative URL**, because it's relative to the document in which it appears. You can also use **absolute URLs**, such as **http://example.com/styles/base.css** (assuming that's where your style sheet lives, of course!).

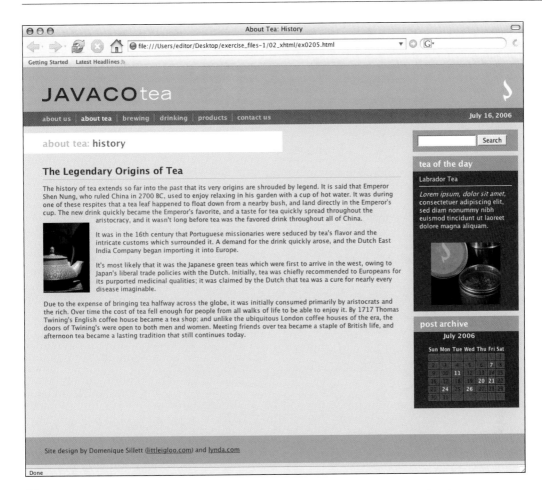

4 Save and close **ex0205.html**, switch to your browser, and reload **ex0205.html**.

Thanks to the changes you made, everything is styled. Congratulations, you've just imported your first external style sheet!

So, are you limited to only one imported style sheet? Not at all. As you'll see in the next exercise, it's possible to have a number of imported style sheets and add regular rules to the same embedded style sheet containing the imports. You might add those rules after your imports in case you have a couple of page-specific rules that add to or override the rules you're importing.

6 | Importing Multiple Style Sheets

In this exercise, you will import multiple style sheets into an XHTML document. In addition, you will see how you must place regular rules with respect to the imports.

1 In a browser, open **ex0206.html** from the **02_xhtml** folder you copied to your desktop, as shown in the illustration here.

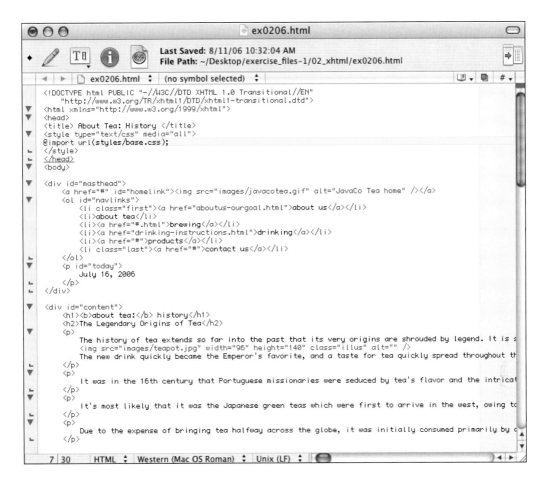

```
<!DOCTYPE html PUBLIC "-//W3C//DTD XHTML 1.0 Transitional//EN"
    "http://www.w3.org/TR/xhtml1/DTD/xhtml1-transitional.dtd">
<html xmlns="http://www.w3.org/1999/xhtml">
<head>
<title> About Tea: History </title>
<style type="text/css" media="all">
@import url(styles/base.css);
</style>
</head>
<body>

<div id="masthead">
    <a href="#" id="homelink"><img src="images/javacotea.gif" alt="JavaCo Tea home" /></a>
    <ol id="navlinks">
        <li class="first"><a href="aboutus-ourgoal.html">about us</a></li>
        <li>about tea</li>
        <li><a href="#.html">brewing</a></li>
        <li><a href="drinking-instructions.html">drinking</a></li>
        <li><a href="#">products</a></li>
        <li class="last"><a href="#">contact us</a></li>
    </ol>
    <p id="today">
        July 16, 2006
    </p>
</div>

<div id="content">
    <h1><b>about tea:</b> history</h1>
    <h2>The Legendary Origins of Tea</h2>
    <p>
        The history of tea extends so far into the past that its very origins are shrouded by legend. It is s
        <img src="images/teapot.jpg" width="96" height="140" class="illus" alt="" />
        The new drink quickly became the Emperor's favorite, and a taste for tea quickly spread throughout th
    </p>
    <p>
        It was in the 16th century that Portuguese missionaries were seduced by tea's flavor and the intrica
    </p>
    <p>
        It's most likely that it was the Japanese green teas which were first to arrive in the west, owing to
    </p>
    <p>
        Due to the expense of bringing tea halfway across the globe, it was initially consumed primarily by c
    </p>
```

2 Open **ex0206.html** with your text or HTML editor. Near the beginning of the file, find the following block of code:

```
<head>
<title> About Tea: History </title>
<style type="text/css" media="all">
@import url(styles/base.css);
</style>
</head>
```

3 Edit the block as follows:

```
<head>
<title> About Tea: History </title>
<style type="text/css" media="all">
@import url(styles/base.css);
@import url(styles/secondary.css);
</style>
</head>
```

Now you have two style sheets being imported. The first, base.css, is quite long, as you saw in a previous exercise. The second, secondary.css, has only two rules:

```
body {
  background: #E3EDC2 url(slant.gif) center repeat;
}
#sidebar div {
  background: #6B7549;
}
```

The first rule adds a graphic to the background of the page. The second alters the boxes in the page's sidebar to have an olive green background.

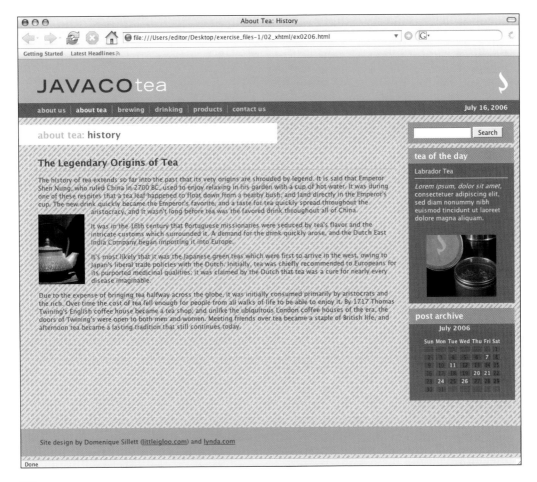

4 Save **ex0206.html**, switch to your browser, and reload **ex0206.html**.

Note the changes to the page background and to the color of the boxes in the sidebar (from dark gray to dark olive green). These changes came about because of the second imported style sheet. The two imported style sheets are effectively combined into one large style sheet, and the result of that combination is what you see onscreen. (You'll see the details of how style sheets combine in Chapter 3, *"Selectors and the Cascade."*)

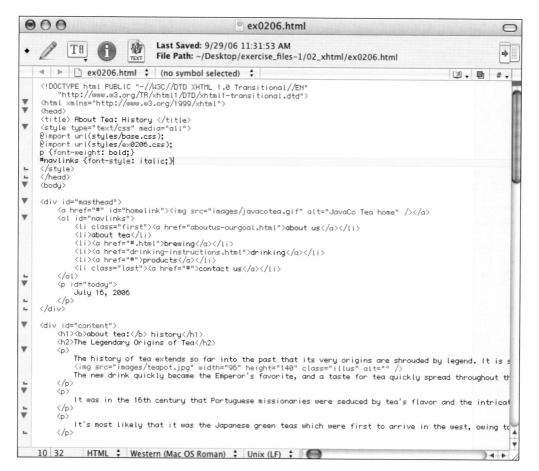

5 Return to your text or HMTL editor. Edit the style sheet as follows:

```
@import url(styles/base.css);
@import url(styles/ex0206.css);
p {font-weight: bold;}
#navlinks {font-style: italic;}
```

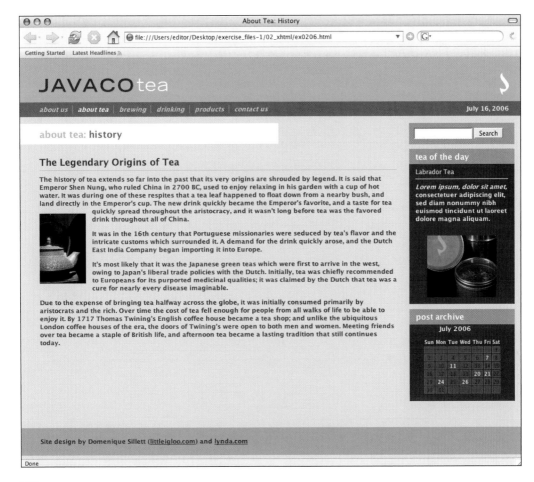

6 Save and close **ex0206.html**, switch to your browser, and reload **ex0206.html**.

Now you've added some rules to the embedded style sheet, and they combine with the imported styles the same way as the two imported styles combined in Step 5. Just because this style sheet contains imports doesn't make it any more or less of a style sheet, so adding normal rules is fine. Keep in mind, any rules you add (such as the ones you added in this exercise) *must* come after any imports—the first code in any style sheet has to be the import directives.

Although they relied on an embedded style sheet to operate, the style sheets you imported in this exercise were certainly a lot easier to deal with than embedding base.css in the XHTML document, as you did in Exercise 4. Importing an external style sheet keeps all the styles in one file and all the markup in another, which makes maintaining both much easier.

Importing style sheets is just one way you can work with external style sheets. Next, you'll learn how to link to external style sheets.

Restricting Imported Style Sheets for Specific Media

In theory, you can restrict imported style sheets to specific media. For example, you could write the following:

```
@import url(styles/base.css) screen, print;
@import url(styles/ex0206.css) screen;
```

As a result, **base.css** would apply when viewing the page onscreen and when printed, and **ex0206.css** would apply only when viewing onscreen. The only flaw in this is a complete lack of support for media descriptors in Internet Explorer for Windows, prior to and including Internet Explorer 6.

7 | Linking to an External Style Sheet

In this exercise, you will use a specialized XHTML element to link an XHTML document and an external style sheet.

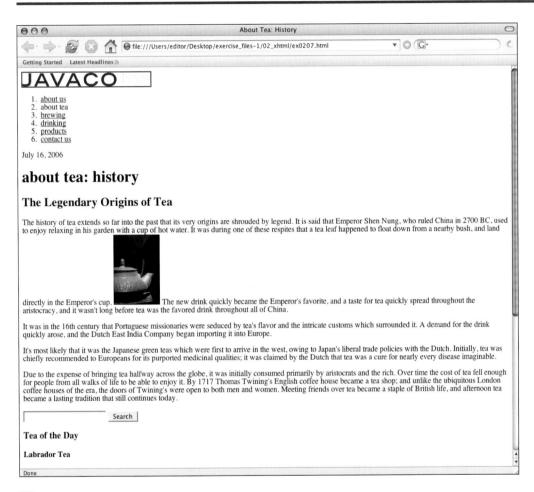

1 In a browser, open **ex0207.html** from the **02_xhtml** folder you copied to your desktop, as shown in the illustration here.

As in the previous exercise, when you open the file in a browser, you'll see no formatting—just plain text, the Javaco tea logo, and a small photo. As in the previous exercise, this XHTML file doesn't have a style sheet associated with it. You'll fix that in this exercise by linking to an external style sheet.

2 Open **ex0207.html** with your text or HTML editor. Near the beginning of the file, find the following block of code:

```
<head>
<title> About Tea: History </title>
</head>
```

```
000                           ex0207.html
```

Last Saved: 8/11/06 10:31:56 AM
File Path: ~/Desktop/exercise_files-1/02_xhtml/ex0207.html

ex0207.html   (no symbol selected)

```
<!DOCTYPE html PUBLIC "-//W3C//DTD XHTML 1.0 Transitional//EN"
    "http://www.w3.org/TR/xhtml1/DTD/xhtml1-transitional.dtd">
<html xmlns="http://www.w3.org/1999/xhtml">
<head>
<title> About Tea: History </title>
<link rel="stylesheet" type="text/css" href="styles/base.css" media="all" />
</head>
<body>

<div id="masthead">
    <a href="#" id="homelink"><img src="images/javacotea.gif" alt="JavaCo Tea home" /></a>
    <ol id="navlinks">
        <li class="first"><a href="aboutus-ourgoal.html">about us</a></li>
        <li>about tea</li>
        <li><a href="#.html">brewing</a></li>
        <li><a href="drinking-instructions.html">drinking</a></li>
        <li><a href="#">products</a></li>
        <li class="last"><a href="#">contact us</a></li>
    </ol>
    <p id="today">
        July 16, 2006
    </p>
</div>

<div id="content">
    <h1><b>about tea:</b> history</h1>
    <h2>The Legendary Origins of Tea</h2>
    <p>
        The history of tea extends so far into the past that its very origins are shrouded by leger
        <img src="images/teapot.jpg" width="96" height="140" class="illus" alt="" />
        The new drink quickly became the Emperor's favorite, and a taste for tea quickly spread thr
    </p>
    <p>
        It was in the 16th century that Portuguese missionaries were seduced by tea's flavor and th
    </p>
    <p>
        It's most likely that it was the Japanese green teas which were first to arrive in the wes\
    </p>
    <p>
        Due to the expense of bringing tea halfway across the globe, it was initially consumed prin
    </p>
</div>

<div id="sidebar">
```

6 1   HTML   Western (Mac OS Roman)   Unix (LF)

3 Edit the block as follows:

```
<head>
<title> About Tea: History </title>
<link rel="stylesheet" type="text/css" href="styles/base.css" media="all" />
</head>
```

Before you continue to the next step, look at the code required to link an external style sheet and compare that to what you saw in the previous exercise. Notice two of the attributes and values, **type="text/css"** and **media="all"**, are the same as they were when you embedded a style sheet in Exercise 4. Notice the **href** attribute is similar to the **url()** attribute you created for an imported style sheet in Exercises 5 and 6— its value provides the location of the external style sheet.

The newcomer here is **rel**, with its value of **stylesheet**. The **rel** attribute defines the relationship of the targeted file to the current file. The attribute-value combination **rel="stylesheet"** says "the file at which this **link** element is pointing (base.css) is a style sheet for the document in which this **link** element sits (ex0207.html)."

As with embedded style sheets, you must place **link** elements within the **head** element. If you put them elsewhere, you're just asking for trouble.

Note: Spaces have special meaning in XHTML. When you type **stylesheet** as the **rel** attribute, make sure it is all one word; do not put a space between the words *style* and *sheet*, or it will not work as shown.

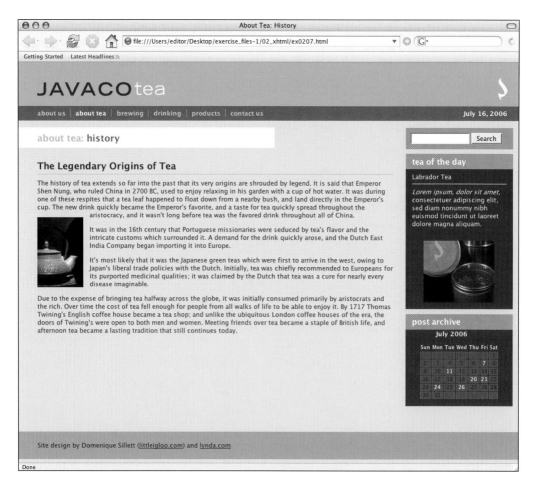

4 Save **ex0207.html**, switch to your browser, and reload **ex0207.html**.

As you no doubt expected, it's all styled. You should be pleased—you've just created your first link between an XHTML document and an external style sheet. Next, you'll link a second external style sheet.

5 Return to your text or HTML editor. Add the following line below the **link** element you added in Step 4:

```
<link rel="stylesheet" type="text/css" href="styles/secondary.css" media="all" />
```

Now you have ex0207.html linking to two style sheets, both of which are applied to the document. This is just like when you imported two style sheets into the document in Exercise 6, only here you're linking to two style sheets. Though the mechanism differs, the styling result is the same.

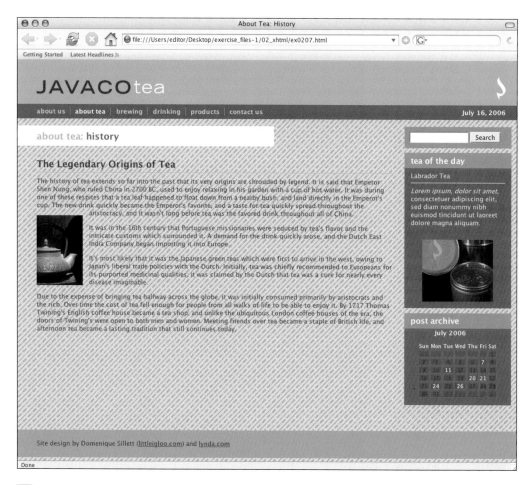

6 Save and close **ex0207.html**, switch to your browser, and reload **ex0207.html**.

Visually, you've hit the same ending point as in Step 6 of Exercise 6. If you want to add boldfacing to paragraphs and italicize the navigation links, you'd need to either link to another style sheet with those rules or embed a style sheet with those rules.

So, why can you use either linking or importing? It's a difference of languages. The link element is a feature of XHTML and can (in theory) be used for a good deal more than just linking style sheets to pages. The @import directive is a feature of CSS and allows style sheets to import other style sheets. Wait—style sheets can import other style sheets? Why? Don't fret, you'll learn more in the next section.

NOTE: **Linking Versus Importing**

One difference between linking and importing is that you can link only from an XHTML document, whereas any style sheet can have one or more `@import` directives. There are a few other differences also worth mentioning.

First, not all browsers cache imported style sheets. This is particularly true of Internet Explorer for Windows, which at least a few of your site's visitors will be using. If you have a lot of style sheets and are importing them all, you may be forcing more downloads for your users.

Second, it's easy to script `link` elements; it's much, much harder to script imports. If you're working on a site where you will add scripting actions to switch style sheets on or off, it's best to link your style sheets.

Finally, you can define sets of style sheets, and even alternate style sheets, but only if you link them. The result is that the site can have different themes or skins. Developers rarely do this, largely because only a few browsers (the most famous being Firefox) can natively handle alternate style sheets, and almost nobody knows where to find the alternate style features. You can simulate this capability in script-based ways for other browsers, but again, developers rarely do this. Over time, it has become fairly clear that the vast majority of users will ignore a site's theme feature, and of those who do play with it, the vast majority will ignore it after the first time they play with it.

Managing Style Sheets

The previous exercises may have already convinced you of this, but it's worth saying anyway—one of the primary advantages of CSS is the use of external style sheets. If you have a Web site with ten, a hundred, a thousand, or even a *million* pages, you can style the whole site with a single, external style sheet. Similarly, you can manage the presentation of an entire site with a small collection of style sheets.

A natural question to ask is, which is best? Should you just have one style sheet or a few? If you have a few, how should you organize them? How many style sheets are too many?

In the end, these questions don't have simple, universal answers. The right answer depends on the site and almost as much on you, the author of the CSS. The next few sections discuss different approaches in the hopes of teaching you how to answer these questions for yourself and for your site.

Creating one style sheet, using it for many pages

The simplest way to organize your CSS is to create a single, external style sheet that every page on the site uses (either by linking or by importing) using the techniques you learned in this chapter.

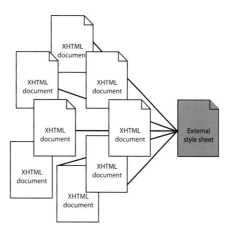

The obvious advantage is that you can implement a change to the site's appearance—a different font, a new set of colors, even changes to the layout—by editing this one style sheet. From the user's perspective, the first time they visit a page on your site, the style sheet is downloaded and cached (stored locally), the same way images are cached. So for them, the site seems faster because they don't have to download a different style sheet when they visit other pages on your site. If you inserted an embedded style sheet into every page, then it would add to the size of every page. Effectively, users would have to download it every time.

Although a single style sheet for an entire Web site may seem like the obvious answer, some drawbacks can start to emerge over time. Most seriously, it can be difficult to maintain more than one page layout from a single style sheet. It isn't impossible, and if you're going to have only two or three different page layouts—say, one layout for the home page, one for inner pages, and a special one for a sign-up form—then the maintenance isn't too difficult. However, for more complex sites, where you have many pages with many different layouts, the complications start to add up quickly. The more complex the site's layout (and the more types of page layouts it allows), the larger a single style sheet will become. If allowed to expand a bit here and a bit there, you can end up with a style sheet weighing in at thousands of lines of text and 50 KB or more, which is hard to manage and can put a lot of strain on your server's bandwidth, as that .css file is downloaded by every user. Anytime you see a style sheet this size (or bigger), you should look at ways to make the file smaller by simplifying the CSS or by moving some of the content to another style sheet. It isn't always possible to make a large style sheet smaller, but it is *nearly* always possible.

I don't want to give you the wrong impression—people can and do run entire Web sites with one CSS file, and some of the sites are fairly complex. When you're starting out, it's likely the best approach to take, because that way you have only one CSS file to worry about. Just keep in mind that as your CSS skills and Web site expand, you may want to use more than one style sheet. You'll learn techniques for managing multiple style sheets in the following sections.

Using sectional styles

Closely related to the "one-style-sheet-for-everything" approach is the idea of having one basic style sheet that acts as the site's default style sheet and having section-specific style sheets for the various areas of the site. With this approach, each section's style sheet overrides whatever parts of the basic style sheet need to be altered and adds anything new that is specific to the section.

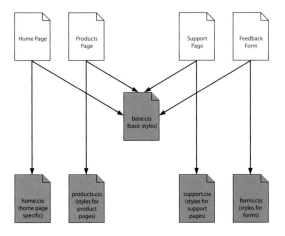

The classic example of this approach is to have a single basic style sheet and then have color-changing style sheets for each of the site's sections. That way, the Products area can be in reds and oranges, Support can be in blues and grays, and so on.

The advantage is that you can control a whole Web site from a central point while still being able to vary the look of various parts of the site. The only real disadvantage is that if you ever change your XHTML markup, you'll have to coordinate CSS changes across multiple files, but that's a relatively small drawback. Usually major markup changes accompany redesigns, in which case you're usually starting over with the CSS anyway.

Using modularized styles

The concept of using multiple style sheets gets a different spin when you use what are sometimes called **modular style sheets**. In this case, instead of breaking up styles based on the areas of the site, you instead break them up by areas of the design.

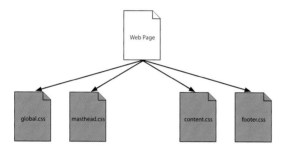

For example, as shown in the illustration here, one style sheet would handle all the "global" styles, such as headings, paragraphs, link colors, and so forth. A second style sheet would handle the masthead, a third style sheet would handle the presentation of the main page content, and a fourth style sheet would handle the footer styles.

The advantage is that when you update an area of the layout, you can load the style sheet that affects just that area, which allows you to concentrate more fully on the styles in question.

A downside is that this approach can prove unwieldy, especially if you have several modules to style. If you were to link to all the style sheets necessary on every page, you could have five or six **link** elements in each page. While it's certainly more efficient than embedding all those styles, it's still kind of clumsy.

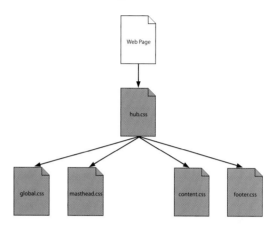

One way to avoid this is to collect all the style modules you know will apply to every page, such as the masthead, main content, and footer, and import them all from a linked style sheet, as shown in the illustration here. This reduces the number of **link** elements in your pages, and when and if you decide to add modules, you can simply add another **@import** declaration to the linked style sheet.

Since **@import** is a CSS feature, it can appear in any style sheet, whether embedded or external. You can't use a **link** element in an external style sheet because it would involve placing XHTML in a CSS file—something every browser will simply ignore or, worse, cause some or all of the external style sheet to be ignored.

A variation on this approach is to use imports to chain external style sheets together and link only to the last style sheet in the chain. This is a little more complicated and isn't suited to every site, but it can be quite powerful.

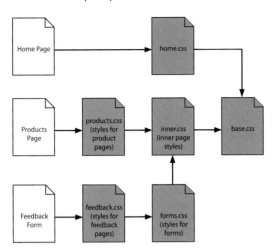

For example, a feedback form might link to a style sheet called **feedback.css**. At the top of **feedback.css** would be an import declaration importing **forms.css**. In turn, **forms.css** would import **inner.css** (for any inner pages, those behind the homepage), which would import **base.css** (the basic style sheet for the whole site). In the meantime, the homepage of the site would link to **home.css**, which would import **base.css**.

This approach requires any given page to have only one `link` element. It also requires knowing what style sheets exist and how they chain together; thus, the organizational challenges are a bit greater.

Understanding why external style sheets rock

As you can see, when you work with external style sheets, you have many choices for how to manage the style sheets. You might ask, why bother when you could just embed all your style sheets and then know exactly what you have on hand? Working with external style sheets is just more efficient. The obvious benefit is that you can edit once and update all pages, but you should consider other factors too, including bandwidth consumption and server load. Consider what happens when a user comes to the homepage of a CSS-driven site. The user's browser downloads the XHTML file and then downloads all the external file references—images, scripts (if any), and style sheets. All those external resources are stored on the user's hard drive in a cache (pronounced "cash," by the way).

Then the user clicks a link to another page on the same site. The browser dutifully downloads that XHTML file and then checks all the external files it references against the cache.

If the style sheet (or other external resources, for that matter) doesn't change for the entirety of the user's visit to the site, the user will have to download the style sheet only that one time. After that, the browser will ask the server whether it has been changed, and the server will say "no," so the style sheet won't be downloaded again.

The advantage over old-school HTML table design, where the presentation of every page was baked into the page structure, is significant. This is why embedding style sheets is generally discouraged—you'd be forcing the style sheet to be downloaded in its entirety for every page, which would make the user experience for your site rather slow and unpleasant. That's just not right!

Encountering High-Traffic Exceptions

Although everything I said in the previous section is true, it's also false for certain cases. It has been found that for incredibly high-traffic sites (and here I'm talking about the Yahoos and eBays of the world), external style sheets are a less efficient use of server resources than embedded style sheets. The reason is that all of those "has this changed?" questions drain more server resources than sending out larger files with embedded style sheets.

One could argue that the solution is to buy more servers, but you could just as easily argue that in these rare cases, the best thing to do is embed the style sheets. It makes each page bigger than it would be otherwise and forces more bandwidth consumption onto the users. On the other hand, it makes the site faster because the servers don't have to work as hard.

For more than 99 percent of all Web sites, it's more efficient to externalize style sheets. But if you ever find yourself in charge of a site that gets millions of page views per hour, remember this little sidebar, and check to see whether embedding would make more sense for you.

In this chapter, you learned some of the basic terms of CSS and how they relate to each other. You experimented with the various ways of associating a style sheet (or several style sheets) with an XHTML document, including embedding, linking, and importing. You saw a number of approaches to organizing external style sheets, as well as the benefits for working with external style sheets versus embedded style sheets.

What happens if the order of two style sheets is switched or if two rules try to set different values for the same property on a given element? What if one rule says a paragraph should be red and another says it should be blue? These are all excellent questions I'll answer in Chapter 3, *"Selectors and the Cascade."*

3

Selectors and the Cascade

In this chapter, I'll cover selectors in some detail. Understanding selectors is essential to writing good CSS (**C**ascading **S**tyle **S**heets). A selector offers the ability to apply a set of styles to all elements of the same type. For example, say you wanted to change the color of all your headers (not just one) from green to orange. You can accomplish this with a single line of CSS code. Imagine the alternative—going through the painstaking process of reviewing the markup and changing the color of each header element individually.

I'll start by introducing the different kinds of selectors before diving into each exercise. Then, I'll discuss how style conflict resolution works, how you can use the `!important` declaration to troubleshoot style conflicts, and how inheritance impacts your final document. These are important concepts, and I encourage you to study this chapter thoroughly and refer to it as necessary as you proceed through the rest of the book.

Understanding Selectors

Several kinds of selectors exist: element selectors and ID selectors are two of the most common.

Element selectors

An XHTML (e**X**tensible **HTML**) document consists of elements and the contents of those elements, so it makes sense you would at least be able to apply styles to those elements. An **element selector** is simply a selector that applies to a type of element. While working through Chapter 2, *"Understanding CSS,"* you worked with a number of element selectors.

For example, suppose you wanted to style all paragraphs consistently. The rule to do that would look like this:

```
p {font-family: Arial, Verdana, sans-serif;}
```

The selector **p** just means "apply the declarations in this rule to any **p** element." Whether the document has one **p** element or one thousand, every one of them will be matched by the element selector **p**. If the document doesn't have any **p** elements, then the selector won't match any elements, and the declarations won't be applied to anything.

Another example would be if you wanted to draw a 3-pixel red border around the outside of all your tables. Again, you would use an element selector:

```
table {border: 3px solid red;}
```

Because they are so basic, element selectors are sometimes referred to as "simple" selectors. This distinguishes them from the more complex selectors you'll see in the next several sections of this chapter.

ID selectors

Before discussing how to write an ID selector, it's important to quickly cover what exactly an ID selector matches. XHTML allows any element (except for the **html** element) to be given an **id** attribute, such as this:

```
<div id="example">Here's an example.</div>
```

The value of an element's **id** attribute, which is usually referred to as the element's **ID**, is what's matched by an ID selector. To match the previous bit of markup, you would write this selector:

```
#example
```

Simple enough. It's just the ID value you want to match preceded by an octothorpe (#), with no space between the two.

Technically, **#example** means "any element whose **id** attribute has the value **example**." Thus, the selector would still match the previous markup even if you changed the **div** to a **p**, an **h1**, or anything else. As long as the ID remained, the match would still occur.

If you have a situation where you want to restrict the selector to match only a certain type of element with the ID, then you add the element name before the octothorpe. For example:

```
div#example
```

NOTE:

Octo-what?

Yes, the # symbol is really called an **octothorpe**. Other common names are the number sign, the pound sign (but the British find this confusing and annoying), the hash symbol (which can confuse the DEA), and the tic-tac-toe symbol (which makes a great deal of sense but isn't easy to type more than once or twice).

In case you're curious, the word *octothorpe* is derived from *octo*, meaning "eight" in Latin and referring to the eight points that stick out (two on each side), and from *thorpe* in honor of the famous early 20th-century athlete Jim Thorpe. No kidding!

This now means "any `div` element whose `id` attribute has the value `example`." If the ID value appears on a different element type, then the selector won't match it.

The most important fact to know about IDs in XHTML is this: In any given XHTML document, every ID value *must* be unique. In other words, if you have an element in your document with an ID of `example`, then no other element anywhere else in that document can have an ID of `example`.

For this reason, IDs are usually employed to label sections of a page layout. Here's an example document skeleton showing how you can use IDs in this way:

```
<div id="masthead">…</div>
<div id="main">
   <div id="content">…</div>
   <div id="sidebar">…</div>
</div>
<div id="footer">…</div>
```

Because each area of a layout is going to be unique—most pages don't have more than one footer, after all—IDs are well suited to this kind of labeling.

Think of an ID like your Social Security number (or the local equivalent). It's unique to you, and any information pertaining to that number pertains only to you. Thus, if your number is 123-456-7890 and the government announces that the next leader of the free world will be the person with the number 123-456-7890, that's just like an ID selection. Only one person gets the leadership, just like the unique ID gets the style.

Class selectors

Like IDs, you can use classes to "label" elements in a document. Classes are different from IDs in two ways. The primary is that you must add a class to an element via the `class` attribute, like this:

```
<li class="first urgent"><a href="
aboutus-ourgoal.html>about us</a></li>
```

Words appearing in an element's `class` attribute are usually referred to simply as the element's **class**. As you can see in this example, you can actually have multiple words in an element's `class` attributes and address them separately in the style sheet. These words are what are matched by class selectors. To match the previous bit of markup, you would write this selector:

```
.first
```

It's just the class value you want to match preceded by a period (.), with no space between the two.

Technically, **.first** means "any element whose **class** attribute contains the word **first** in its value." The actual element type doesn't matter in this case. If you wanted to restrict the match to just **p** elements with a class of **first**, then you'd write this:

```
p.first
```

VIDEO: **id_selectors.mov**

To learn more about ID selectors, check out **id_selectors.mov** in the **videos** folder on the **CSS HOT CD-ROM**.

TIP: **Maintaining ID Uniqueness**

Although it's clear that having repeated IDs within a document is not permitted, most browsers will let you get away with it. Despite this, you should never repeat IDs within a document. It's a bad habit and one that browsers might one day punish. It's also unnecessary, since you can have multiple elements share a common "label" in another way, as you'll see later in the chapter.

Then add your rules. You could add another class selector, **.urgent**, and add a different set of rules. It doesn't matter in which order you list them. (The order styles are in can matter, but I will discuss this later in this chapter.) This isn't a common need—sometimes called **multiclassing** in a document—but it can come in handy. A classic example is when you're creating a portal page, and you have form fields wrapped in a **div** and each **div** has its own class. For all the boxes that require user input, such as a box to enter a ZIP code to find the local weather forecast, you could have a class of **user allowed**, which would allow you to style these particular form fields differently. That's a situation where multiclassing would come in handy.

Let's spend some time discussing a few best practices when it comes to class selectors. It can be tempting to "overclass" on the off chance you may need them someday. In the following example, these list items contain links and navigations links, all the list items contain classes of **nav** links, and the **a** elements inside them also contain **class** links.

```
</style>
</head>
<body>

<div id="masthead">
    <a href="#" id="homelink"><img src="images/javacotea.gif" alt="JavaCo Tea home" /></a>
    <ol id="navlinks">
        <li class="navlink"><a class="navlink" href="aboutus-ourgoal.html">about us</a></li>
        <li class="navlink">about tea</li>
        <li class="navlink"><a class="navlink" href="#.html">brewing</a></li>
        <li class="navlink"><a class="navlink" href="drinking-instructions.html">drinking</a></li>
        <li class="navlink"><a class="navlink" href="#">products</a></li>
        <li class="navlink"><a class="navlink" href="#">contact us</a></li>
    </ol>
    <p id="today">
        July 16, 2006
    </p>
</div>
```

This is really inefficient. You don't need to have all this class linking. You could remove all this and just have the plain elements. How are you supposed to select those? That's coming up later in the chapter, but the short answer is that you use the primary ID on the element **<ol id ="navlinks">** that encloses all the other elements. It's an understandable urge to class everything, but it's an urge that needs to be

VIDEO: **class_selectors.mov**

To learn more about ID selectors, check out **class_selectors.mov** in the **videos** folder on the **CSS HOT CD-ROM**.

TIP: **Maintaining Case Consistency**

XHTML defines ID values to be case-sensitive; that is, the capitalization matters. Thus, the ID **Example** is different than **example**, and both are different from **EXAMPLE**. Most browsers do enforce this rule, so always make sure to keep your capitalization consistent. If your XHTML has **id="searchBox"**, then the CSS has to say **#searchBox**, not **#searchbox**.

restrained. You risk bloating your document, making it that much harder to maintain. As shown in the illustration here, it's much cleaner.

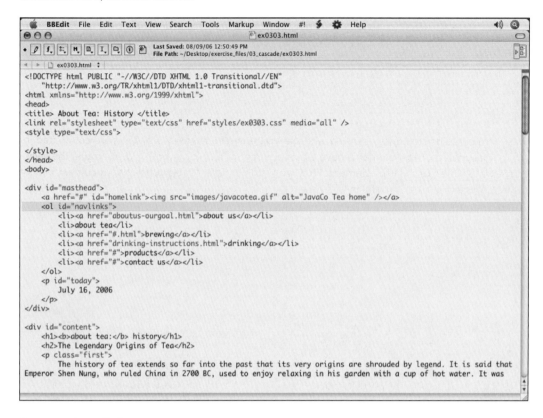

Descendant Selectors

In this section I'll discuss descendent selectors, but first I'll talk about document structure. I don't exactly mean the order in which you write your elements, but instead the structure that's created by those elements. For example, look at this very (very!) simple XHTML document:

```
<!DOCTYPE html PUBLIC "-//W3C//DTD XHTML 1.0 Transitional//EN"
  "http://www.w3.org/TR/xhtml1/DTD/xhtml1-transitional.dtd">
<html xmlns="http://www.w3.org/1999/xhtml">
<head>
  <title>Simple Document</title>
</head>
<body>
  <h1>Simple Document Title</h1>
  <p>Simple paragraph.</p>
  <ul>
    <li>Simple list item.</li>
    <li>Simple list item.</li>
    <li><em>Simple</em> list item.</li>
    <li>Simple list item.</li>
  </ul>
```

```
<div id="summary">
   <p>Simple paragraph.</p>
   <p>Simple <em>paragraph</em>.</p>
   <ul>
      <li><em>Simple</em> list item.</li>
      <li>Simple list item.</li>
   </ul>
</div>
</body>
</html>
```

Every document contains elements—starting with the **html** element. All these elements are connected in parent-child relationships. Most elements have either a parent or a child, or both. For example, the **body** and **head** are the children of the **html** element. Now, you could abstractly represent that document in a lot of ways, but the one that's most useful in CSS terms is a tree diagram.

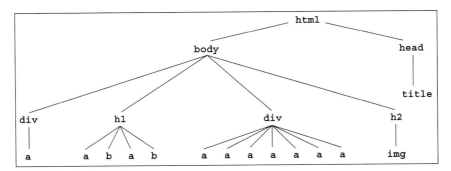

Hierarchical data structures in the computer science world are typically represented as a "tree"—it's the kind of tree that grows downward, more like a root system, but still a tree. The illustration shown here presents a tree view of an XHTML document. At the root of everything is the **html** element. Descending from that root are all the other elements of the document. To one side, you see the **head** and to the other, the **body**. Descending from the **body** are all the elements that eventually get drawn in a browser.

When discussing relationships in document trees, I'll use four terms often:

Ancestor: An element that is on a path between an element and the root element in the document tree.

Descendant: The inverse of ancestor; an element on a path that descends from a given element.

Parent: A direct ancestor; that is, the element directly above an element in the document tree.

Child: A direct descendant; that is, an element directly below an element in the document tree.

Did you notice how I have used the word *descending* throughout this section? I used it intentionally, because it's key to how you create descendant selectors.

Suppose you want to make the summary paragraphs red. Here's how:

```
div p {color: red;}
```

Yes, there's a space there, and it's on purpose. This is a descendant selector: It selects elements based on their relationship to a parent element. The way to read this is actually backward: "Select any **p** element that is a descendant of a **div** element." The space between **div** and **p** is what indicates the relationship "is a descendant of."

You can figure out whether an element descends from another element by tracing up the document tree. Consider all the paragraphs in your tree.

Put your finger on any **p** element, and trace upward along the lines until you reach the root. If your finger passes over a **div** along the way, then it's an ancestor of the **p**, and by definition that means the **p** is a descendant of the **div**.

Similarly, if you wanted to put all the **em** (emphasis) elements that are descendants of the **div** in bold, you'd write the following:

```
div em {font-weight: bold;}
```

Again, trace up the tree from every **em** element, and if there's a **div** between it and the document tree's root, then the selector will match it.

1 | Using ID Selectors

In this exercise, you'll work with ID selectors. Remember, you assign IDs in the markup, and the most important point to bear in mind when it comes to ID selectors is that you can have only one instance of a given ID in a document.

1 Copy the **03_cascade** folder from the **CSS HOT CD-ROM** to your desktop. Double-click the **03_cascade** folder to open it so you see the exercise files inside.

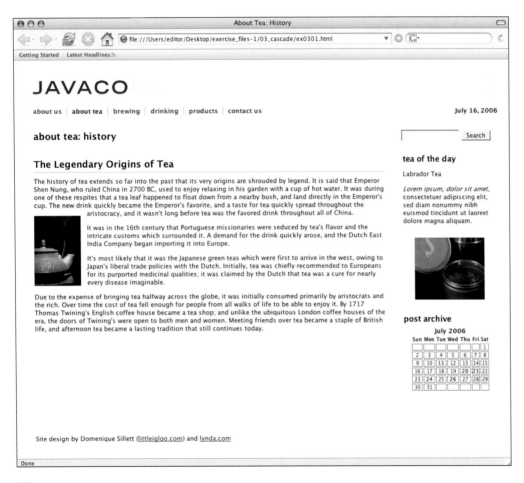

2 In a browser, open **ex0301.html** from the **03_cascade** folder you copied to your **desktop**, as shown in the illustration.

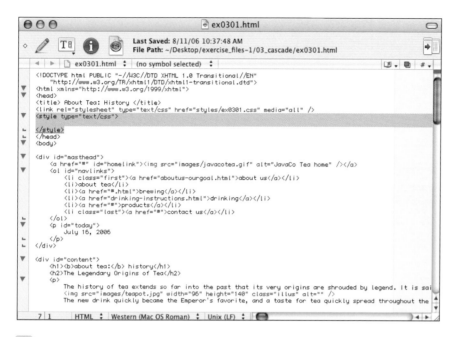

3 Open **ex0301.html** with your text or HTML (**H**yper**T**ext **M**arkup **L**anguage) editor. Near the beginning of the file, find the following block of code, as shown in the illustration:

```
<style type="text/css">
</style>
```

This is the embedded style sheet you'll be working with in this exercise. The first step is to add a rule that styles the masthead.

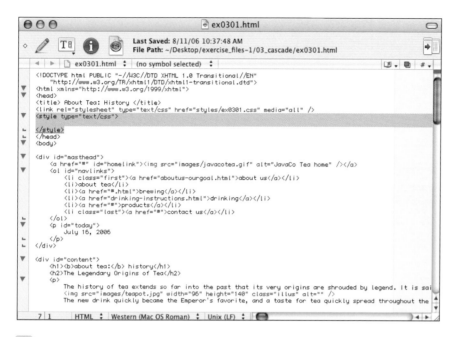

4 After the `<style type="text/css">` line, type the following:

`#masthead {background: green;}`

The rule you just added has a selector that says "select any element whose **id** attribute has a value of **masthead**." Because the XHTML source has only one such element (remember that IDs have to be unique!), you know that the green background will show up there only.

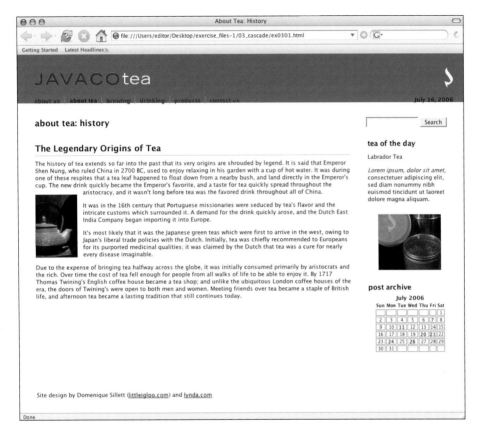

5 Save **ex0301.html**, switch to your browser, and reload **ex0301.html**.

There's the green. It's filling the background of the masthead, just as planned.

6 Return to your text or HTML editor. Add the following rules to the style sheet:

```
#navlinks {background: silver;}
#sidebar {border: 1px solid gray;}
```

Here, you've added two rules, each of which selects a different ID value. As before, the actual element types don't really matter, because ID values are unique. Regardless of whether the element with an ID of **navlinks** is a **div** or an **ul** or an **ol** or a **table**, **#navlinks** will select it. (As it happens, it's an **ol**.)

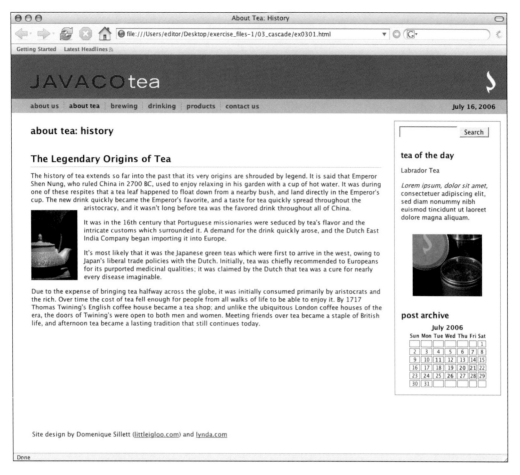

7 Save **ex0301.html**, switch to your browser, and reload **ex0301.html**.

The navigation area now has a silver background, and the sidebar has a border around it. This is kind of nice, in a bold, minimalist fashion, don't you think? Now, just to prove a point, you'll add some element names.

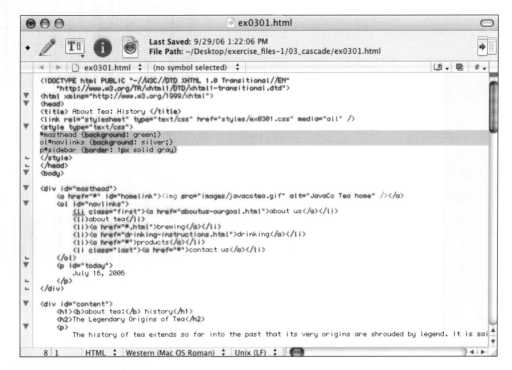

```
<!DOCTYPE html PUBLIC "-//W3C//DTD XHTML 1.0 Transitional//EN"
    "http://www.w3.org/TR/xhtml1/DTD/xhtml1-transitional.dtd">
<html xmlns="http://www.w3.org/1999/xhtml">
<head>
<title> About Tea: History </title>
<link rel="stylesheet" type="text/css" href="styles/ex0301.css" media="all" />
<style type="text/css">
#masthead {background: green;}
ol#navlinks {background: silver;}
p#sidebar {border: 1px solid gray}
</style>
</head>
<body>

<div id="masthead">
    <a href="#" id="homelink"><img src="images/javacotea.gif" alt="JavaCo Tea home" /></a>
    <ol id="navlinks">
        <li class="first"><a href="aboutus-ourgoal.html">about us</a></li>
        <li>about tea</li>
        <li><a href="#.html">brewing</a></li>
        <li><a href="drinking-instructions.html">drinking</a></li>
        <li><a href="#">products</a></li>
        <li class="last"><a href="#">contact us</a></li>
    </ol>
    <p id="today">
        July 16, 2006
    </p>
</div>

<div id="content">
    <h1><b>about tea:</b> history</h1>
    <h2>The Legendary Origins of Tea</h2>
    <p>
        The history of tea extends so far into the past that its very origins are shrouded by legend. It is sai
```

8   Return to your text or HTML editor. Edit the style sheet as follows:

```
#masthead {background: green;}
ol#navlinks {background: silver;}
p#sidebar {border: 1px solid gray;}
```

Here you've added some element names. Now, instead of selecting any element with an ID of navlinks, you're selecting any **ol** element with an ID of navlinks; similarly, instead of selecting any element with an ID of sidebar, you're selecting any **p** element with that ID.

WARNING:

Avoiding Trouble with Spaces

A fairly common mistake is to accidentally put a space between the element and the ID descriptor. Doing so would make the last rule in Step 8 look like this:

```
ol #navlinks {background: silver;}
```

See that space there before the octothorpe? Its presence *completely* changes the meaning of the selector. Return to your browser, and reload the document—there's no silver background. The selector no longer refers to an **ol** element with an ID of navlinks. Instead, it now will select any element with an ID of navlinks that's a descendant of an **ol** element.

And what does being a descendant of another element mean? You'll find out all about it later in the section "Understanding Descendant Selectors."

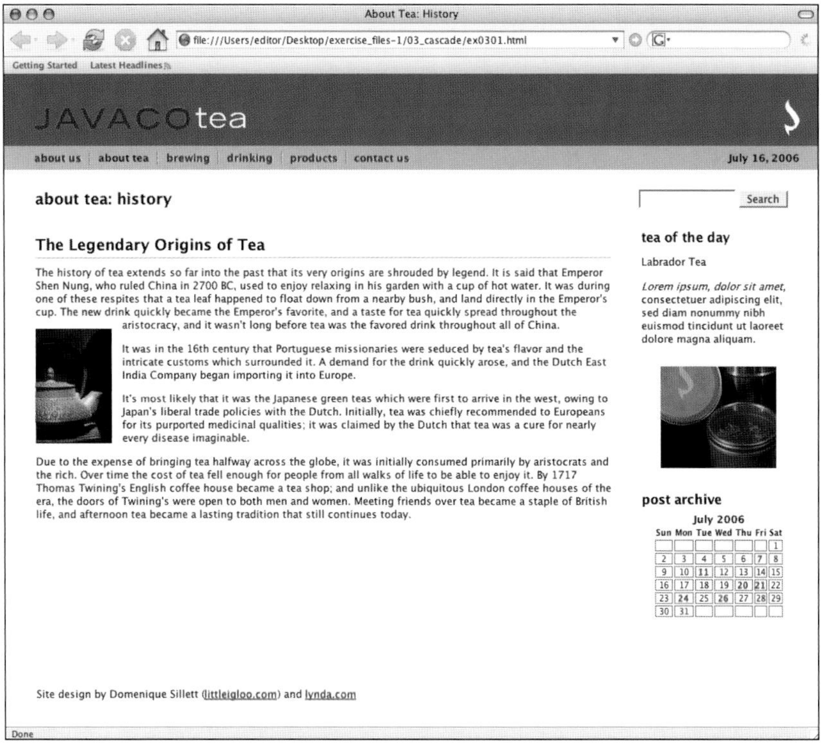
About Tea: History
file:///Users/editor/Desktop/exercise_files-1/03_cascade/ex0301.html
Getting Started   Latest Headlines
JAVACOtea
about us | about tea | brewing | drinking | products | contact us
July 16, 2006
about tea: history
Search
The Legendary Origins of Tea
The history of tea extends so far into the past that its very origins are shrouded by legend. It is said that Emperor Shen Nung, who ruled China in 2700 BC, used to enjoy relaxing in his garden with a cup of hot water. It was during one of these respites that a tea leaf happened to float down from a nearby bush, and land directly in the Emperor's cup. The new drink quickly became the Emperor's favorite, and a taste for tea quickly spread throughout the aristocracy, and it wasn't long before tea was the favored drink throughout all of China.
It was in the 16th century that Portuguese missionaries were seduced by tea's flavor and the intricate customs which surrounded it. A demand for the drink quickly arose, and the Dutch East India Company began importing it into Europe.
It's most likely that it was the Japanese green teas which were first to arrive in the west, owing to Japan's liberal trade policies with the Dutch. Initially, tea was chiefly recommended to Europeans for its purported medicinal qualities; it was claimed by the Dutch that tea was a cure for nearly every disease imaginable.
Due to the expense of bringing tea halfway across the globe, it was initially consumed primarily by aristocrats and the rich. Over time the cost of tea fell enough for people from all walks of life to be able to enjoy it. By 1717 Thomas Twining's English coffee house became a tea shop; and unlike the ubiquitous London coffee houses of the era, the doors of Twining's were open to both men and women. Meeting friends over tea became a staple of British life, and afternoon tea became a lasting tradition that still continues today.
tea of the day
Labrador Tea
Lorem ipsum, dolor sit amet, consectetuer adipiscing elit, sed diam nonummy nibh euismod tincidunt ut laoreet dolore magna aliquam.
post archive
July 2006
Sun Mon Tue Wed Thu Fri Sat
Site design by Domenique Sillett (littleigloo.com) and lynda.com
Done

9 Save and close **ex0301.html**, switch to your browser, and reload **ex0301.html**.

The silver background stays in place, but the sidebar's border disappears.

That's because the element with an ID of `sidebar` is not a `p`; it's a `div`, so the selector fails to match it, and the border style just doesn't get added. The silver background stayed because the element with an ID of `navlinks` is indeed an `ol`, so `ol#navlinks` matches it. If you wanted to include the sidebar, you would include an element of `div#sidebar` or just `#sidebar`.

Congratulations! You finished the first exercise on selectors. In the next exercise, you'll start working with class selectors.

*always use lower case

NOTE:

Learning All About Capitalization

If you were to change this selector to `ol#NavLinks {background: silver;}` and return to the Web page in the browser, you still won't see a silver background. Why? Because ID names are case-sensitive. In the markup, `navlinks` is all lowercase. To make sure the selector matches the element, you need to change the markup either in the XHTML or in the selector. It doesn't matter what kind of capitalization you use with your IDs—all lowercase, all uppercase, or mixed—as long as it is consistent throughout your documents. Some older browsers ignored these inconsistencies, notably earlier versions of Internet Explorer for Windows, but that led to some sloppiness and the need for further corrections down the road. Do not do this. Nowadays, if your capitalization is not consistent, your styles will not be applied to the resulting Web page.

2 | Using Class Selectors

This exercise will allow you to explore the value of class selectors firsthand. Using a class selector, you will be able to apply style changes to one or many unrelated elements in a document, provided they are assigned to a class.

1 In a browser, open **ex0302.html** from the **03_cascade** folder you copied to your desktop, as shown in the illustration.

2 Open **ex0302.html** with your text or HTML editor. Near the beginning of the file, find the following block of code:

```
<style type="text/css">
</style>
```

This is the embedded style sheet where you'll be working in this exercise. The first step is to add a rule that styles based on a class value.

3 After the **<style type="text/css">** line, type the following:

```
li.first {background: yellow;}
```

WARNING:

Avoiding More Trouble with Spaces

As with IDs, a fairly common mistake is to accidentally put a space between the element and the class descriptor. When you're selecting specific kinds of elements based on their class names, you need to have the element name and class name snuggled right up against that period. Otherwise, the rule will fail.

4 Save **ex0302.html**, switch to your browser, and reload **ex0302.html**.

A yellow background appears behind the "about us" link in the nav bar. The rest of the page background has not changed, because the "about us" link is the only **li** element with a **class** attribute that contained the word **first**.

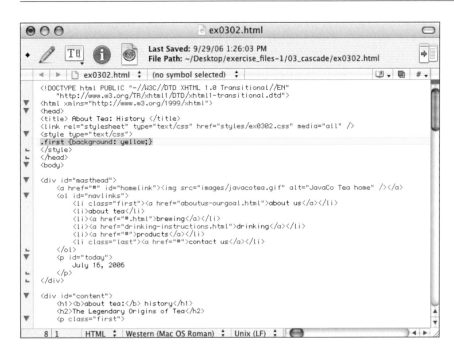

5 Return to your text or HTML editor. Edit the first rule in the style sheet as follows:

```
.first {background: yellow;}
```

Now you've removed the element restriction. Now *any* element with a class of **first** will get a yellow background.

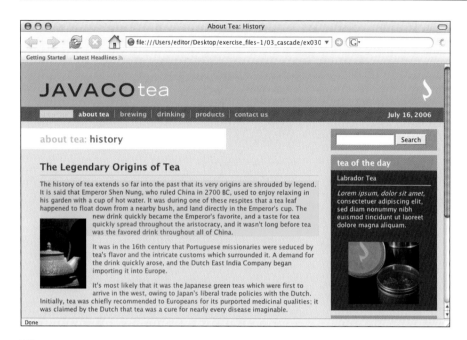

6 Save **ex0302.html**, switch to your browser, and reload **ex0302.html**.

The first paragraph on the page now has a yellow background—and if you were to scroll down in your XHTML document, it would have a class of **first**.

NOTE:

ID Versus Class Selectors

Earlier, I mentioned there were two primary differences between ID and class selectors. The first was that classes had to be assigned in the markup. Well, remember how IDs have to be unique within a document? Classes do not. This is the second critical difference that exists between IDs and classes. You can apply a given class to as many or as few elements as you want. In fact, you could give every single element in a document the same class. It would be a completely pointless exercise, but it's certainly possible.

Think of a class like your name. Many people throughout the world share that name with you, right? So if your name is Joe Smith, and if the results of a lottery meant that anyone with the name Joe Smith gets 100 dollars, that's like a class selection. Everyone in the class Joe Smith is selected (regardless of nationality, ethnicity, age, and so on) and gets a hundred dollars. That's just like selecting all the elements (regardless of their type) based on a class and applying styles to them all.

7   Return to your text or HTML editor. Insert a new line and add the following rule to your style sheet:

`.tue {background: orange;}`

The rule you just added puts an orange background on elements whose **class** attribute values contain the word **tue**. This is short for Tuesday, and you may guess that this will have an effect on the calendar.

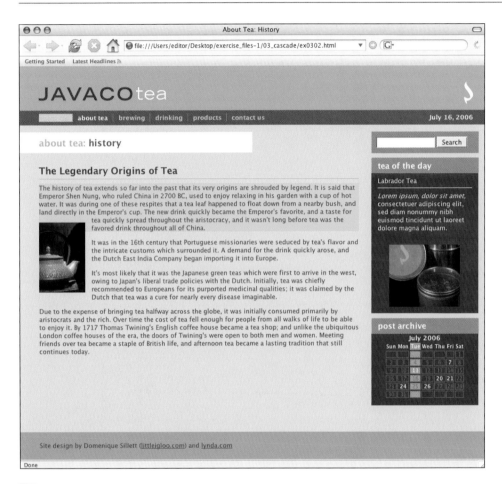

8   Save **ex0302.html**, switch to your browser, and reload **ex0302.html**.

You were right! Because all the cells in the calendar table are classed according to the day of the week, all the Tuesday cells—including the "Tue" header at the top—are selected by **.tue**.

9 Return to your text or HTML editor. Edit the second rule in the style sheet as follows:

```
td.tue {background: orange;}
```

Having the orange on the "Tue" header looked kind of ugly, so here you restricted the selector so that it matches only **td** elements with a class of **tue**. Any other elements, including **th** elements, will not be selected no matter what class they have.

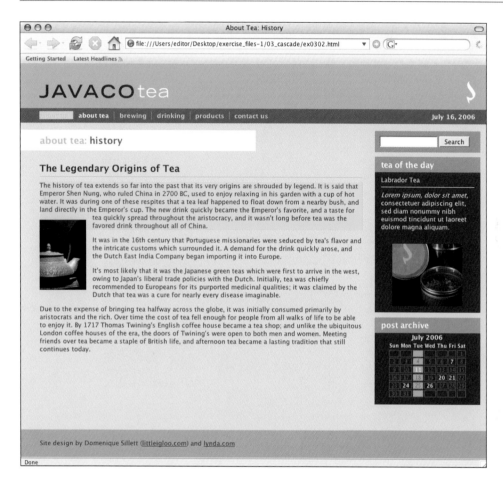

10 Save and close **ex0302.html**, switch to your browser, and reload **ex0302.html**.

The orange is confined to the **td** cells.

In this exercise, you learned how to apply single, simple class selectors. In the next exercise, you'll learn how to use a grouped selector to apply the same styles to a series of elements.

3 | Using Grouped Selectors

So far, you've seen only single selectors. In every rule you've written, a single selector went with the declaration block. That's fine for simple rules, but what if you want to apply the same set of styles to a set of elements? You could class them all the same, but that would get messy. It's much easier to use a grouped selector, which is a comma-separated list of simple selectors in the same rule.

To pick a basic example, suppose you wanted to set a consistent indentation for all three kinds of XHTML lists: unordered, ordered, and definition. You would write this like so:

```
ul, ol, dl {margin-left: 2em; padding-left: 0;}
```

See how that works? The selector means "select all **ul**, all **ol**, and all **dl** elements." This will cause the declarations to be applied to all those element types.

You can group any kind of selector, not just element selectors. If you had to set a color for links with a class of **more**, all tables on your page, and a paragraph with an ID of **today**, you'd write the following:

```
a.more, table, p#today
```

In this exercise, you'll apply a style to a group of header elements. This is particularly useful when working with text-heavy documents.

1 In a browser, open **ex0303.html** from the **03_cascade** folder you copied to your desktop. It should appear as shown in the illustration.

2 Open **ex0303.html** with your text or HTML editor. Near the beginning of the file, find the following block of code:

```
<style type="text/css">
</style>
```

This is the embedded style sheet where you'll be working for this exercise.

---

3 After the `<style type="text/css">` line, type the following:

```
h1 {text-transform: uppercase;}
h2 {text-transform: uppercase;}
h3 {text-transform: uppercase;}
h4 {text-transform: uppercase;}
h5 {text-transform: uppercase;}
h6 {text-transform: uppercase;}
```

You just added a rule that alters the heading elements so their text is all in uppercase letters, regardless of the capitalization of the text in the XHTML source.

4 Save **ex0303.html**, switch to your browser, and reload **ex0303.html**.

You'll notice the headers, from "About Tea: History" to "Tea of the Day," are now uppercase.

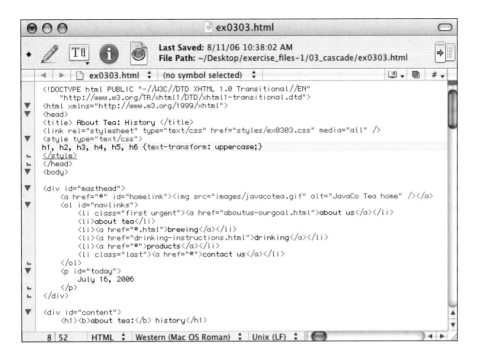

```
                                                ex0303.html
   ● ● ●
   ◆        T⬚  ℹ   🌐    Last Saved: 8/11/06 10:38:02 AM              ⇥▤
                              File Path: ~/Desktop/exercise_files-1/03_cascade/ex0303.html
      ◀ ▶  📄 ex0303.html ⬙  (no symbol selected)  ⬙                          📖 ▾ 🗐   # ▾
   ▼  <!DOCTYPE html PUBLIC "-//W3C//DTD XHTML 1.0 Transitional//EN"
   ▼     "http://www.w3.org/TR/xhtml1/DTD/xhtml1-transitional.dtd">
         <html xmlns="http://www.w3.org/1999/xhtml">
         <head>
         <title> About Tea: History </title>
         <link rel="stylesheet" type="text/css" href="styles/ex0303.css" media="all" />
   ▼     <style type="text/css">
         h1, h2, h3, h4, h5, h6 {text-transform: uppercase;}
   ⌊     </style>
   ⌊     </head>
   ▼     <body>

   ▼     <div id="masthead">
   ▼        <a href="#" id="homelink"><img src="images/javacotea.gif" alt="JavaCo Tea home" /></a>
            <ol id="navlinks">
               <li class="first urgent"><a href="aboutus-ourgoal.html">about us</a></li>
               <li>about tea</li>
               <li><a href="#.html">brewing</a></li>
               <li><a href="drinking-instructions.html">drinking</a></li>
               <li><a href="#">products</a></li>
               <li class="last"><a href="#">contact us</a></li>
   ⌊        </ol>
   ▼        <p id="today">
               July 16, 2006
   ⌊        </p>
   ⌊     </div>

   ▼     <div id="content">
            <h1><b>about tea:</b> history</h1>                                     ▲
                                                                                   ▼
      8 | 52    HTML ⬙ | Western (Mac OS Roman) ⬙ | Unix (LF) ⬙  ◉━━━━        ◀▶/
```

5 After the `<style type="text/css">` line, delete the header declaration, and type the following instead:

```
h1, h2, h3, h4, h5, h6 {text-transform: uppercase;}
```

This grouped selector radically simplifies the document and, as you will see in the next step, is rendered the same by your browser.

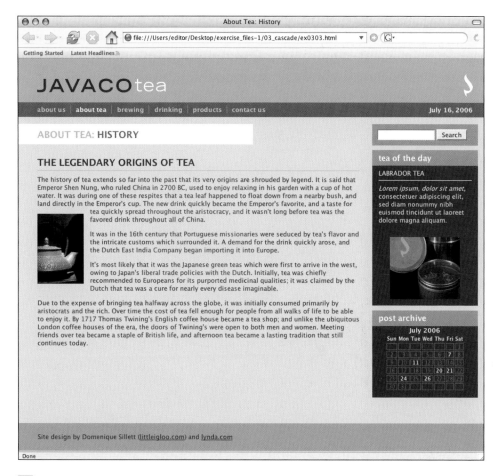

6 Save **ex0303.html**, switch to your browser, and reload **ex0303.html**.

---

7 Return to your text or HTML editor. Add the following rule to the style sheet:

`th, td {background: #A0C63A;}`

The rule you've just created selects all **th** (table header) and **td** (table data, more usually called a **table cell**) elements and fills in a green background color.

8 Save and close **ex0303.html**, switch to your browser, and reload **ex0303.html**.

Perhaps that wasn't the best choice of a background color for the calendar, but it nicely illustrates that tables are often composed of two different kinds of cells, and styling both consistently is a snap using grouped selectors.

In this exercise, you learned how to simplify your style sheet by using grouped selectors:

```
h1, h2, h3, h4, h5, h6 {text-transform: uppercase;}
```

As far as a browser is concerned, you typed the following:

```
h1 {text-transform: uppercase;}
```

```
h2 {text-transform: uppercase;}
```

```
h3 {text-transform: uppercase;}
```

```
h4 {text-transform: uppercase;}
```

```
h5 {text-transform: uppercase;}
```

```
h6 {text-transform: uppercase;}
```

To the browser, it doesn't matter which of those two approaches you take. The six-rule sequence is treated exactly the same as the one-rule grouped selector. And who wants to do all that typing?

Recognizing That Blocks Are Groups, Too

Another instance of grouping in CSS exists, and that's the declaration block, which I covered in Chapter 2, *"Understanding CSS."* Consider this simple little rule:

```
p {font-style: italic; color: red; margin: 1em;}
```

To a browser, this is exactly like typing the following:

```
p {font-style: italic;}
```

```
p {color: red;}
```

```
p {margin: 1em;}
```

Using grouped selectors with a declaration block reaps you even more savings. For example:

```
h1, h2 {font-weight: bold; color: navy;}
```

That's equivalent to the following:

```
h1 {font-weight: bold; }
h1 {color: navy;}
h2 {font-weight: bold;}
h2 {color: navy;}
```

You can see why I'm not using more complicated examples. The expanded lists would go on for pages!

Using Descendant Selectors

In this exercise, you'll use descendant selectors to italicize elements of a Web page and then start to limit exactly where the italics show up on the Web page.

1 In a browser, open **ex0304.html** from the **03_cascade** folder you copied to your desktop, as shown in the illustration here.

A quick glance at the page reveals that none of the text is italicized.

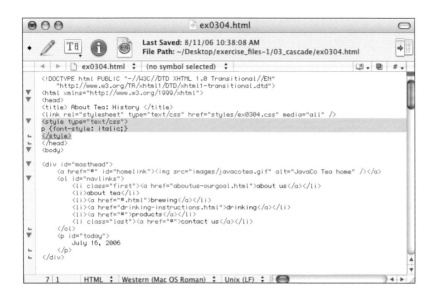

2 Open **ex0304.html** with your text or HTML editor. Near the beginning of the file, type the following after **<style type="text/css">**:

```
p {font-style: italic;}
```

3 Save **ex0304.html**, switch to your browser, and reload **ex0304.html**.

Notice the text is now italic.

4 Return to **ex0304.html** in your text or HTML editor, and edit the first line of the style sheet (the **p {font-style: italic;}** line) as follows:

```
#masthead p {font-style: italic;}
```

One of the ancestors of the **p** element enclosing the date is the **div** that has an ID of **masthead**. By adding that ID to the selector, you're saying that the declaration block of this rule should be applied to any **p** element that **descends** from (that is structurally nested inside of) any element with an ID of **masthead**.

5 Save **ex0304.html**, switch to your browser, and reload **ex0304.html**.

Now, the only italic text is the date.

6 Return to your text or HTML editor. Edit the first line of the style sheet (the **#masthead p {font-style: italic;}** line) as follows:

```
#sidebar p {font-style: italic;}
```

You just changed the descendant relationship. Now, only **p** elements that descend from the element with an ID of **sidebar** will be selected.

7 Save **ex0304.html**, switch to your browser, and reload **ex0304.html**.

The date is no longer italic, since it isn't in the sidebar. Instead, the sidebar paragraph in the "tea of the day" section is being italicized. But what if you want to italicize both of them?

8 Return to your text or HTML editor. Edit the first line of the style sheet (the `#sidebar p {font-style: italic;}` line) as follows:

`#masthead p, #sidebar p {font-style: italic;}`

Here you created a grouped selector of two descendant selectors. This comes out to mean "select any **p** element that descends from an element with an ID of **masthead** *and* select any **p** element that descends from an element with an ID of **sidebar**."

9 Save and close **ex0304.html**, switch to your browser, and reload **ex0304.html**.

In this exercise, thanks to the grouped descendant selectors, both the date and the sidebar paragraphs are italicized. The paragraphs in the main content area of the page are not affected, since none of them is a descendant of the `masthead` or `sidebar` element. In the next exercise, I'll discuss specificity and style conflict resolution, but first I'll discuss the origins of styles.

Looking for the Sources of Styles

Where does style come from? A combination of three sources. The first, and the one that probably interests you the most, is from the author of the Web page. The second comes from **user styles**, or **reader styles**. The person who is viewing your page may have a style sheet associated with the browser they are using and may have the font appear larger on the pages they visit or have all the links underlined. This is a particularly useful feature for users with vision problems, color blindness, and so on. User style sheets are very rare; most people don't even realize they're there, but keep it in mind. The third source is common—user **agent styles**, otherwise known as **browser styles**. This is a style behavior built into the browser.

The Sources of Style

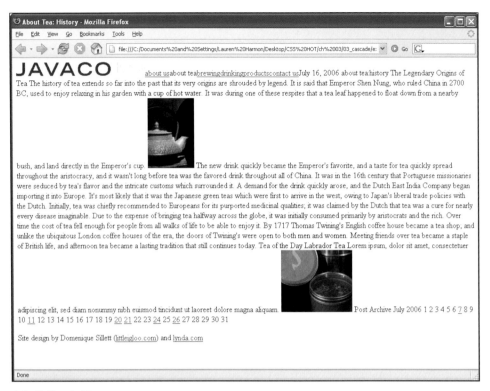

A Really Unstyled Page

You might not think much style is built into a browser, but let's take an "unstyled" page as an example, like the one shown in the illustration here.

Nothing is being applied here by default, except for the hyperlink treatment, the default colors, and the default fonts that come from the browser preferences, which are turned into style rules. But as you can see, paragraphs don't look like paragraphs, and headings don't look like headings. The text is all running together. If you look below the last image, that's table markup. But the browser is displaying the text as if there were no elements at all. This is really unstyled—except for the browser preference settings, which are the most basic (and third and final) source of styles to keep in mind when you're styling your document.

When the style sheets conflict, and inevitably they do—the user style sheet and the author style sheet, for example—the browser has to pick one of the two. This is usually resolved by the **cascade**. The first step is to consider the sources—author styles usually trump user styles, but the second step in the resolution process is specificity, which I will discuss in the next exercise.

VIDEO: **style_sources.mov**

To find out more about the sources of styles and how they are resolved in the cascade, check out **style_sources.mov** in the **videos** folder on the **CSS HOT CD-ROM**.

---

5 | Resolving Style Conflicts with Specificity

In this exercise, I'll discuss specificity, the heart of conflict resolution in CSS. If you have two rules that absolutely conflict in a single document, **specificity** is CSS's way of assigning priority to the rules.

---

1 In your text or HTML editor, open **ex0305.html** from the **03_cascade** folder you copied to your desktop. Near the beginning of the file, find the following block of code:

```
<style type="text/css">
</style>
```

---

2 Type the following after the leading **<style>** tag:

```
li {background: red;}
li {background: green;}
```

This presents an obvious conflict. Which color is going to appear? You can't have both. It would be nice if the browser would resolve them, maybe with stripes or candy-cane style, but it doesn't.

3 Save **ex0305.html**, return to your browser, and reload the page.

The answer is: green! Why? Because green was the last declaration.

---

4 Return to your text or HTML editor, and modify the **li {background: red;}** line as follows:

```
body li {background: red;}
```

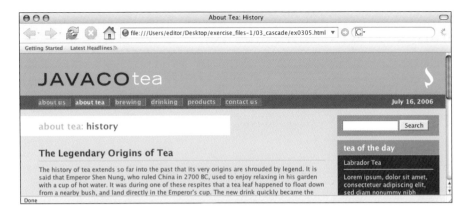

5 Save **ex0305.html**, return to your browser, and reload the page.

The background is now red. The reason for this is specificity. According to the CSS specification, an element selector has a specificity of 1, class selectors have a specificity of 10, and ID selectors have a specificity of 100. When you add descriptors or other attributes to the selector, the specificity increases. The list item **li** has one element descriptor, **li**, so the specificity of that is 0,0,1,0, being that there is one element descriptor. The specificity of the **body li** is 0,0,0,2, because it has two element descriptors. When rules are in conflict, the rule with the selector of the highest specificity "wins." The order of the items no longer matters, when the specificity differs.

---

6 Return to your text or HTML editor, and type the following under the last list item (**li**):

```
li.first {background: yellow;}
```

7 Save **ex0305.html**, return to your browser, and reload the page.

You discover the list item with the class of **first** is yellow. That's not because it's last but because it has a higher specificity. It has one element descriptor and one class descriptor. The specificity is 0,0,0,1 for the element descriptor and 0,0,1,0 for the class descriptor. 0,0,1,1 is a higher specificity than 0,0,0,2 (for **body li**). The reason why only the first list item is yellow is because it's the only element that has a class of **first**.

8 Return to your text or HTML editor, and type the following after the **li.first** list item:

```
li.last {background: yellow;}
```

9 Save **ex0305.html**, return to your browser, and reload the page.

Now, both the first and last list items have yellow backgrounds.

10 Return to your text or HTML editor, and type the following after the **li.first** list item:

```
#navlinks li {background: fuchsia;}
```

So, the specificity of this will be 01 for the ID (**navlinks**) and 1 for the element (**li**).

11 Save **ex0305.html**, return to your browser, and reload the page.

All the list items are now fuchsia. The specificity of the **#navlinks** selector outweighs all the others.

12 Return to your text or HTML editor, and modify the **li** list item as follows:

```
li {background: green; font-style: italic;}
```

13 Save **ex0305.html**, return to your browser, and reload the page.

The background of the list items is still fuchsia, but the fonts are now all italic. This is because none of the rules has any conflicting font style declarations with higher specificities. The specificity resolution kicks in only when conflicts exist. But you have one more way to affect specificity: using the inline **style** attribute, which you'll test in the next step.

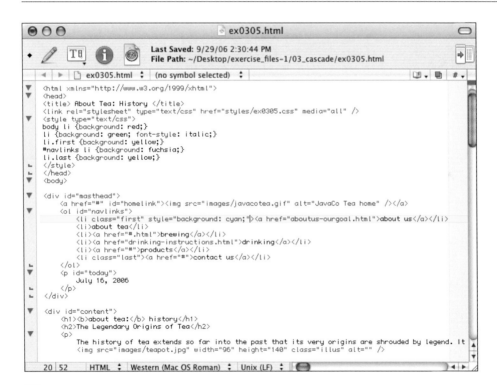

14 Return to your text editor, and scroll down through the HTML to the following:

```
<li class="first"><a href="aboutus-ougoal.html">aboutus</a></li>
```

Modify it as follows, as shown in the illustration:

```
<li class="first" style="background: cyan;"><a href="aboutus-ougoal.html">aboutus</a></li>
```

The specificity of this style attribute value is 1,0,0,0. That's higher than 0,1,0,1, the specificity of the `#navlinks li` rule.

15 Save and close **ex0305.html**, return to your browser, and reload the page.

The element with the in-style attribute wins. The first list item background is cyan. The specificity of an inline style attribute always overrides the author style sheet, because these rules start with 1, and rules in the style sheet begin with 0. This is not recommended, because it defeats the purpose of using style sheets at all; however, it is there if you need it.

In this exercise, you explored specificity and how specificity helps resolve declaration conflicts. It is not the most intuitive concept but is important to understanding CSS. In the next exercise, you'll learn how using the `!important` declaration can aid you in finding these conflicts.

6 | Using the !important Declaration

In this exercise, you'll use the **!important** declaration to root out and resolve style conflicts.

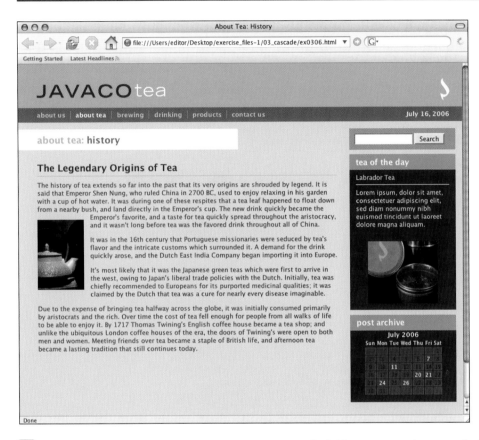

1 In a browser, open **ex0306.html** from the **03_cascade** folder you copied to your desktop, as shown in the illustration.

2 Open **ex0306.html** in your text or HTML editor. Near the beginning of the file, find the following block of code:

```
<style type="text/css">
</style>
```

3 Type **h1 {background: green;}** between the style tags.

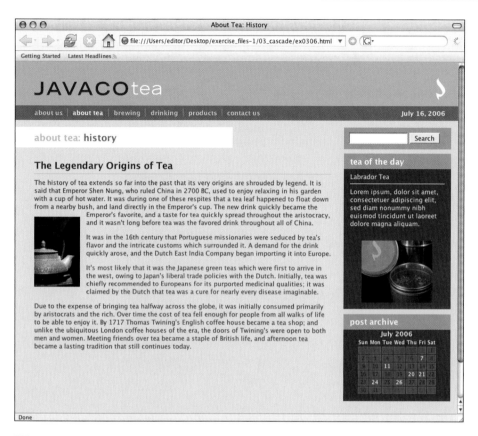

4 Save **ex0306.html**, return to your browser, and reload the page.

There's no change! What's happening? Let's find out in the next step.

5 Return to your text or HTML editor, and modify the **h1** declaration as follows:

```
h1 {background: green !important;}
```

6 Save **ex0306.html**, return to your browser, and reload the page.

Aha! The background of our header is now green. What this tells you is that somewhere in your style sheet, you have a rule that is setting that white background, and it has a higher specificity than the **h1** declaration. In effect, you're using `!important` as a diagnostic tool. The `!important` declaration overrides all the unimportant declarations, no matter how high the specificity of their selector. No matter what their source is, they will lose out to this `!important` declaration. So now that you know what the problem is, you can dig into the style sheet to resolve it.

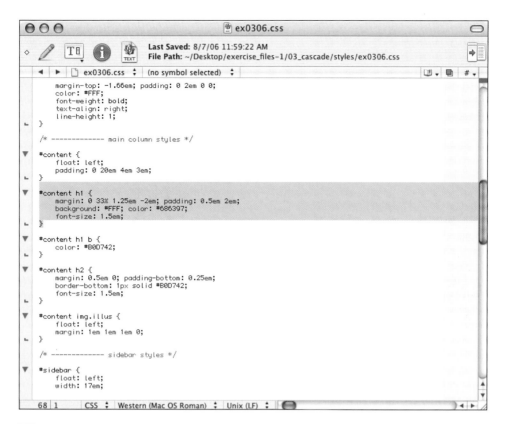

```
        margin-top: -1.66em; padding: 0 2em 0 0;
        color: #FFF;
        font-weight: bold;
        text-align: right;
        line-height: 1;
}

/* ------------ main column styles */

#content {
        float: left;
        padding: 0 20em 4em 3em;
}

#content h1 {
        margin: 0 33% 1.25em -2em; padding: 0.5em 2em;
        background: #FFF; color: #686397;
        font-size: 1.5em;
}

#content h1 b {
        color: #B0D742;
}

#content h2 {
        margin: 0.5em 0; padding-bottom: 0.25em;
        border-bottom: 1px solid #B0D742;
        font-size: 1.5em;
}

#content img.illus {
        float: left;
        margin: 1em 1em 1em 0;
}

/* ------------ sidebar styles */

#sidebar {
        float: left;
        width: 17em;
}
```

7 In a browser, open the file **ex0306.css** (in your text or HTML editor) from the **styles** folder in the **03_cascade** folder you copied to your desktop. Find the following declaration:

```
#content h1 {
    margin: 0 33% 1.25em -2 em; padding: 0.5em 2em;
    background: #FFF; color: #686397;
    font-size: 1.5em;
}
```

This rule determines the background color of the header. You can reduce the specificity either in your external style sheet or in your HTML document. Let's do the latter; you may not want to override this in every document tied to your style sheet.

---

8 Return to your text or HTML editor, and modify the **h1** declaration as follows:

```
#content h1 {background: green;}
```

This will increase the specificity of this declaration.

9 Save and close **ex0306.css**, return to your browser, and reload the page.

The "about tea" heading is again green—without using `!important`. You found your conflict and were able to resolve it.

In this exercise, you used the `!important` declaration to troubleshoot specificity problems. If you used this declaration, reloaded your Web page, and saw no change, you would know the problem was not a specificity conflict. In that case, you may want to check your declaration statement for spelling errors. It happens to me all the time. Also important to note about the `!important` declaration is that you should not leave it in the pages you publish to the Web. It fixes your problem temporarily, but you might find in the future you want to override the particular style someplace else and therefore will need to use yet another `!important` because the original problem was never fixed. Never leave `!important` in your style sheets, if you can avoid it. That's `!important` in a nutshell: Any declaration that is important always wins over unimportant declarations. Only when you have two conflicting `!important` declarations do you return to using the cascade resolution mechanisms such as specificity and declaration order.

7 | Understanding Inheritance

In this exercise, you'll explore a core feature of CSS called **inheritance**, which is the mechanism by which properties and values are propagated down the document tree. By applying styles to core elements, you can see this propagation in action.

1 In a browser, open **ex0307.html** from the **03_cascade** folder you copied to your desktop, as shown in the illustration here.

2 Open **ex0307.html** in your text or HTML editor. Add the following line of code between the **style** tags as follows:

```
<style type="text/css">
body {color: orange;}
</style>
```

3 Save **ex0307.html**, return to your browser, and reload the page.

Voila! The text changes to orange. You specifically set the **body** element to be orange but didn't touch any of the other elements. But the text of the sidebar, for example, is orange. Why?

NOTE:

Inheritance and the Document Tree

Computers are notoriously short on intuition, so the computer doesn't automatically understand your every desire. It needs a mechanism to apply properties throughout elements—that mechanism is inheritance.

The document structure is key to inheritance. When you apply a property to an element like the **body**, that value is propagated down the structure or document tree. It spreads downward from the **body**. Child elements receive properties from their parents. Not all properties are inherited. The exceptions are pretty obvious—borders, margins, and padding, and other properties that cannot be applied to all elements in the same way. The properties that are inherited, such as font color, size, family, are sensible.

You may have noticed in the previous step that the link colors didn't change. Why? Inheritance works only when there is no competition. Inherited values have no specificity. Not even zero—none at all. Inherited values will always lose to directly assigned values. The color of the links (blue) is coming from the browser style sheet, and that value overrides any inherited properties and values.

4 Return to your text or HTML editor, and type the following after the first (**body**) rule:

`#sidebar {color: teal;}`

By assigning a specific property value to the `sidebar` element, you will override the inherited properties set up in the first rule in your style sheet.

5 Save **ex0307.html**, return to your browser, and reload the page.

The sidebar text should now appear teal, as shown in the illustration here. This includes all the headings and borders. Why? Well, this property is propagated down the `sidebar` element tree to its descendent elements.

6 Return to your text or HTML editor, and modify the first rule (**body**) as follows:

`body {color:orange !important;}`

Ordinarily, the `!important` declaration would override any other style rules. Let's see whether this happens here.

7 Save and close **ex0307.html**, return to your browser, and reload the page.

There is no change. The links stay blue. As the orange value is inherited, the specificity is lost and the importance is lost.

In this exercise, you learned how the mechanism of inheritance works to propagate property values to descendent elements in a document and how inherited values are overridden. Often times, people will confuse the cascade in CSS with inheritance, assuming that the properties cascade down the document tree. But as you saw previously in this chapter, the cascade is actually the set of conflict resolution mechanisms used to determine how disparate styles are brought together to arrive at a final presentation style sheet. The process of having one style propagate to child elements is inheritance, not the cascade.

8 | Revealing Unstyled Documents

This exercise will show how to modify the settings of the Firefox browser to reveal documents in their truly unstyled state. This shows how much browser settings really do impact how the user perceives your Web site and the importance they play in the cascade.

1 Mac users, start by opening the **Finder** application. Windows users, proceed directly to Step 6.

2 Ensure Firefox is not running on your computer. Choose **Applications > Firefox**, right-click, and choose **Show Package Contents**.

3 Navigate through **Contents / Mac OS** to the **Res** folder.

4 Choose **Sort by Kind** to view all the CSS files together. The files that most directly relate to Web page presentation are **forms.css**, **html.css**, and **quirk.css**. The **ua.css** file is actually for the user agent.

5 **Ctrl+click** to multiple-select these files, and then drag them to the **Trash**. Minimize your **Finder** window.

Mac users, skip the next step. It's for Windows users only.

6 Windows users, ensure Firefox is not running on your computer; then choose **Start > Search**. Select **Search All Files and Folders** for the file name **html.css**. As shown in the illustration here, it should appear in **C:\Program Files\Mozilla Firefox\res**. Delete the file by selecting it and hitting the **Delete** key or by right-clicking and choosing **Delete**. Close the **Search Results** window.

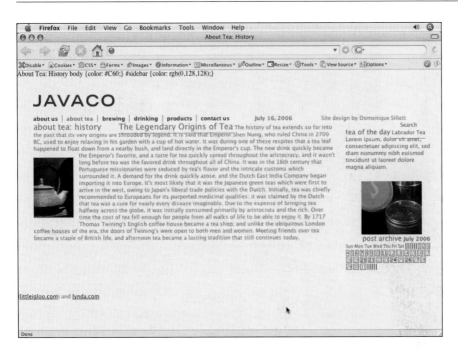

7 This step applies to both Windows Mac users. In a browser, open the **ex0308.html** file from the **03_cascade** folder you copied to your desktop, as shown in the illustration here.

This is the Web page without any user agent styles applied. There are still some styles applied, but you'll remove them in the next step.

8 Open the **ex0308.html** file in your text or HTML editor. Delete the following block of code:

```
<link rel ="stylesheet" type="text/css" href="styles/ex0307.css" media="all" />
<style type ="text/css">
body {color: #C60;}
#sidebar {color: rgb(0,128,128);}
```

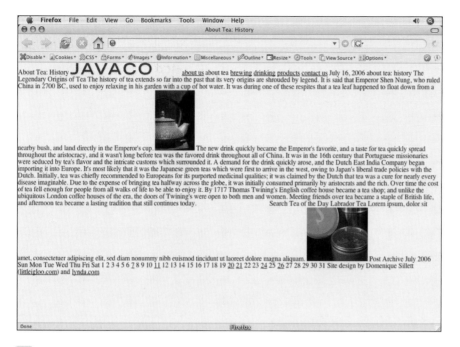

9 Save and close **ex0308.html**, return to your browser, and reload the page.

Here you go. This page is now almost completely unstyled. The exception is the link styling, which is derived from the browser preferences.

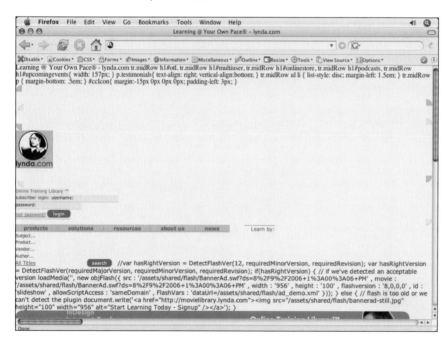

At this point, I recommend you browse the Web and check out some of your favorite sites such as lynda.com, for example. Script elements, like JavaScript, are ordinarily set to Display None, but you removed these settings, so you will see snippets of code appear, and so forth. Also, items such as forms will not work—presentation-wise at least. For example, your cursor may not completely align with the address bar.

---

10 Quit Firefox. Then, depending on your operating system, do the following:

Mac users: Reopen your resources directory (the **res** folder) by choosing **Window > res**. Open the **Recycle Bin** icon on your desktop. Multiple select the three CSS files in the **Recycle Bin**, and drag these to the open resource directory window.

Windows users: Go to the **Recycle Bin** to locate **html.css**, right-click, and select **Restore**. Alternatively, you can copy and paste it to the following location: **C:\Program Files\Mozilla Firefox\res**.

---

11 Open **ex0308.html** from the **03_cascade** folder you copied to your desktop. This should launch Firefox again.

The Web page should appear as it did the first time you opened it, with minimal styling.

---

12 Navigate to **lynda.com** by entering **www.lynda.com** in your address bar.

Everything should be back to normal! No JavaScript, no missing form fields, and so on.

In this exercise, you learned how to modify your browser settings to remove the built-in styles. Most users are unlikely to modify their settings in this way—it kind of ruins the visual experience. However, it's useful to know just how important the browser (or user agent, as I've referred to it elsewhere) preferences and defaults are that affect your final document. It is a critical element in the cascade.

In this exercise, you'll learn how to associate a user style sheet with your browser so it will apply to every Web page you visit.

1 In a browser, open **ex0309.html** from the **03_cascade** folder you copied to your desktop, as shown in the illustration here.

I took this screen shot using Safari on a Mac, and although I generally use Mozilla Firefox, Safari makes it really easy to apply a user style sheet. I've also included instructions in this exercise for Windows users working with Internet Explorer.

2 Depending on what operating system you're using, follow these steps:

Mac users: Open Safari, click the **Safari** menu item, select **Preferences** and then select the **Advanced** tab. From the **Style Sheet** pop-up menu, choose **Other**. In the window that opens, navigate to the **03_cascade** folder you copied to your desktop. Navigate to the **Styles** folder, select **ex0309.css**, and click **Choose**. Close the Safari **Preferences** dialog box.

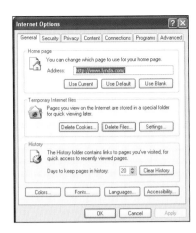

Windows users: Open Internet Explorer. Choose **Tools > Internet Options**, and select the **General** tab. Click the **Accessibility** button. In the **Accessibility** dialog box that opens, turn on the **Format documents using my style sheet** check box, and then click the **Browse** button. Navigate to the **03_cascade** folder you copied to your desktop. Navigate to the **Styles** folder, select **ex0309.css**, and click **Open**. In the **Accessibility** dialog box , click **OK**, and then click **OK** again to close the **Internet Options** dialog box.

You'll notice that the page just changed. That's because you have applied the user style sheet. Let's take a look at the contents of the style sheet.

3 Open **ex0309.css** in your text or HTML editor.

You'll notice the style sheet has applied a background and text colors, as well as some text decoration. You have made all these declarations `!important`, as discussed previously, to make sure they override the author style guide.

4 In a browser, type **www.lynda.com** in the navigation bar.

Well, isn't this interesting? You might just wander around the Internet for a bit to see how the user agent preferences interact with different sites.

---

5 To remove the user style sheet, do the following depending on your operating system:

Mac users: Click the **Safari** menu item, and select the **Advanced** tab. From the **Style Sheet** drop-down list, choose **None Selected**. Close the Safari **Preferences** dialog box, which will restore the page default settings. Close Safari.

Windows users: Choose **Tools > Internet Options**, and click the **Accessibility** button. Turn on the **Format documents using my style sheet** check box, and click **OK**. Click **OK** to close the **Internet Options** dialog box, which will restore the default settings. Close Internet Explorer.

---

6 Close Firefox and close **ex0309.css** in your text or Web editor.

This was a short exercise, but I hope you learned the importance of user style sheets and how they can affect your document presentation. They are yet another important element in the cascade.

Moreover, I hope you've enjoyed this chapter. I covered some key concepts, including selectors and the important elements of the cascade. In the next chapter, you'll explore how to use CSS to modify page layout, including tables and columns. I find this to be one of the biggest incentives for using CSS—getting rid of that pesky table markup. See you there!

4

Using CSS to Affect Page Layout

You can use CSS (**C**ascading **S**tyle **S**heets) for much more than styling fonts and backgrounds. You can use it to modify the entire presentation layer. If you're migrating from straight XHTML (e**X**tensible **HTML**) or HTML (**H**yper**T**ext **M**arkup **L**anguage), you know page layout using table-based designs has some notable drawbacks.

Specifically, table-based designs are cumbersome, are hard to maintain when layering or nesting, require more coding, and lead to larger file sizes. If you wanted to create a simple border and background for a paragraph, you'd have to create a table and assign all its attributes just for a single cell wrap. With CSS, you can create a border and background for a paragraph with as little as three lines of code.

In this chapter, you'll learn the basics of the CSS box model, including margins, padding, and borders, which are all alternatives to those complicated tables. Then you'll practice placing some images by using simple floating techniques and creating some columns by floating content. A few of the exercises deal with the quirks of floats, such as column drop and containers, and you'll see multiple solutions to these problems in a variety of design scenarios. Finally, you'll work with some display attributes and learn how to manipulate how, where, and when your elements appear onscreen.

1 | Introducing the CSS Box Model

In this exercise, you'll work with the CSS box model. Every CSS element generates a box, whether it's a contiguous box or not. For example, a paragraph or text block usually forms a rectangular shape—a simple element box. An image generates an element box, as does a header or a footer element. This is the foundation of layout and determines how the browser reads the position of the elements on the page. In addition to a basic width, every element box has margins, padding, and borders, which you can manipulate to various effects. In this exercise, you'll start by adding margins and then work your way to padding and borders.

---

1 Copy the **04_layouts** folder from the **CSS HOT CD-ROM** to your desktop.

---

2 In a browser, open **ex0401.html** from the **04_layouts** folder you copied to your desktop, as shown in the illustration here.

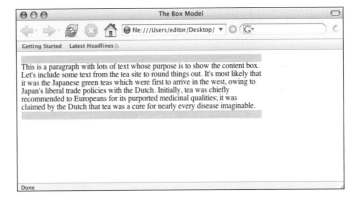

Notice what is happening here. Margins are always transparent, but with a little bit of trickery, I've created a way in which you can actually see the margins of this element box. In the markup, I've wrapped another element around the paragraph and put a background image on the wrapping element so it shows through the margins. You wouldn't ordinarily do this— that's what borders are for, after all—but for the purposes of this exercise, wherever you see the gray crosshatch, it's actually a margin of the paragraph.

Of all the box model properties, margin reside the furthest from the actual content area of the element, as shown in the illustration here. Padding is always positioned directly next to the content, while borders fit between the padding and margins.

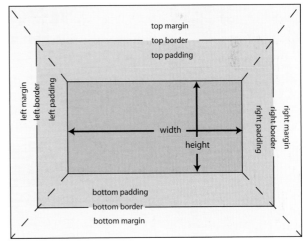

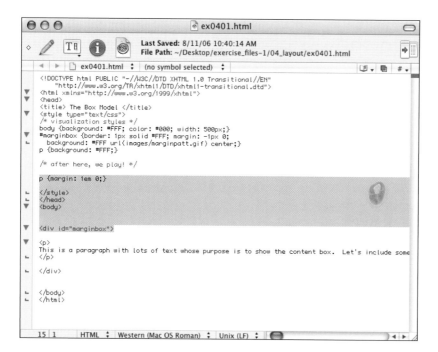

3 Open **ex0401.html** in your text or HTML editor. Find the following block of code:

```
p {margin: 1em 0;}
</style>
</head>
<body>
<div id="marginbox">
```

The rule at the beginning of this block establishes the margin width. This is in the embedded style sheet. Note the wrapping `div` in the markup, which lets you visualize the margin on the page.

---

4 Modify the **p {margin...}** rule as follows:

```
p { margin: 50px;}
```

---

5 Save **ex0401.html**, switch to your browser, and reload **ex0401.html**.

There you go. That's 50 pixels of margin applied to the top and bottom. Again, this is an image showing through the margins. Margins are not directly visible—I have made them implicitly visible here to help illustrate their use. In fact, I don't recommend creating a background for the margin elements in actual practice.

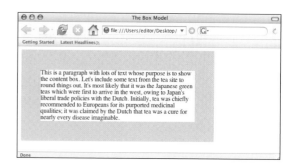

6 Modify the **p {margin...}** rule as follows:

```
p { margin: 1em;}
```

7 Save **ex0401.html**, switch to your browser, and reload **ex0401.html**.

The margins now appear on all four sides. Note, an **em** is a unit of measurement in CSS related to the font size of the paragraph. A margin of 1 em in this case is equal to the font size of this paragraph. An em-based measurement will always scale with changes in the font size. You will change the font size of this paragraph in the next step so you can see this relationship in action.

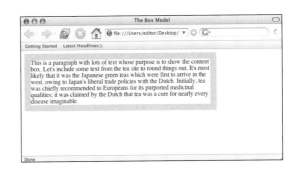

8 Return to your text or HTML editor, and modify the **p {margin...}** rule as follows:

```
p { margin: 1em; font-size: 10px;}
```

9 Save **ex0401.html**, switch to your browser, and reload **ex0401.html**.

Now, 10 pixels is an uncomfortably small font size to read, but then again, it's easy math. The 1 em margins are automatically calculated to be 10 pixels wide. Now, you'll add borders and padding in the next few steps.

10 Return to your text or HTML editor, and modify the **p {margin...}** rule as follows:

```
p { margin: 1em; border: 1px solid #000;}
```

11 Save **ex0401.html**, switch to your browser, and reload **ex0401.html**.

Here you can see the effects of the border on a page. Borders, unlike margins, can be visible or invisible, depending on the color and line weight/thickness values you specify.

Note: The border goes around the content but inside the margin of an element.

12 Return to your text or HTML editor, and modify the **p {margin...}** rule as follows:

```
p { margin: 1em; border: 1px solid #000; padding: 1em;}
```

13 Save **ex0401.html**, switch to your browser, and reload **ex0401.html**.

Here you can see the effects of padding on a page. **Padding** appears between the border and the content. In the next step, you'll modify the width of the paragraph element and see how this affects its box model properties.

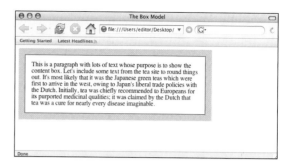

NOTE:

Ems Versus Pixels

I prefer ems over pixels for margins and padding because, as I mentioned, they scale with changes to the font size. If the user were to use a browser command—in Firefox, this is **Cmd+plus** or **Cmd+minus** (Mac) and **Ctrl+plus or Ctrl+minus** (Windows)— or set their browser preferences to automatically increase or decrease the font size of a Web page they were viewing, the em-based margins and padding would scale accordingly. I have even done em-based borders, although borders are typically pixel based (1 or 2 pixels in my experience, although they might be larger) since they are a design element of the page.

When I do use an em-based border, it is usually on only one or two sides of an element. I might do a thicker top border, such as .33 em, and the border will scale with the text size, which can be visually pleasing because it maintains the original proportions of the page.

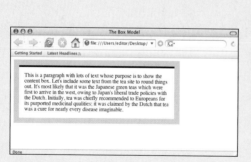

This is the same content, border, margin, and padding elements, with a top border set at .33 em at its original font size.

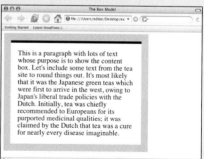

Ex0401.html, after increasing the font size within the browser

14 Return to your text or HTML editor, and modify the **p {margin...}** rule as follows:

```
p {margin: 10px; border: 1px solid #000; padding: 10px; width: 300px;}
```

15 Save **ex0401.html**, switch to your browser, and reload **ex0401.html**.

So, what's going on here? You set the width of the **p** element to 300 pixels. Instead of filling out the entire width of its parent element, **body**, which is 500 pixels wide, you've overridden that value by assigning it in this declaration. However, it's inter-esting to note, if you were to count the pixels from one border of this paragraph to the other, it would actually be greater than 300 pixels. Setting the **width** value to 300 pixels is actually setting the width of the content area of the paragraph element—the text. The **width** value doesn't include the padding or borders, 20 pixels and 2 pixels, respectively.

Then there are the margins, such as the 10-pixel margin on the left. OK, that jives with the code. But then on the right, a wide margin appears. Why? Well, since you defined a content area width of 300 pixels, the overall box does not fill the entire width of the parent element; therefore, the right margin expands to fill the "leftover" space.

Margin expansion takes place for elements that have normal flow. **Normal flow** means they are plain ele-ments that have text, and they're not floated, positioned, or laid out in any particular way. Elements that are floated, which I will discuss in the next exercise, don't experience this kind of margin expansion. But don't worry about this just yet! You can align your normal flow elements and work around the impact of margin expansion, which you will do in the next step.

16 Return to your text or HTML editor, and modify the **p {margin...}** rule as follows:

```
p {margin: 10px 10px 10px auto; border: 1px solid #000; padding: 10px; width: 300px;}
```

Here, you are assigning values for the top, right, and bottom margins and leaving the left margin at **auto**. This should move the text box, which is the content, to the right side.

17 Save **ex0401.html**, switch to your browser, and reload **ex0401.html**.

And voila! The margin expansion happens on the left side of the text box, because that's the margin you set to **auto**. Now, let's try to center this element.

18 Return to your text or HTML editor, and modify the **p {margin...}** rule as follows:

```
p {margin: 10px auto 10px auto; border: 1px solid #000; padding: 10px; width: 300px;}
```

The order in which values are assigned to the top, right, bottom, and left sides of a box model element are as listed here: top, right, bottom, left.

---

19 Save and close **ex0401.html**, switch to your browser, and reload **ex0401.html**.

Now the margin expansion is distributed on both sides of the text box.

Remember, the margins are visible here because of my bit of trickery, but ordinarily, you wouldn't see those gray areas. The text block would simply be centered within the boundaries of the content area.

Congratulations! You have just reviewed the CSS box model and learned how to apply borders, padding, and margins. One of the most important lessons to keep in mind from this exercise is that if you hard-code the **width** value, you are setting the width of the content area only, not including the borders or padding; in addition, the margins will expand automatically to fill whatever space the content does not. You have to manipulate the margin values to center the element correctly. However, in the next exercise, you will learn to float elements and avoid having to perform this calculation.

2 | Creating Simple Floats

In this exercise, you'll review simple **floating**, which is the act of taking an image or another type of element, putting it on one side of the Web page, and letting text flow around it. This is a common effect, used both on the Web and in print. Before the advent of CSS, you could perform text wrapping only with basic images and occasionally tables, using the `align` attribute. However, with CSS, you can float complex images, paragraphs, and more. You'll start by floating a simple image.

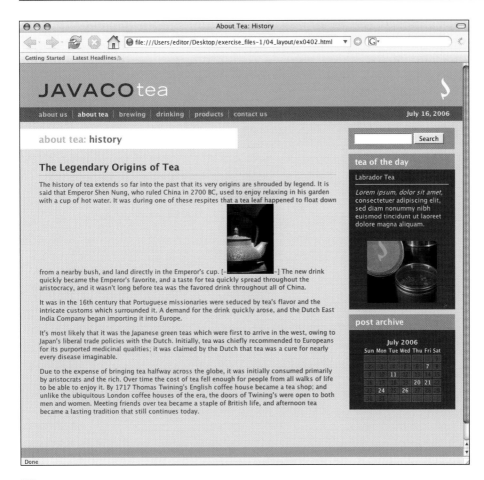

1 In a browser, open **ex0402.html** from the **04_layout** folder you copied to your desktop, as shown in the illustration here.

See how the image of a teakettle is suspended between lines of text in the paragraph? This is how an image would appear if it didn't have floating applied to it. I've added some brackets and hyphens on both sides of the image so, after you float it, you can compare the new image location to the original placement.

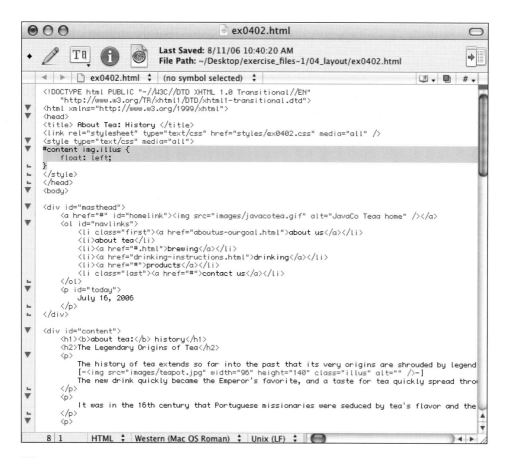

2 Open **ex0402.html** in your text or HTML editor. As shown in the illustration here, after the leading style tag (**<style type ="text/css" media="all">**), type the following:

```
#content img.illus {
    float: left;
}
```

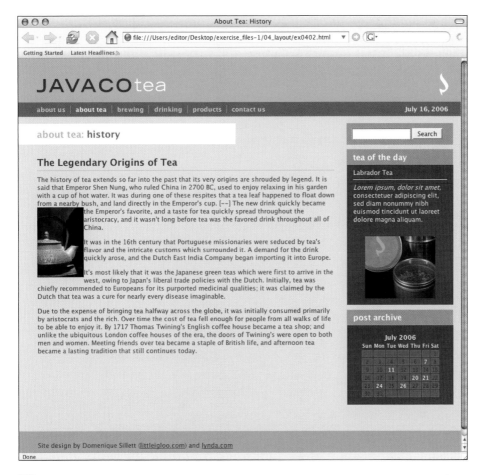

3 Save **ex0402.html**, switch to your browser, and reload **ex0402.html**.

The image, the little teapot, has floated to the left. You can see the square brackets I added denoting its original location are still in the middle of the paragraph. The image is still embedded there in the paragraph, at least in the document source, but by using CSS, you have floated it to the left.

So, the text is now flowing around the image; however, it is still kind of tight—squashed right up against the image. In the next step, you will fix this by adding a margin to the image.

NOTE:

Learning About the Origin of Float

The term **float** comes from when it was originally added to a browser, Netscape 1.1, way, way "back in the day." It was described as "you can float an image to one side." You can float **left**, **right**, or **none**. (The default value is **none**; otherwise, everything on the page would float by default!) You cannot float to center. **float** is not an inherited property, and you can apply it to any element.

---

4 Return to **ex0402.html** in your text or HTML editor, and modify the **#content** rule as follows:

```
#content img.illus {
    float: left;
    margin: 10px 10px 10px 10px;
}
```

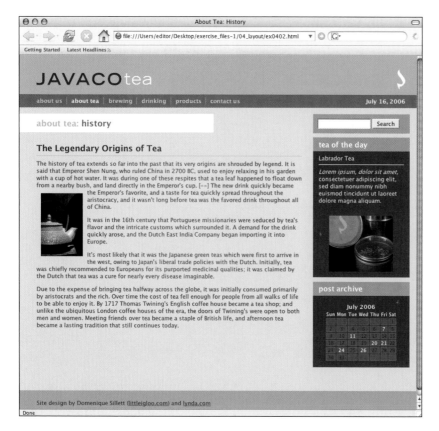

5 Save **ex0402.html**, switch to your browser, and reload **ex0402.html**.

That looks much nicer! The image has a little breathing room. You have applied the margin directly to the image element, and the text elements cannot overlap that. However, the picture is no longer aligned with the left edge of the text. You'll fix this in the next step.

6 Return to **ex0402.html** in your text or HTML editor, and modify the **#content** rule as follows:

```
#content img.illus {
    float: left;
    margin: 10px 10px 10px 0;
}
```

Tip: When you assign a 0 value, you never have to follow it with a measurement, such as **em** or **px**.

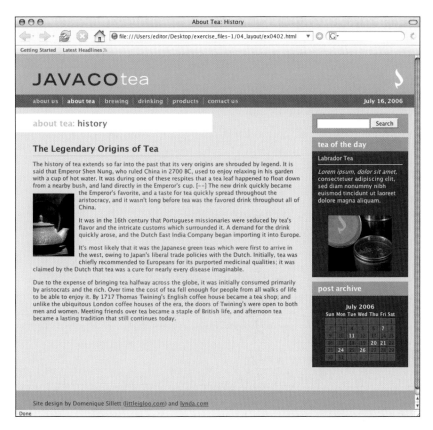

7 Save **ex0402.html**, switch to your browser, and reload **ex0402.html**.

The top, right, and bottom margins are still keeping the text away from the visible portion of the image, but it is now cleanly aligned with the left edge of the text around it.

8 Return to **ex0402.html** in your text or HTML editor, and modify the **#content** rule as follows:

```
#content img.illus {
    float: left;
    margin: 1em 1em 1em 0;
}
```

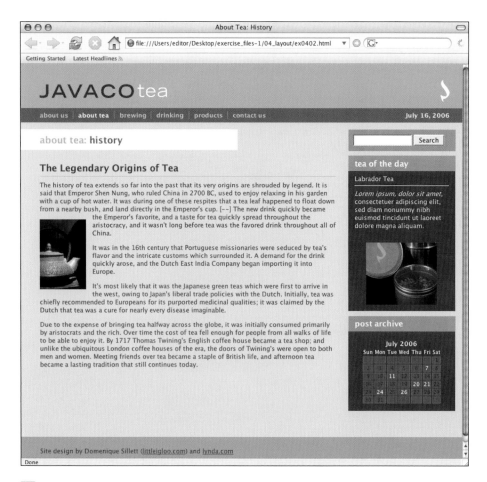

9 Save and close **ex0402.html**, switch to your browser, and reload **ex0402.html**.

Now, you won't see a terribly big difference in terms of placement. However, with the em-based margins and with 1 em being equal to the font size of the element (and images do have font sizes, but typically you don't see much happen as a result), if the user changed the font size, the image margins on this teapot would scale along with it.

So, do you want to give an image em- or pixel-based margins? An image is, after all, pixel based, in terms of height and width, but then the image is usually surrounded by text, and you might want to scale it with that text. There's really no right answer. It's more a question of what sort of design effect you want and your personal preferences.

Congratulations on finishing another exercise! That's simple floating. You can move an element to the right or left, and the other content will float around it. In the next few exercises, you'll proceed to more advanced applications of floating. You can use floats for much more than just moving images and aligning text. In the next exercise, I'll show you how to use a float to create columns.

3 | Using Floats for Page Layout

In this exercise, you'll work with a version of the Javaco site with the columns removed, and you'll reintroduce them using CSS floats. This is a great way to avoid those pesky HTML tables.

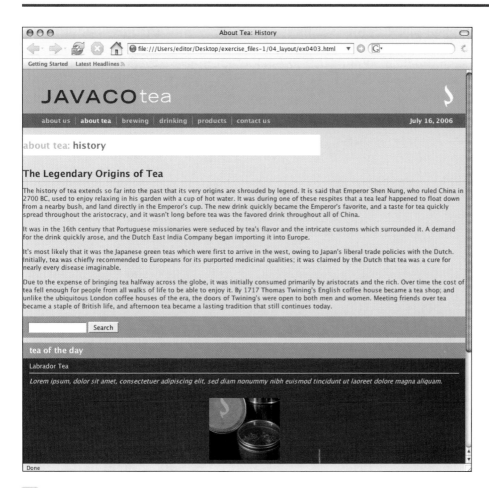

1 In a browser, open **ex0403.html** from the **04_layout** folder you copied to your desktop, as shown in the illustration here.

This is the good old Javaco site without the content in columns, which is why it might look a bit weird.

2 Open **ex0403.html** in your text or HTML editor.

Scroll through the markup, and notice the two **div** elements. One **div** with an ID of **content** (**<div id="content">**) encloses all the main content. You can think of this **div** as what will be the left column. The second **div** is **<div id="sidebar">**, which denotes that the content should be placed to the side, and in this design, this is on the right. In the next step, you will first float the content **div**.

3 Scroll to the beginning of the document, and after the leading style tag, `<style type="text/css">`, type the following:

```
#content {
    float: left;
    width: 40em;
}
```

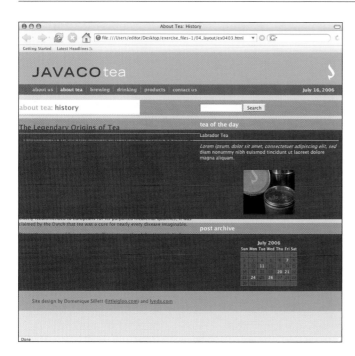

4 Save **ex0403.html**, switch to your browser, and reload **ex0403.html**.

As strange as the page looked when you began, it looks even stranger now—but this is only temporary. If you squint, you can see that the content **div** is indeed on the left, instead of taking up the whole width of the document.

Next, you'll float the sidebar.

5 Return to **ex0403.html** in your text or HTML editor, and modify the style sheet as follows:

```
#content {
    float: left;
    width: 40em;
}
#sidebar {
    float: right;
    width: 17em;
}
```

6 Save **ex0403.html**, switch to your browser, and reload **ex0403.html**.

There you go. The sidebar is now floated on the right, and the main content is on the left.

NOTE:

The Incredible Shrinking Float

Unfortunately, floats do have a quirk. As shown in the illustrations here, if you make the browser window smaller by clicking and dragging the bottom-right corner of the window, the **div** elements get closer and closer together until, all of the sudden, the sidebar disappears!

Going...

And gone....

continues on next page

The Incredible Shrinking Float *continued*

Well, actually, the sidebar doesn't disappear; it just drops below the content **div**. The way floats work is, if you have two floats next to each other, they are pretty good neighbors. They align nicely—until they don't have enough room. At the point where they are squeezed so close they cannot align without overlapping, the float that comes second in the document markup will drop below the first. As soon as you make the window bigger, the floats will align horizontally again; however, this isn't a desirable effect. Don't worry. Before this exercise is through, you'll discover how to work around this little quirk.

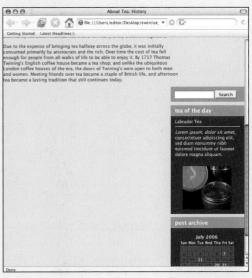

7 Return to **ex0403.html** in your text or HTML editor, and modify the style sheet as follows:

```
#content {
    float: left;
    width: 40em;
}
#sidebar {
    float: left;
    width: 17em;
}
```

Yes, you are floating both elements to the left. Are they on a collision course? No. Remember, floats will never overlap with other elements on the page. (This has one exception, but you'll get to that later in this exercise.)

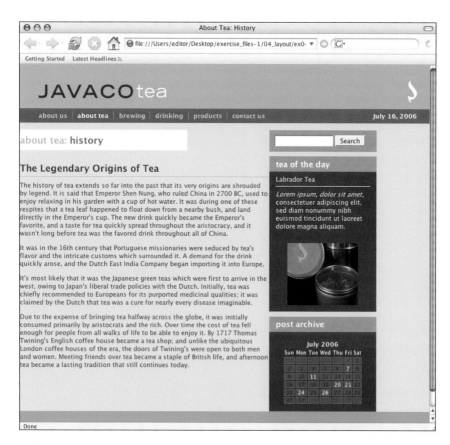

8 Save **ex0403.html**, switch to your browser, and reload **ex0403.html**.

This content **div** floats to left, leaving space for the sidebar **div** to float to the left as well, right up against the content **div**. Now they both have room to be next to each other, but again, if you make the window smaller, the second float, the sidebar **div**, will drop to the bottom.

Also notice, this time the sidebar floats to the left, per the instructions in the style sheet. But what if you have a float mysteriously dropping below another, even though there appears to be enough space in the browser window? In the next step, I'll show you how to diagnose this problem.

9 Return to **ex0403.html** in your text or HTML editor, and modify the style sheet as follows:

```
#content {
    float: left;
    width: 40em;
    background: #FFA;
}
#sidebar {
    float: left;
    width: 17em;
}
```

10 Save **ex0403.html**, switch to your browser, and reload **ex0403.html**.

Here you can see the content `div` now has a yellow background. It can be any color you want, provided it's highly visible. Whatever the color, the background establishes the exact width of the contents and as you will see in the next exercise, makes the padding allowances visible and aids in fixing column drop.

In this exercise, you worked through the basics of column layouts in CSS. You created columns using floats. However, you still have a problematic gap between the columns and the dropping of the second float. You'll address that in the next exercise.

4 | Fixing Column Drop

In this exercise, you'll practice working with padding and negative margins to avoid the problem of dropped floats, and then you'll finish by closing that gap between the two column floats.

1 In a browser, open **ex0404.html** from the **04_layout** folder you copied to your desktop, as shown in the illustration here.

This page might look similar to where you left off in the previous exercise. It has two columns, with one to the left and one to the right, and it has a variable amount of space in the middle. That space won't change unless the user changes the browser window, which few people rarely do during active browsing. However, they might set up their viewing preferences beforehand. Someone who is browsing in a window maximized at 1024 x 768 will see as much of a gap as shown in the illustration here. Someone using a 800 x 600 window will see a much smaller gap. Maybe that's OK with you, but for consistency's sake, you'll fix this next. The first step is to remove the width from the content **div** completely.

2 Open **ex0404.html** in your text or HTML editor. Find the following block of code, and delete the `width` property and its value:

```
#content {
    float: left;
    width: 40em;
    background: #FFA;
}
```

3 Save **ex0404.html**, switch to your browser, and reload **ex0404.html**.

You will discover that because the content has no width restrictions, the float expands until there is no room for the sidebar. Now the content `div`, although it's a floated column, is taking up the entire width of the browser window—basically the entire width of its parent, the `body` element. You might be thinking this doesn't do much good, does it? Actually, it does.

You'll address this in a moment, but first you'll add some padding to the content `div`.

4 Return to **ex0404.html** in your text or HTML editor, and modify the **#content** rule as follows:

```
#content {
    float: left;
    padding: 0 20em 4em 3em;
    background: #FFA;
}
```

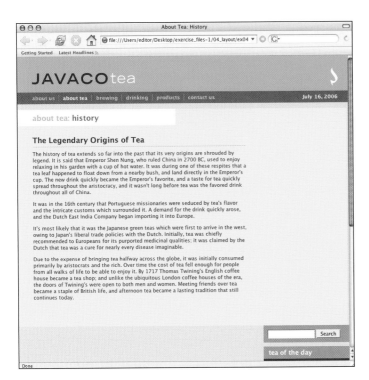

5 Save **ex0404.html**, switch to your browser, and reload **ex0404.html**.

The content is still consuming most of the page width, dropping the second float, the sidebar, down below it. However, now you have enough padding on the right side of the content that it pushes the text to the left. The right-side padding is wide enough for the sidebar to fit there. If you could get the sidebar to sit inside it, you wouldn't have any more problems. The two `div` elements would be side by side again. So, how do you get the sidebar there? That's in the next step!

---

6 Return to **ex0404.html** in your text or HTML editor, and modify the **#sidebar** rule as follows:

```
#sidebar {
    float: right;
    width: 17em;
    margin: 0 9px 4em -18em
}
```

By assigning a negative margin, you can exploit the way the CSS algorithms work. This tricks the browser into thinking this float has no width (actually, a width of -1 em in this case, mathematically) and will allow it to fit next to the second float, not to drop below it.

---

7 Save **ex0404.html**, switch to your browser, and reload **ex0404.html**.

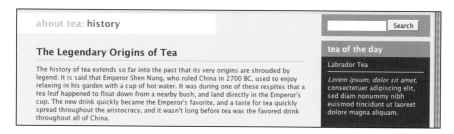

The sidebar is now tucked next to the content **div**. The two columns are once again reunited—side by side at last. In fact, you can see they are actually overlapping. The yellow background on the content **div** makes this clear. How did this work?

The float algorithms in CSS are written so that if you haven't given your floated element a width, the size is automatically determined by the contents and the limits of the space on the page. The element will contract and expand as necessary to fill the size of the browser window. So first, you purposefully did not specify a width for the content **div** for just this reason—so it could expand and contract to fit the limits of the browser window. However, you did specify a width for the padding of this element—just wide enough for the sidebar.

Second, you assigned the sidebar a *negative margin greater than its assigned width*. From a CSS point of view, that element no longer has a width. And as long as a float has no width, mathematically at least, there is always room for it. Be careful, though: If you don't give enough padding to the first float, the content will expand and can slide under the second, as shown in the illustration here.

The importance of the padding on the first float is obvious. If you reduce it, say from 20 em to 3 em, the text will expand and slide right under the sidebar. Floats don't ordinarily overlap, but the browser isn't recognizing the second float since you made it effectively null and void by reducing its width to -1 (a width of 17 minus a negative margin of 18 = -1). So, do a little math beforehand, and figure out exactly how much space your second float needs so you can build your padding for the first float and build the negative margins for the second float from there.

Also, remember to leave a little extra space in your right padding to create a consistent gap between the two floats. You assigned 20 em of right padding to the content **div**, and since the assigned width of the sidebar is 17 em, that leaves a difference of 3 em. You will have a consistent distance between the two columns no matter how the window is resized, as you can see in the illustration here.

---

8 Return to **ex0404.html** in your text or HTML editor, and modify the **#content** rule as follows:

```
#content {
    float: left;
    padding: 0 20em 4em 3em;
}
```

You're almost finished. In this step, you are removing the little diagnostic tool, the yellow background, so you can preview the finished site.

9 Save and close **ex0404.html**, switch to your browser, and reload **ex0404.html**.

Congratulations! You restored the sidebar column to its rightful place.

In this exercise, you worked a little more with margins and padding to manipulate page layout. You'll learn more about negative margins in Chapter 7, *"Using Margins and Borders to Create Whitespace and Separation."* It is really features such as negative margins that allow for some creative design and layout effects. However, if you're thinking about using negative padding to the same effect, please don't! Padding can never be less than zero.

In the next exercise, you'll work with another layout property, `clear`, which is closely related to `float`. In fact, designers often use the two properties together.

5 | Clearing Essentials

In this exercise, you'll practice using the **clear** property to move normal flow elements, the footer in this case, in relationship to floated elements on a Web page.

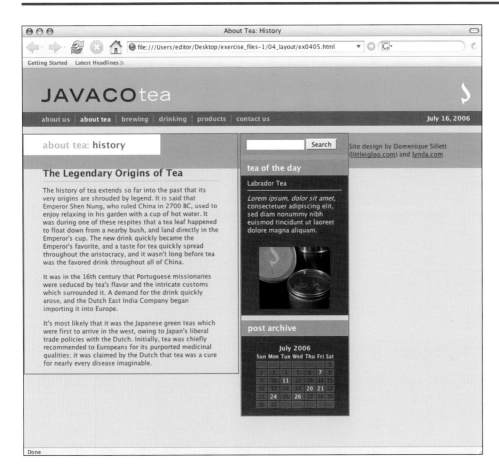

1 In a browser, open **ex0405.html** from the **04_layout** folder you copied to your desktop, as shown in the illustration here.

In this document, I've floated the two columns to the left and given them explicit widths. This is a step back from the previous two exercises, where the elements were finally starting to align according to the design comp, but you'll resolve this during the course of this exercise. Also, notice the mysterious green stripe at the top of the page. That's actually the footer, all the way at the top of the document. Also, the footer content is being squashed to the right. So, you'll now perform a few fixes to move that footer down—first by floating the sidebar to the right.

Open **ex0405.html** in your text or HTML editor. Find the following block of code in the style sheet:

```
#sidebar {
    float: left;
    width: 17em;
}
```

And change it to the following:

```
#sidebar {
    float: right;
    width: 17em;
}
```

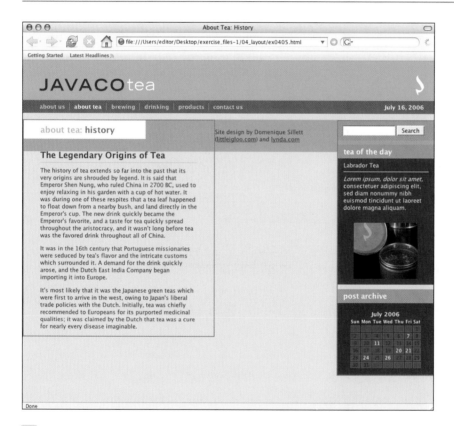

3 Save **ex0405.html**, switch to your browser, and reload **ex0405.html**.

No luck. The content of the footer is now simply floating between the two floats. You need to push the footer down below them. Fortunately, you can do this in CSS. It's called `clear`.

4 Return to **ex0405.html** in your text or HTML editor, and add the following rule after the **#sidebar** rule:

```
#footer {
    clear: left;
}
```

`clear: left` essentially means you want this element (ID of **footer**) to be pushed down, or cleared down, below any left floating elements.

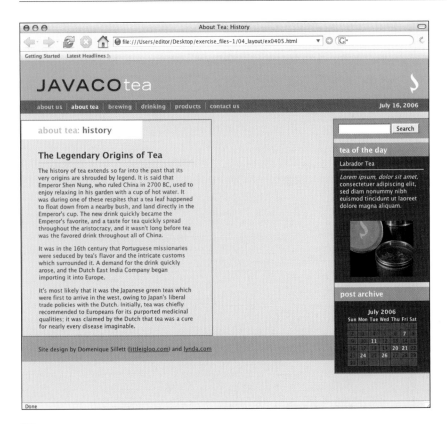

5 Save **ex0405.html**, switch to your browser, and reload **ex0405.html**.

And the footer has dropped! It is cleared to the left, below any left floated element like the content **div** but not under any right floated elements. As you can see, it's still sliding under the sidebar. If you want it to clear both the left and right floated elements—well, you'll do that in the next step.

6 Return to **ex0405.html** in your text or HTML editor, and modify the **#footer** rule as follows:

```
#footer {
    clear: right;
}
```

7 Save **ex0405.html**, switch to your browser, and reload **ex0405.html**.

Now the footer has dropped below both elements. However, this is a little misleading. It has cleared both elements simply because the sidebar column is longer. But what if the content `div` got bigger, maybe flowing onto another page where you're using the same styling? You'd have an overlap problem again. Let's try something else.

---

8 Return to **ex0405.html** in your text or HTML editor, and modify the **#footer** rule as follows:

```
#footer {
    clear: both;
}
```

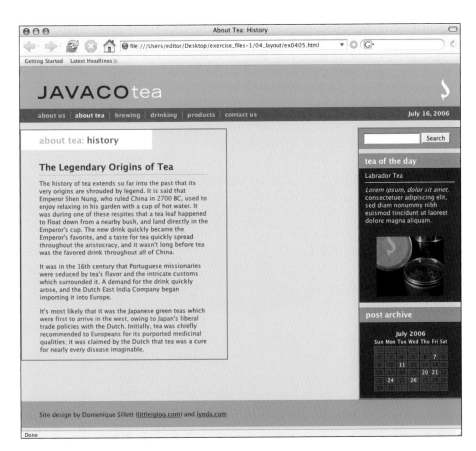

9 Save and close **ex0405.html**, switch to your browser, and reload **ex0405.html**.

`clear: both` means "clear this element below any floated element," basically either right floats or left floats. You don't see much of a difference now, but no matter how the left or right columns increase in size, the footer will appear below the longest column.

NOTE:

Using Margins Between Cleared and Floated Elements

The way **clear** actually works is that the top margin of the cleared element is automatically overridden and set so that only the visible portions of the element will show below the floats. If you were to set a top margin width, it would be overruled by the **clear** declaration. If you decide you want a space between your floated columns and the footer, add a bottom margin to your floated elements. Make sure to add this to all floats because their size might change and the margin might no longer be inserted if it is placed on the shorter float.

Congratulations! This was a short exercise but an important one. The reason why floats are used so commonly is because of the **clear** declaration. It is a simple but powerful command. Whereas floats allow you to align elements to the left and right, **clear** moves other elements below the floats. In the next exercise, you will review container **div** elements.

6 | Containing Floats

In this exercise, you will add a container to the Javaco Web page. Containers are useful for adding border elements and margins to a page, which you can't do on a plain background. As you might have guessed, container elements also "hold" your other content elements. However, working with containers, a normal flow object, and floats, as you have in previous exercises, can be a bit tricky. I'll show you two methods of reconciling these elements in this exercise.

1 In a browser, open **ex0406.html** from the **04_layout** folder you copied to your desktop, as shown in the illustration here.

What you see here is a situation where I have removed the floated columns and instead enclosed the content **div** and sidebar **div** in a container **div**. Let's locate this element in the markup.

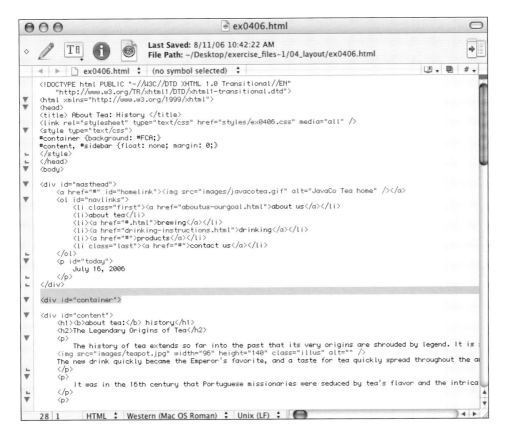

```
<!DOCTYPE html PUBLIC "-//W3C//DTD XHTML 1.0 Transitional//EN"
    "http://www.w3.org/TR/xhtml1/DTD/xhtml1-transitional.dtd">
<html xmlns="http://www.w3.org/1999/xhtml">
<head>
<title> About Tea: History </title>
<link rel="stylesheet" type="text/css" href="styles/ex0406.css" media="all" />
<style type="text/css">
#container {background: #FCA;}
#content, #sidebar {float: none; margin: 0;}
</style>
</head>
<body>

<div id="masthead">
    <a href="#" id="homelink"><img src="images/javacotea.gif" alt="JavaCo Tea home" /></a>
    <ol id="navlinks">
        <li class="first"><a href="aboutus-ourgoal.html">about us</a></li>
        <li>about tea</li>
        <li><a href="#.html">brewing</a></li>
        <li><a href="drinking-instructions.html">drinking</a></li>
        <li><a href="#">products</a></li>
        <li class="last"><a href="#">contact us</a></li>
    </ol>
    <p id="today">
        July 16, 2006
    </p>
</div>

<div id="container">

<div id="content">
    <h1><b>about tea:</b> history</h1>
    <h2>The Legendary Origins of Tea</h2>
    <p>
        The history of tea extends so far into the past that its very origins are shrouded by legend. It is
        <img src="images/teapot.jpg" width="96" height="140" class="illus" alt="" />
        The new drink quickly became the Emperor's favorite, and a taste for tea quickly spread throughout the a
    </p>
    <p>
        It was in the 16th century that Portuguese missionaries were seduced by tea's flavor and the intrica
    </p>
    <p>
```

2 Open **ex0406.html** in your text or HTML editor, and scroll down to find the start and end tags for the container **div**. Naturally, it will have an ID of `container`.

The container **div** begins right above the content and ends just below the sidebar.

---

3 Scroll up to the style sheet, and review the rules set for the container. The background color is set to **#FCA**.

The reason the columns aren't floating is because I've written a rule, **#content, #sidebar {float: none;**
margin: 0;}, to override the built-in float styles in the external style sheet (**ex0406.css**). The external style sheet says to float these elements, but I've embedded a rule to set **float** to **none**. You'll get rid of that rule now.

---

4 Modify the embedded style sheet rules as follows:

```
#container {background: #FCA;}
/*
#content, #sidebar {float: none; margin: 0;}
*/
```

Commenting in CSS

The /* and */ characters indicate the start and end of a comment block. Comments in HTML are written using the <!– and –!> start and end tags; in CSS you use /* and */. Programmers use comments to summarize code or to explain parts of it, such as where a revision might be required. The **compiler** (the program that translates the source code into a form usable by the user) ignores any text within the comments. In Web programming, the compiler is the browser.

Commenting is not usually recommended in published Web pages, simply because it is easy for the user to view the comments. However, comments can be useful when you want to disable a line or block of code but retain that line or block for future use, like you did here in Step 4. The browser will ignore, or not **translate**, this rule, even though it is maintained in the source code.

5 Save **ex0406.html**, switch to your browser, and reload **ex0406.html**.

The columns floated into place, but the container has disappeared. Why did that happen? The container collapses to have no height at all because it no longer contains any normal flow elements. Remember, the normal flow of the document would be the unfloated, unpositioned, generic flow of the document, as shown in the illustration here.

But the document is mostly non-normal flow. You floated the content, and you floated the sidebar. The only normal flow items are the footer and some aspects of the masthead, which are not included in the container. So again, the container **div** has no normal flow content, and it therefore has no height.

Why is the CSS specification written this way? Consider the teakettle image you floated to the left. Remember, that's an image inside the first paragraph that has been floated to the left. It's sticking out of that paragraph. If it didn't—if elements always increased in size to contain floats inside them—you'd have the first paragraph and then a huge gap followed by the second paragraph. Why? Well, the first paragraph would have to expand to contain the floated image. That would be horrible.

Floats were originally intended to float images or other elements to the sides of a content area and then have text flow around them, as you observed in Exercise 2. That's how they're written—floats were not designed to interfere with the size of normal flow elements. But when you start to use floating in a more advanced way, for designing layout, creating columns, and so forth, you might still want them to interact with normal flow elements, such as the container **div**.

You can address this in a couple of ways. Perhaps the most obvious way is to use floated elements, which do increase in size to contain other floated elements. So if you float the container **div**, it should reappear. You'll try that in the next step.

6 Return to **ex0406.html** in your text or HTML editor, and modify the **#container** rule as follows:

```
#container {background: #FCA;
    float: left;}
```

7 Save **ex0406.html**, switch to your browser, and reload **ex0406.html**.

The container element is back. However, this solution has a potential problem. The size of the container float is not constrained by the width of the content area. Watch what happens when you add a border to the container.

8 Return to **ex0406.html** in your text or HTML editor, and modify the **#container** rule as follows:

```
#container {background: #FCA;
    float: left; border: 2px solid red;
    width: 100%;}
```

9 Save **ex0406.html**, switch to your browser, and reload **ex0406.html**.

It's kind of hard to see, so I've circled it in the illustration here; by adding the border, you have expanded the contents beyond the width of the browser window. If you recall from Exercise 1 in this chapter, width is the content width, and any borders or padding beyond that are added to it. Now, this page extends 4 pixels beyond the browser window, with 2 pixels extra border width on each side. That's not really what you want. You can accomplish this in another way—return the container to the normal flow but have it contain the floats.

---

10 Return to **ex0406.html** in your text or HTML editor, and modify the **#container** rule as follows:

```
#container {background: #FCA;
    border: 2px solid red;
    overflow: auto;}
```

In this step, you are removing the **width** declaration as well as the **float** declaration, returning the container element to normal flow, and adding overflow.

11 Save and close **ex0406.html**, switch to your browser, and reload **ex0406.html**.

The container has snapped back within the page boundaries. By returning it to normal flow and not explicitly giving it a width of 100 percent, it expands as much as it can, including the margins, padding, and so forth.

So, the container now fits nicely in the document window. But wait, if the container is back in the normal flow and the content and sidebars are floated, how is it still visible? This is because of the **overflow: auto** declaration. This property controls how content is drawn if it happens to be taller than its actual parent. For example, **overflow: hidden** will clip any content that was longer or wider than the container **div**. What does this have to do with the floats and container relationship? Well, it's an obscure corner of the CSS specification that happens to be written to the effect that **overflow: auto** means "normal flow elements increase in size to contain floats." If you're interested, you can do more research on overflow in the CSS specification and really crawl through all the ins and outs, but I happen to think of this as just another quirk of CSS.

In this exercise, you reviewed the two methods for working with floats and containers. First, you floated the container. Second, you didn't float it and set it to be **overflow: auto**. In the next exercise, the last one in this chapter, you'll review display order for list items and other elements.

7 | Displaying Elements

In this exercise, you'll look at the kind of display values elements can have. Display can affect how list items appear, the color and shape of text backdrops, and even whether elements appear on the page.

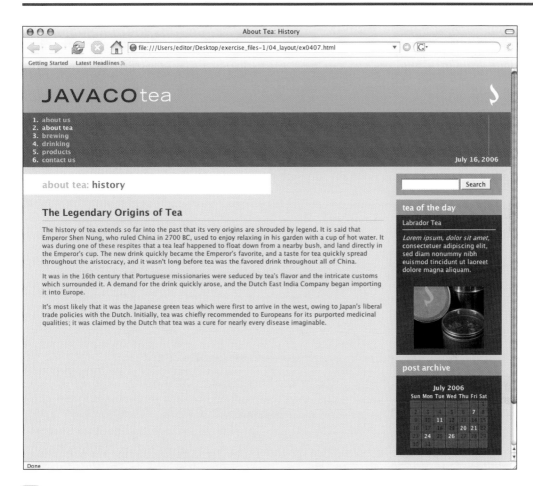

1 In a browser, open **ex0407.html** from the **04_layout** folder you copied to your desktop, as shown in the illustration here.

You can see the list items in the navigation bar on the Javaco page have become an ordered list, items 1–6 on the navigation bar. However, you want it to be a horizontal navigation bar.

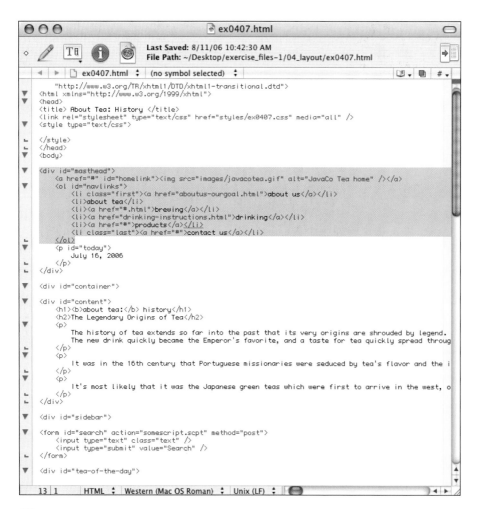

2 Open **ex0407.html** in your text or HTML editor.

You can see the various list items in the markup, under the `masthead` element with the ID `navlinks`. They are in an ordered list already. By default, these list items generate layout boxes known as **block boxes**. This is the same kind of box generated by a `div` element, a paragraph, or a heading. They span side to side and don't let any other element sit next to them. Hyperlinks and spans generate what are known as **inline boxes**. You can have a bunch of them on the same line of text, and they can wrap from line to line, if necessary. Here, you will want these list items, which are generating block boxes, to act more like spans. Luckily, you can do this through some simple instructions in the style sheet.

3 Between the `<style..>` start and end tags, type the following:

```
#navlinks li {
    display: inline;
}
```

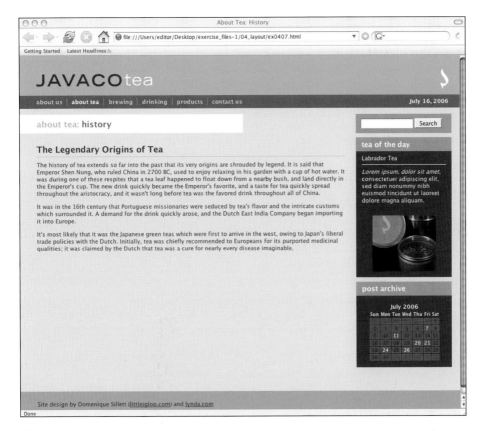

4 Save **ex0407.html**, switch to your browser, and reload **ex0407.html**.

How simple was that? With one rule, you've transformed block boxes to inline boxes. You can create the other aspects, such as the vertical separators, using borders, as I will discuss in Chapter 7, *"Using Margins and Borders to Create Whitespace and Separation"*.

This looks great in Firefox. However, this is still an ordered list. In a couple of browsers, even if you make the list items inline, they might still generate their markers, which were the numbers 1–6 you saw when you first opened the page in your browser. You'll suppress these markers in the following step.

---

5 Return to **ex0407.html** in your text or HTML editor, and modify the **#navlinks** rule as follows:

```
#navlinks li {
    display: inline;
    list-style: none;
}
```

If you are using a browser other than Firefox and see the markers after adding the inline display declaration, you might want to save your HTML document, return to your browser, and reload the page to see the effect of this change. Since I'm using Firefox, I'll skip that step here. Now, one other display value is of primary interest, and that's an inline box. You'll add one in the next few steps.

---

6 Return to your text or HTML editor, and after the first rule, add the following:

```
#content h1 b {
    background: #000;
}
```

You might recall that a **b** element appears inside the **h1** to set the color of the "about tea" text. A **b** element is inline, and by default, it generates an inline box. You'll set the background to black so it is visible.

---

7 Save **ex0407.html**, switch to your browser, and reload **ex0407.html**.

There's the black background on that inline box.

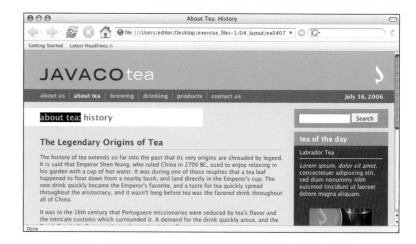

---

8 Return to **ex0407.html** in your text or HTML editor, and modify the **#content** rule as follows:

```
#content h1 b {
    background: #000;
    display: block;
}
```

9 Save **ex0407.html**, switch to your browser, and reload **ex0407.html**.

There you go. The **b** element is now generating a block box. If you have experience with XHTML or HTML, you might think this means the **b** element has gone from being an inline element to block element. It hasn't. The only change is in the kind of box being displayed. You'll probably use one other value for the display attribute fairly often, `display: none`. You'll practice using it now.

---

10 Return to **ex0407.html** in your text or HTML editor, and modify the **#content** rule as follows:

```
#content h1 b {
    background: #000;
    display: none;
}
```

11 Save **ex0407.html**, switch to your browser, and reload **ex0407.html**.

`display: none` quite simply means "do not display a box for this element." And when you hit Reload, the **b** element disappears. It generates no box and has no effect on the page layout. This value primarily hides elements that need to appear later, such as pop-up menus, which can be concealed in their unhovered state by using this declaration. (You could also use `visibility: hidden`, by the way.) The other reason you might use `display: none` is for features such as printing—suppressing the display of page elements in print. I will discuss printing and print formatting further in Chapter 9, "Styling for Print."

Congratulations! You've completed the last exercise in this chapter. Don't forget to check out Appendix A, "CSS 2 Properties," for descriptions of all the properties and values mentioned in this chapter.

Layout is one of the core elements of Web design, and I hope I've shown that CSS can make this part of your job much easier—and it doesn't have to involve a single table! In the next chapter, you'll start working with backgrounds and color.

5

Setting Foreground and Background Properties

In this chapter, you'll learn how to use CSS (**C**ascading **S**tyle **S**heets) to color elements on your Web pages. Though I won't address color theory in this chapter, you will learn some useful techniques to take your page design to the next level. You'll review different color values, learn to color both foreground and background elements, and add and control background images in elements. Though you can achieve a lot of these effects using simple XHTML (e**X**tensible **HTML**), CSS offers greater control, such as the precise positioning of repeated background images and the ability to specify colors for several different elements on the page, from list headings to hyperlinks to form backgrounds, without having to dig into the markup. Using CSS instead of XHTML also allows you to change colors for elements on the fly, which can be a godsend if you have a whimsical client or have to refresh a site regularly. You'll start in the first exercise by taking a step back to an unstyled version of the Javaco page and adding color to a few of the foreground elements.

1 | Adding Foreground Colors

In this brief exercise, you'll see how easy it can be to change the foreground color of elements using CSS. In CSS terms, the foreground is composed of elements such as text, images, and borders—the content present on the top level of the page.

1 Copy the **05_color** folder from the **CSS HOT CD-ROM** to your desktop.

2 In Firefox, open **ex0501.html** from the **05_color** folder you copied to your desktop, as shown in the illustration here.

This is one of the Javaco Web pages you've been working with up to this point but with most of the colors removed. The colors remaining on the page are there primarily because of your browser's settings. Now you'll examine these settings in Firefox.

You'll use Firefox specifically in this exercise because it offers an easy way to access the browser style sheet. If you haven't yet, download it for free at www.mozilla.com/firefox.

3 Open the Firefox Preferences by choosing **Firefox > Preferences** (Mac) or **Tools > Options** (Windows). Select the **Content** tab, and then click **Colors** under **Fonts & Colors**.

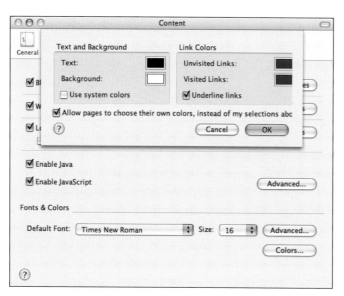

Here you can see the default colors for the text (black), the background color (white), the unvisited link color (blue), and the visited link color (purple) on the Web pages you visit. Firefox defaults to these colors if the Web page hasn't specified any other colors.

---

4 Click **Cancel**, and close the Firefox **Preferences** (Mac) or **Options** (Windows) dialog box.

JAVACO

about us | about tea | brewing | drinking | products | contact us

about tea: history

5 Click the **brewing** link at the top of the page.

This link doesn't go anywhere right now, but notice that the color changes from blue to purple. When you clicked it, you changed it from an unvisited link to a visited link, and therefore Firefox changed the color based on its own internal style sheet, which you viewed in the previous step by opening the Preferences (Mac) or Options (Windows) dialog box.

Now you'll change this page's style sheet to have it use different colors for text.

---

6 Open **ex0501.html** with your text or HTML (**H**yper**T**ext **M**arkup **L**anguage) editor, and place your cursor between the opening and closing **`<style>`** tags, as shown in the illustration here. Type the following:

```
p {color:teal;}
```

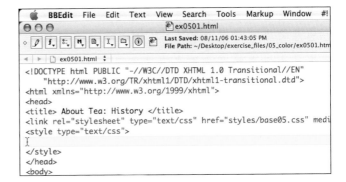

about us | about tea | brewing | drinking | products | contact us   July 16, 2006

about tea: history

Search

The Legendary Origins of Tea

tea of the day

Labrador Tea

The history of tea extends so far into the past that its very origins are shrouded by legend. It is said that Emperor Shen Nung, who ruled China in 2700 BC, used to enjoy relaxing in his garden with a cup of hot water. It was during one of these respites that a tea leaf happened to float down from a nearby bush, and land directly in the Emperor's cup. The new drink quickly became the Emperor's favorite, and a taste for tea quickly

 spread throughout the aristocracy, and it wasn't long before tea was the favored drink throughout all of China.

Lorem ipsum, dolor sit amet, consectetuer adipiscing elit, sed diam nonummy nibh euismod tincidunt ut laoreet dolore magna aliquam.

It was in the 16th century that Portuguese missionaries were seduced by tea's flavor and the intricate customs which surrounded it. A demand for the drink quickly arose, and the Dutch East India Company began importing it into Europe.

It's most likely that it was the Japanese green teas which were first to arrive in the west, owing to Japan's liberal trade policies with the Dutch. Initially, tea was chiefly recommended to Europeans for its purported medicinal qualities; it was claimed by the Dutch that tea was a cure for nearly every disease imaginable.

Due to the expense of bringing tea halfway across the globe, it was initially consumed primarily by aristocrats and the rich. Over time the cost of tea fell enough for people from all walks of life to be able to enjoy it. By 1717 Thomas Twining's English coffee house became a tea shop; and unlike the ubiquitous London coffee houses of the era, the doors of Twining's were open to both men and women. Meeting friends over tea became a staple of British life, and afternoon tea became a lasting tradition that still continues today.

post archive

July 2006

Sun Mon Tue Wed Thu Fri Sat

7 Save **ex0501.html**, switch to your browser, and reload **ex0501.html**.

Notice that all the regular paragraph text on the page is now teal. That's how easy it is to change the foreground text color—just add the **color** property to the element you want to change. You'll try coloring another text element next.

8 Return to your text or HTML editor. Insert a new line after the rule you just added, and type the following:

```
h2 {color: orange;}
```

9 Save **ex0501.html**, switch to your browser, and reload **ex0501.html**.

The **h2** element text is now orange. Also note that the border underneath the text is now orange as well.
In the next step, you'll see why that happened.

---

10 Return to your text or HTML editor. Open the
base05.css file from the **05_color/styles** folder. This is the
external style sheet you are using as the base for the Web
page. Scroll through the code to find the **h2** rule, as shown
in the illustration here.

```
h2 {
    margin: 0.5em 0; padding-bottom: 0.25em;
    border-bottom: 1px solid;
    font-size: 1.5em;
```

Notice that this **h2** rule contains a property called **border-bottom**, specifying that the bottom border should
be 1 pixel and solid. But you should also notice that no color has been specified here. In this case, the
border draws its color from the foreground of the element, **h2**.

If this is the effect you want, you're all set. If not, you can make the border color different from its parent
element.

---

11 Close **base05.css**, and return to **ex0501.html**. Place
your cursor after **h2 {color: orange;**, and type the following:

border-color: black;

```
<style type="text/css">
p {color: teal;}
h2 {color: orange; border-color: black;}
</style>
```

---

12 Save **ex0501.html**, switch to your browser, and reload **ex0501.html**.

There you go! The bottom border is now black.

---

13 Close **ex0501.html** in your browser and in your text or HTML editor.

In this exercise, you changed the color of the text and a few other foreground elements, such as the
heading and border. This was pretty simple, but keep in mind, working with multiple style sheets, such
as an internal and external style sheet, creates some added challenges. In the next exercise, you'll learn
how to change the background of elements. But first, make sure to check out the tip about defining
colors in CSS. You used color keywords in this exercise, but you can specify colors in several other ways.

Defining Colors in CSS

In the previous exercise, you specified the color of elements by using the actual names of colors, such as black, orange, teal, and so on. This is fine if you want to use a specific color that has a name. But you have actually five ways to specify colors in CSS. You'll want to learn and understand at least a few of these methods so you'll be able to apply colors without traditional names to your elements.

Keyword: You can use keyword color definitions, also known as **named colors**, when you need to pick from only a small, basic set of colors. To use a named color, it must exist in the CSS 2.1 specification. As of this writing, 17 named colors are available in the specification, as shown in the following chart:

CSS 2.1 Keyword Colors

maroon	red	orange	yellow	olive	purple
fuchsia	white	lime	green	navy	blue
aqua	teal	black	silver	gray	

Any browser claiming to be CSS compliant should be able to properly display these keyword colors. Specifying a color using a keyword looks like this:

`h1 {color: maroon;}`

Hexadecimal: If you've been working in Web design for some time now, you're most likely familiar with hexadecimal colors. Hexadecimal (hex) colors are defined by stringing together three pairs of numbers and letters in the range from 00 through FF. The generic syntax for this notation is `#RRGGBB`, where RR is the value for red, GG is the value for green, and BB is the value for blue. Therefore, the hexadecimal notation for white is `#FFFFFF`; red, green, and blue are at the full values. The hexadecimal notation for black is `#000000`; basically, this is the complete absence of red, green, and blue. Specifying a color using a hexadecimal value looks like this:

`h1 {color: #FFA500;}`

If you're using a Mac, you'll see the Apple DigitalColor Meter program in your Applications/Utilities folder. You can use this program to find the hexadecimal value of any color on your screen. Unfortunately, Windows doesn't offer a similar built-in utility, but a program such as Adobe Photoshop offers a color picker that can give you the hexadecimal value of any color you like.

Short hex: As mentioned, each pair of digits in a hexadecimal number describes the color level of red, green, and blue. CSS also offers a shorthand hexadecimal notation style you can use if you have a value in which all three pairs match. For example, the color orange is written as `#FF6600`, but it can also be written as `#F60`. When a browser comes across this type of notation, it knows to expand this three-digit number into

continues on next page

Defining Colors in CSS *continued*

matching pairs to produce **#FF6600**, or orange. You cannot use short hex for colors that don't contain a matching pair. For example, you can't write a short hex version of **#CA3701**. Hexadecimal and short hex colors have no functional difference; it's a matter of personal choice. Specifying a color using a short hex value looks like this:

`h1 {color: #C30;}`

RGB decimal: Similar to the way hexadecimal values span a range from 00 through FF, where 00 is no value and FF is full value, RGB (**R**ed, **G**reen, **B**lue) decimal values span a range from 0 through 255. For example, white is represented as **255, 255, 255**, and black is represented as **0, 0, 0**. Specifying a color using RGB decimal values looks like this:

`h1 {color: 204, 51, 0;}`

RGB percent: It's also possible to express colors in percentage notations, which can be useful if for some reason you want to specify that a color be exactly 25.7 percent red, 43 percent green, and 98.2 percent blue. RGB percentages span a range from 0 through 100 percent, where 0 is no value and 100 is the full value. Therefore, white is expressed as **100%, 100%, 100%**, and black is expressed as **0%, 0%, 0%**. Specifying a color using RGB percentage values looks like this:

`h1 {color 80%, 20%, 0%;}`

As you can see, you can express colors using CSS in many ways. Each of these offers different levels of variation and precision, and you can decide to use one or another depending on your design specification. The choice is entirely up to you.

VIDEO:

colors.mov

To learn more about the various ways to define colors in CSS, check out **colors.mov** in the **videos** folder on the **CSS HOT CD-ROM**.

2 | Adding Color to Elements' Backgrounds

In the previous exercise, you learned how to change the color of an element's foreground. In this exercise, you'll start examining the ways in which to add solid colors to your backgrounds. **Backgrounds** are pretty self-explanatory—they're the backdrop for the foreground of elements and include both the content area and the padding (because, as you may remember from the previous chapter, background shows through padding). Generally, it's considered good practice to assign a background color wherever you assign a foreground color, especially when you are working with objects with some transparency. So, let's get started.

1 In a browser, open **ex0502.html** from the **05_color** folder you copied to your desktop.

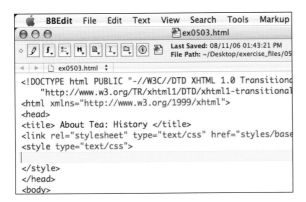

2 Open **ex0502.html** with your text or HTML editor, as shown in the illustration here.

When starting with CSS, one of the first techniques people want to learn is how to set the background color of an entire page. In old school HTML, you accomplish this by adding a `color` attribute to the `body` tag. In CSS, you essentially do the same.

3 After the leading **<style>** tag, insert a break, and type the following:

```
body {background-color: #E3EDC2;}
```

4 Save **ex0502.html**, switch to your browser, and reload **ex0502.html**.

This changes the background color of the entire page to a light green color, as shown in the illustration here.

With CSS, changing the background color is not that much different from changing it with regular HTML, where you might type **<body bgcolor="#E3EDC2">**. But with CSS, you're not limited to changing the color of only the Web page's body or just a few rows and columns in tables; you can set a background color for just about any element you want.

```
<style type="text/css">
body {background-color: #E3EDC2;}
#masthead {background-color: #ABD240;}
#navlinks {background-color: #686397;}
</style>
</head>
```

5 Return to your text or HTML editor. Here, let's pretend you want to change the background color of the masthead and navigation bar areas of the Web page. (If you scroll a few lines into your markup, you'll see the two elements—the **<div id="masthead">** and **<div id="navlinks">** tags.) Insert a new line after the first rule, and type the following:

```
#masthead {background-color: #ABD240;}
#navlinks {background-color: #686397;}
```

6 Save **ex0502.html**, switch to your browser, and reload **ex0502.html**.

The masthead and navigation areas now have new background colors. It's worth noting that color fills the entire background of the element to which it happens to be applied, but *not* the margin areas of elements. Don't worry about this now, though; I'll discuss margins, padding, and borders in a later chapter.

For now you'll continue coloring the backgrounds of more elements on your page.

---

7 Return to your text or HTML editor. Insert a new line after the **navlinks** rule, and type the following:

```
#sidebar {background-color: rgb(23%, 24%, 18%);}
```

In this step, you're coloring the sidebar area using RGB percentage values, just so you can get some practice defining colors this way.

8 Save **ex0502.html**, switch to your browser, and reload **ex0502.html**.

Voila! You've now colored the sidebar.

Another advantage of working with CSS is that you can create styles for elements that appear only within other elements. For example, the headings in the sidebar area are currently styled with **h3** tags. You can change the style of these tags but limit the change to the **h3** tags appearing only within the sidebar.

---

9 Return to your text or HTML editor. Insert a new line after the **sidebar** rule you just created. You'll use RGB decimal values for this example. Type the following:

```
#sidebar h3 {background-color: rgb(155, 150, 202);}
```

10 Save **ex0502.html**, switch to your browser, and reload **ex0502.html**.

The headings should have a light purplish-blue background. This color adds both contrast and some visual interest!

---

11 Close **ex0502.html** in your browser and in your text or HTML editor.

As this exercise shows, changing the background color of elements is a pretty simple task with CSS. It is more efficient in the short-term and easier to maintain in the long-term. Should you need to change your page color in the future, you know exactly where to find the code. In the next exercise, you'll move on from simple solid colors and start applying images to backgrounds.

---

3 | Adding Background Images

Now that you know the basics of setting foreground and background colors for elements, you'll look at the slightly more interesting and advanced topic of adding images to the background of your elements. Adding images is similar to changing the background color, but you should keep a few other important issues in mind, as you'll explore in this exercise.

1 In a browser, open **ex0503.html** from the **05_color** folder you copied to your desktop, as shown in the illustration here.

This version of the Javaco Web page has already been styled with background colors. Notice the gray color filling the main body of the page. You'll add a background image in the following steps.

2 Open **ex0503.html** with your text or HTML editor, as shown in the illustration here. Notice the rule here applies the gray background color to the **#content** area.

```
<style type="text/css">
#content {
    background-color: rgb(85%,85%,85%);
}
</style>
</head>
```

Now you'll add the rule to insert a background image in this element. To do this on your own site, you'll of course need to prepare an image and place it in your Web site's images folder. When you create the background image style, you'll add a URL (**U**niform **R**esource **L**ocator) reference to the location of the image. This can be either a relative link or an absolute link. In the next step, you'll insert an image called curl-gray.gif, which is currently stored in the images folder in the 05_color folder.

---

3 Insert a new line after the **#content** area's **background-color** rule, and type the following:

`background-image: url(images/curl-gray.gif);`

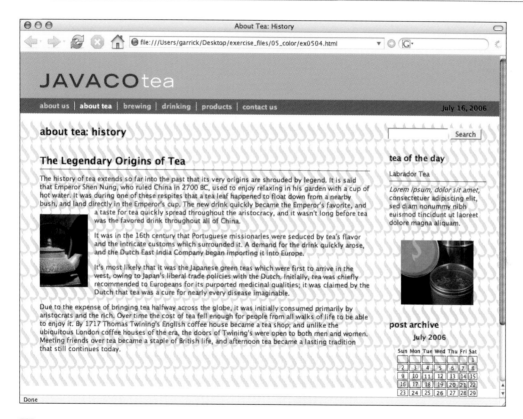

---

4 Save **ex0503.html**, switch to your browser, and reload **ex0503.html**.

And there's your background image. It's the default behavior of background images to continuously repeat themselves throughout the entire background of the element, from left to right and from top to bottom. Also, you no longer see the background color because it's completely obscured by the repeating background image.

---

5 Close **ex0503.html** in your browser and in your text or HTML editor.

N O T E : | **Linking to Images**

The link **images/curl-gray.gif** is a relative URL. **Relative** URLs point to a page in your Web site (versus **absolute** URLs that are used to link to an external resource). Those of you who have worked with XHTML should be familiar with this concept. However, when working with CSS, it's important to note that the address is always relative to the location of the style sheet. In other words, URLs referenced in your style sheets must be relative to the location of style sheet, not to the location of the HTML document. If the style sheet is embedded, these are one and the same, but it's something to look out for when you're using external style sheets.

So, that's how you add an image to the background area of an element. But that's not the only thing you can do with your background images. In the following exercises, you'll learn how to adjust the image's repeat and positioning properties.

4 | Repeating Background Images

In the previous exercise, you added an image to the background element of the **#content** area on the Javaco Web page, and you observed the default behavior of the image repeating itself from top to bottom and from left to right across the entirety of the element's background. In this exercise, you'll learn how to use the property **background-repeat** to control how the image repeats, rather than just letting it tile across the entire element.

1 In Firefox, open **ex0504.html** from the **05_color** folder you copied to your desktop, as shown in the illustration here.

Using CSS, you can have images repeat horizontally (also known as the **X axis**) and vertically (known as the **Y axis**), or you can choose to have images not repeat at all. In the following steps, you'll experiment with different repeat properties. In the next step, you'll begin by having the image repeat only along the horizontal, or X, axis.

2 Open **ex0504.html** with your text or HTML editor. Insert a new line after the **background-image** declaration, and type the following (as shown in the illustration here):

`background-repeat: repeat-x;`

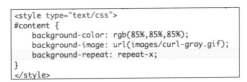
```
<style type="text/css">
#content {
    background-color: rgb(85%,85%,85%);
    background-image: url(images/curl-gray.gif);
    background-repeat: repeat-x;
}
</style>
```

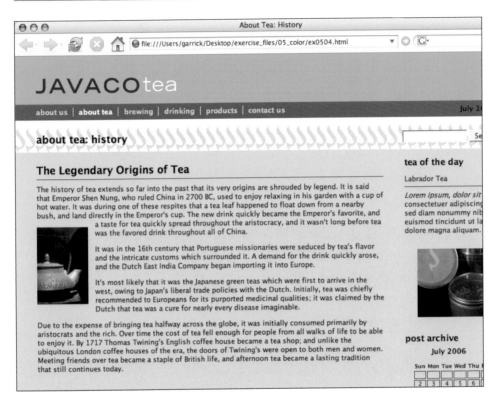

3 Save **ex0504.html**, switch to your browser, and reload **ex0504.html**.

Notice the image now repeats only horizontally. The rest of the content area's background is filled with the gray background color specified in the style sheet.

4 Drag the lower-right corner of the browser window to resize it, and notice how the background image continues to repeat horizontally, regardless of the size of the window.

Now you'll change the style sheet so the background image is restricted to repeating along the vertical, or Y, axis.

5 Return to your text or HTML editor. Change the **x** in the **background-repeat** property to a **y** as follows:

```
background-repeat: repeat-y;
```

6 Save **ex0504.html**, switch to your browser, and reload **ex0504.html**.

As expected, the background image now repeats only from top to bottom, and you see the background color in the area where the image does not appear.

You may want to use one more value here. If, for example, you have a large background image that you want to appear only once on your Web page, you can specify that the image should not repeat at all.

7 Return to your text or HTML editor. Change the **background-repeat** property as follows:

```
background-repeat: no-repeat;
```

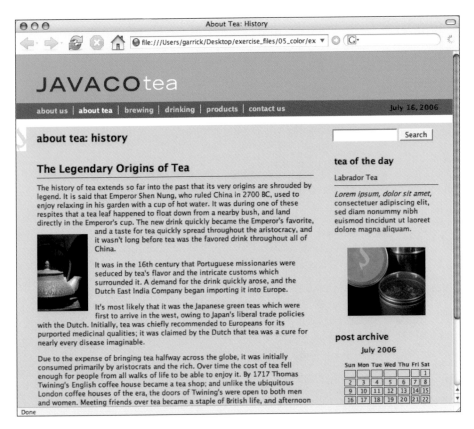

8 Save **ex0504.html**, switch to your browser, and reload **ex0504.html**.

The background image now appears only once in the element. In most cases, you would probably use **no-repeat** with a much larger background image.

---

9 Close **ex0504.html** in your browser and in your text or HTML editor.

You probably noticed that whether you're repeating the image horizontally, vertically, or not at all, the image remains oriented to the upper-left corner of the element. In many cases, this may be fine for what you need, but sometimes you may want to control where the image begins repeating. You'll learn how to do this in the next exercise.

---

5 | Positioning Background Images

Currently, the background image on the Javaco Web page is set not to repeat at all, and it's currently in the default location of being flush to the upper-left corner of the element area. In this exercise, you'll learn how to use the **background-position** property to affect the placement of an image in the background of an element.

---

1 In a browser, open **ex0505.html** from the **05_color** folder you copied to your desktop.

---

2 Open **ex0505.html** with your text or HTML editor. Insert a new line after the **background-repeat** property. Type the following (as shown in the illustration here):

```
background-position: top;
```

```
<style type="text/css">
#content {
    background-color: rgb(85%,85%,85%);
    background-image: url(images/curl-gray.gif);
    background-repeat: no-repeat;
    background-position: top;
}
</style>
```

In this example, **top** is the property's keyword. You can use five available keywords—**top**, **bottom**, **left**, **right**, and **center**—to assign both the horizontal and vertical positions.

---

3 Save **ex0505.html**, switch to your browser, and reload **ex0505.html**.

Notice that the nonrepeating background image is now centered along the top of the element area. If you have only one keyword, the browser assumes the keyword you didn't provide is **center**, which is why the image is centered along the horizontal axis. You could have typed **background-position: top center;** and ended up with the same result. The next step shows another example.

---

4   Return to your text or HTML editor. Change the **background-position** declaration as follows:

```
background-position: right bottom;
```

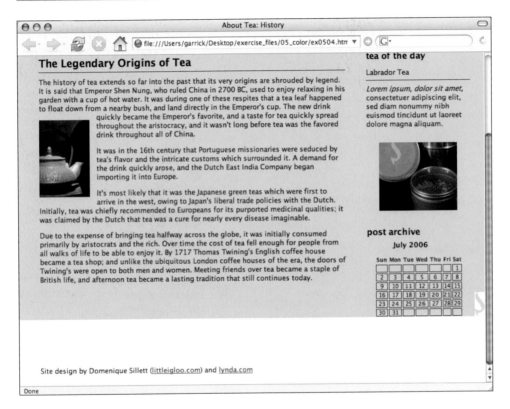

5   Save **ex0505.html**, switch to your browser, and reload **ex0505.html**.

The nonrepeating background image is now aligned to the lower-right corner of the element. It's worth noting that the order of the keywords doesn't matter. You could have also typed the property as **background-position: bottom right;** and achieved the same results.

You're not limited to just placing your images to the top, bottom, left, right, or center of an element. If you want to place an image more precisely at a specific location, you can also use percentage values.

---

6 Return to your text or HTML editor. Change the **background-position** property as follows:

`background-position: 50% 0;`

This will position the image halfway across and flush to the top of the element. However, be aware that, unlike keywords, when using percentages, the order does matter. You need to always specify the horizontal position first, followed by the vertical position.

7 Save **ex0505.html**, switch to your browser, and reload **ex0505.html**.

The result is the same as when you typed **background-position: top;**. But if you typed **background-position: 50% 0;** instead, the image would be centered vertically and flush to the left side of the element. Again, the order of the percentages *does* matter. But similar to using keywords, if you provide only a single percentage, the browser assumes the second, or vertical, position is 50 percent. For example, typing **background-position: 75%;** would result in the image being placed 3/4 of the way across the horizontal axis of the element and halfway down the vertical axis.

Lastly, for those times when you want an image to be absolutely positioned on a page with no chance of moving, regardless of the size of the browser window, you can use pixel-based positioning.

8 Return to your text or HTML editor. Change the **background-position** declaration as follows:

`background-position: 500px 50px;`

9 Save **ex0505.html**, switch to your browser, and reload **ex0505.html**.

10 Drag the lower-right corner of the browser window, and notice that the background image doesn't move at all. It remains exactly at 500 pixels across the X axis and 50 pixels down the Y axis.

You have many, many options when it comes to positioning your background images. If necessary, you can also combine the different types of positioning. For example, **background-position: 75% 50px;** would place the image 3/4 of the way across the element on the X axis and 50 pixels down the Y axis. As the browser window is resized, the image would move freely horizontally but always remain 50 pixels down from the top of the element.

So far you've been playing with the position of a nonrepeating image. But positioning works just the same if the image is repeating. The **background-position** property determines only from where in the element the image originates. You'll now see an example.

11 Return to your text or HTML editor. Change the **background-repeat** and **background-position** rules as follows:

background-repeat: repeat-x;
background-position: 75% 50px;

```
<style type="text/css">
#content {
    background-color: rgb(85%,85%,85%);
    background-image: url(images/curl-gray.gif);
    background-repeat: repeat-x;
    background-position: 75% 50px;|
}
</style>
```

12 Save **ex0505.html**, switch to your browser, and reload **ex0505.html**.

Here it appears as though the image is properly placed 50 pixels down the Y axis. However, it's actually repeating across the entire X axis instead of beginning 3/4 of the way across as you wanted. But this is actually the correct behavior based on the code: `repeat-x` means to repeat across the entire X axis, not just from left to right. So, the image really is originating from 3/4 of the way across the axis, but you can't tell because it's repeating from both the left and the right.

---

13 Return to your text or HTML editor. Change the **background-repeat** declaration as follows:
`background-repeat: repeat-y;`

14 Save **ex0505.html**, switch to your browser, and reload **ex0505.html**.

This time, you can see that the image is repeating across the entire Y axis, not just from top to bottom starting from 50 pixels down. CSS doesn't have any such thing as *repeat left* or *repeat right*—it has only **repeat-x**. And there's no *repeat up* or *repeat down*—only **repeat-y**.

---

15 Close **ex0505.html** in your browser and in your text or HTML editor.

VIDEO: **bgposition.mov**

To learn more about position properties, check out **bgposition.mov** in the **videos** folder on the **CSS HOT CD-ROM**.

Using the Background Shorthand Declaration

In the previous exercises, you learned about the properties for placing an image in the background of an element (**background-image**) and for adjusting the image's repeat (**background-repeat**) and position (**background-position**) settings. But when you use all these properties together, the result is a rather repetitive and unnecessarily verbose declaration set. In this exercise, you'll learn how to express all these items in a single property.

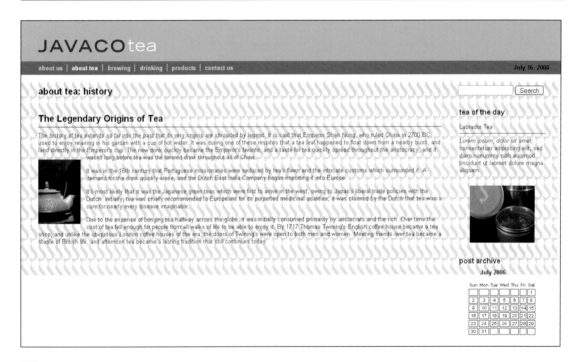

1 In a browser, open **ex0506.html** from the **05_color** folder you copied to your desktop, as shown in the illustration here.

2 Open **ex0506.html** with your text or HTML editor. Review the **#content** rule in the style sheet.

The style properties you see here are similar to what you wrote toward the close of the previous exercise. But you don't need to separate these items into four individual properties, so you'll fix this in the next step.

```
<style type="text/css">
#content {
    background-color: rgb(85%,85%,85%);
    background-image: url(images/curl-gray.gif);
    background-repeat: repeat;
    background-position: 0 0;
}
</style>
```

3 Change the **#content** rule as follows:

```
#content {
background: rgb(85%,85%,85%) url(images/curl-gray.gif) repeat 0 0;
}
```

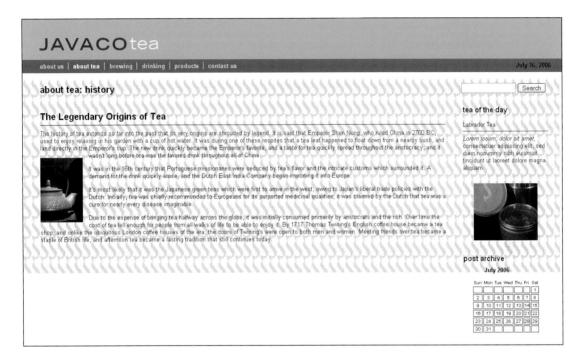

4 Save **ex0506.html**, switch to your browser, and reload **ex0506.html**.

Notice that nothing appears to change in your browser. By using **background:**, you've accessed a "shorthand" version of all those other individual background properties. For the most part, the order of the properties doesn't matter. You can list the repeat values first, followed by the background color, followed by the image URL if you want. It really depends on how you prefer to list them. Just be aware that if you don't include a property (for example, if you don't specify a position), the browser will always use the default property, which in the case of **background-position** is the upper-left corner of the element.

The trick to using the **background** property is to simply list all the properties you want to change, one after another, and exclude any properties you want to set at their default values.

5 Return to your text or HTML editor. Change the **background** rule as follows:

```
background: url(images/curl-gray.gif) no-repeat 50% 75% rgb(85%,85%,0%);
```

Here you are changing not only the value of the properties but the order as well. All the property values and image repetition options you learned in the previous exercises will work with this shorthand declaration, just as if you wrote them individually.

6 Save **ex0506.html**, switch to your browser, and reload **ex0506.html**.

There you go. You changed the background color of the content area to a greenish hue, and the gray curl image is nonrepeating and located 75 percent of the way down the page and halfway in the middle. It's not the most attractive design, but it illustrates the point.

Note: You cannot separate your **background-position** values. In other words, you can't write **background: url(images/curl-gray.gif) no-repeat 50% rgb (85%,85%,0%) 75%;**. This is the exception to the rule about combining property values in any order; however, since **background-position** is a single property, this makes sense.

7 Close **ex0506.html** in your browser and in your text or HTML editor.

Congratulations on finishing this chapter! You cannot underestimate the importance of color in your final composition, and the more controls you have, the better the final result. CSS makes this possible. In the next chapter, you'll look at another important element of page design: typography, including fonts, font sizing, justification, and alignment.

6

Setting Typography

In this chapter, you'll review the essentials of CSS (**C**ascading **S**tyle **S**heets) typography. Now, if you talk to a hard-core typographer, they can get really excited about topics such as leading and kerning, serifs, swashes, and buckles. These are just a few of the many, many elements making up typography (except for buckles, of course—that was a joke). In print design, most designers work with specialized software such as Adobe InDesign and Adobe Illustrator so they have access to a full range of tools and options, such as specialized fonts and type catalogs.

CSS is not quite this advanced. It doesn't have what a typographer would consider real kerning control or leading control. Nevertheless, though CSS has little in the way of advanced typography controls, it does allow you to affect the fonts, font sizes, and other basic elements of the presentation of text and, better yet, apply these universally through your Web page and even an entire site.

1 | Altering Line Height

In this exercise, you'll review the `line-height` property. The simplest definition of **line height** is that it's the vertical distance between lines of text. (Typographers, by the way, refer to the difference between the line height and the font size as the **leading**.) In CSS, line height increases the size of the inline boxes containing the text, actually expanding the content area of the element on the page. In this exercise, you'll start with a basic `line-height` declaration and then review how the different values you can assign—lengths, percentages, and multipliers—affect your composition.

1 Copy the **06_type** folder from the **CSS HOT CD-ROM** to your desktop.

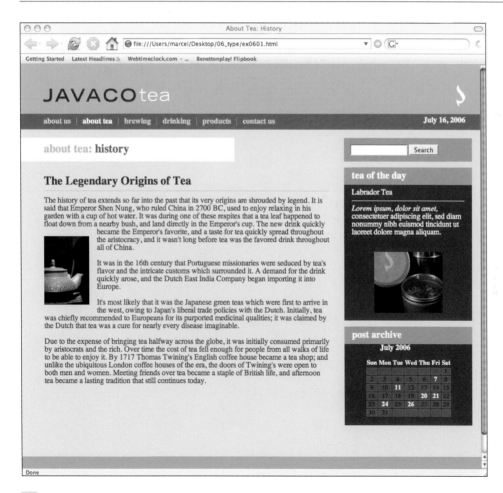

2 In a browser, open **ex0601.html** from the **06_type** folder you copied to your desktop, as shown in the illustration here.

3 Open **ex0601.html** in your text or HTML editor. After the `<style>` start tag, type the following:

`p {line-height: 3;}`

This is one of those rare cases in CSS where you can have a numeric value that doesn't require a unit after it. That's because 3 doesn't mean 3 pixels, 3 inches, 3 millimeters, or even 3 light years. It's simply 3. We call this value a **multiplier**. You'll next see how this translates in your browser.

4 Save **ex0601.html**, switch to your browser, and reload **ex0601.html**.

There you go. The lines of text in the paragraph are now generously spaced. What happened was that this rule used the multiplier to calculate the line height, multiplying the element's font size by 3. That's how a multiplier works. If, for example, the font size were 15 pixels, the line height for these paragraphs would be 45. The best feature of the multiplier is that if the font size were to change, the line height would scale accordingly. Use your shortcut keys (Ctrl+plus or minus [Windows] or Cmd+plus or minus [Mac]) to preview this scaling effect in your browser.

As mentioned in Chapter 4, *"Using CSS to Affect Page Layout,"* you can use another unit of measurement that also supports scaling: ems. You'll try this in the next step.

5 Open **ex0601.html** in your text or HTML editor. Modify the first rule as follows:

```
p {line-height: 3em;}
```

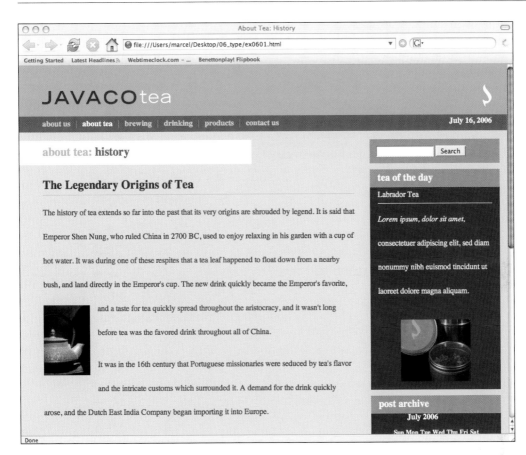

6 Save **ex0601.html**, switch to your browser, and reload **ex0601.html**.

As you can see, 3 ems has essentially the same visual effect here as using a multiplier, because an em scales with the font size in a similar manner.

You can also use length measurements for line height, although it's not recommended. Why? You'll see why in the next step.

7 Open **ex0601.html** in your text or HTML editor. Modify the first rule as follows:

```
p {line-height: 1px;}
```

8 Save **ex0601.html**, switch to your browser, and reload **ex0601.html**.

The paragraphs are now completely compressed. A 1-pixel line height is kind of ridiculous, I admit, but it illustrates the problem with length-based values. They have no relationship to the font size. Even if you were to assign a more normal line height, let's say 15 pixels, if the user were to resize the font to a larger size, 18 pixels even, they'd run into the same problem. Fortunately, CSS doesn't allow negative line height values, or you'd get yourself into more trouble there. Let's move on.

9 Open **ex0601.html** in your text or HTML editor. Modify the first rule as follows:

```
p {line-height: 1em;}
```

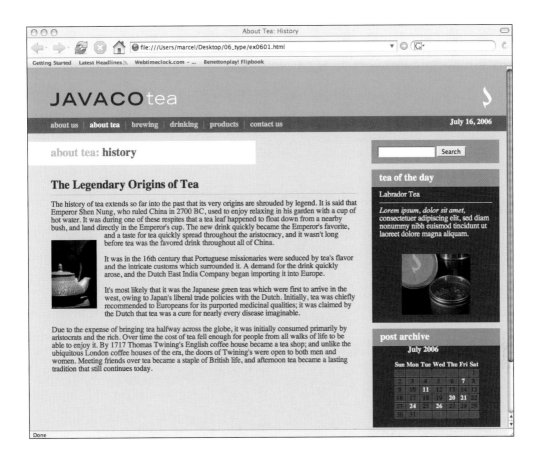

10 Save **ex0601.html**, switch to your browser, and reload **ex0601.html**.

This is a significant improvement over the results from the previous step. However, if you were particularly attuned to the way browsers lay elements out by default, you'd notice this is still a little more crowded than a regular Web page.

That's because the usual default line height for Web pages is somewhere around 1.2 ems. But like so many other properties in CSS, it depends on the individual browser. The CSS specification doesn't explicitly state what the default line height should be. Different written languages (English, Arabic, and so on) have different defaults, and CSS isn't specific to a single language. So instead, the specification generalizes it as "about 1.2 ems." But from browser to browser, you may find some differences. So, don't rely on the defaults if you have a specific line height in mind. Declare it as you have here.

You returned to using ems in this step. Why use ems over multipliers in your `line-height` declarations, if they are nearly equivalent? Well, this is hard to illustrate on the paragraph level, so you'll jump up to the body to see the difference. First, you'll use an em unit of measurement.

---

11 Open **ex0601.html** in your text or HTML editor. Modify the first rule as follows:

```
body {line-height: 1.5em;}
```

This should make the line height of the **body** element 1.5 times the font size of the element.

12 Save **ex0601.html**, switch to your browser, and reload **ex0601.html**.

Notice the line height of the content area text has expanded, but so has the line height of everything else on the page. Why?

Let's say the **body** element's font size is 12 pixels—either set in the markup, specified in a style sheet, or set by the user agent. Per the rule, multiply 12 pixels by 1.5 ems to get a resulting line height value of 18 pixels. That value of 18 pixels would be inherited by not just the paragraph text but by all the descendent elements of the **body** element (which you probably recall from the discussion of inheritance in Chapter 3, *"Selectors and the Cascade"*). This means **h1** elements, paragraphs, links, and so on, would all inherit that exact 18-pixel value, regardless of the font size of their own text.

Now, you'll try the same rule with a multiplier.

13 Open **ex0601.html** in your text or HTML editor. Modify the first rule as follows:

```
body {line-height: 1.5;}
```

14 Save and close **ex0601.html**, switch to your browser, and reload **ex0601.html**.

After you reload, you should notice a small but important change. Instead of inheriting the body's line height (**18px**), the descendent elements instead inherit the multiplier. So, each element calculates their line height using that multiplier and their font size. The **h1** heading, for example, might have a font size of 18 pixels. Times that by the multiplier, 1.5, and the line height for that element is 27 pixels.

Now imagine on this same page you used the 1 em value in the **line-height** declaration and you had a header with a font size of 32 pixels. The resulting line height would still be 18 pixels. But this value would be directly inherited by the header and create the crowding effect you witnessed in Step 8.

Inheritance is why the difference between the multiplier and the em in the **line-height** declaration is important and why I recommend the multiplier so strongly over the em. I strongly discourage using pixel values at all in this context. If you really, really, want you can assign pixel line heights, but again, you could be setting yourself up for a lot of anguish down the road.

In this exercise, you reviewed and practiced setting **line-height** declarations. Moreover, you discovered the importance of using scaling factors, such as multipliers, versus length- or em-based measurements in your style sheets wherever possible. Next, you'll review font faces, font families, and what browser compatibility has to do with it all.

2 | Using Font Families

In this exercise, you'll look at font families and font faces. What's the difference? Essentially, **font families** are collections of **font faces** (also known as typefaces). Verdana is a font family, which includes the faces Verdana bold, Verdana italic, Verdana bold italic, and so on. Font families do not each have the same number of faces. For instance, Microsoft's Tahoma font has no italic face. In this exercise, you'll see what happens to your Web page when you select an unavailable font face. You'll also learn some ways to improve the user experience by assigning fallback fonts as well as how to manage browser discrepancies.

1 In a browser, open **ex0602.html** from the **06_type** folder you copied to your desktop, as shown in the illustration here.

2 Open **ex0602.html** in your text or HTML editor. After the **<style>** start tag, type the following:

```
h1, h2, h3, h4 {font-family: Verdana;}
```

3 Save **ex0602.html**, switch to your browser, and reload **ex0604.html**.

If you look at your headings, "about tea" or "The Legendary Origins of Tea," now they're using Verdana. What happens, technically, is that first the browser uses the font family Verdana and then picks the appropriate font face from within that family. Remember, a font family is a collection of font faces, such as Verdana Bold, Verdana Italic, and so on. Since you haven't specified any additional font attributes, such as `font-style`, `font-weight`, and so on, the browser chooses the default font face: normal, un-italicized text.

Now, you are not limited to specifying just one font family. In fact, that's typically discouraged in Web design, because if that font family does not exist on a user's computer, the browser would select another font, and the page could look completely different from what you intended. What you can do instead is provide a comma-delimited list of fallback fonts for the browser to use. The browser will scroll through the list until it finds a font family it can display. That way, you can choose a variety of related fonts to make your Web page look more consistent across browsers.

4 Return to **ex0602.html** in your text or HTML editor. Modify the style sheet as follows:

```
h1, h2, h3, h4 {font-family: Verdana, Arial, Helvetica, sans-serif;}
#sidebar p {font-family: "Courier New", monospace;}
```

This rule tells the browser "look for Verdana; if you don't have that, then look for Arial; if you don't have Arial, look for Helvetica; and so on." If by some bizarre quirk of fate, this browser is running on a computer with none of these three fairly common fonts, it will display the text in any available sans-serif font. The same thing goes for the sidebar paragraphs. If Courier New is not available on the user's computer, the text will display in any monospace font.

Note that for Courier New, you have placed the name in quotation marks. If a font name is two words, remember to envelope it in either single or double quotation marks so the browser reads it as a single value.

NOTE:

Generic Font Families

Beyond font faces and font families, there is a broad category for fonts in CSS called **generic font families**. Several generic font families exist; the major ones are serif and sans-serif, although CSS also defines cursive, fantasy, and monospace. Every font family may not be available on every user's computer. Available fonts vary between operating systems and can also depend on the kinds of programs the user has installed, since some programs, such as Microsoft Office, come with additional font packs. So, it may be valuable to designate a generic font family for the browser to choose from as a last resort, if the user doesn't have any of the other preferred fonts you've specified installed on their computer.

So, what are the differences between these generic font families? The major difference between the two biggies, serif and sans-serif, for me, comes down to a simple explanation.

> This is a serif font. Can you tell why?
>
> This is a sans-serif font. Can you tell why?

Check out the illustration shown here. Do you notice the little nub that comes down on the lowercase *a* and the way the tail extends on the *y* in the first line? Those are **serifs**, little embellishments on the ends of the strokes in each character. Fonts that have those are called **serif fonts**. Fonts without those are called **sans-serif fonts**. A real expert in typography might be mortified by this simple explanation, but that's the basic difference. Also worth noting, both serif and sans-serif fonts are proportional, meaning that not every character takes up the same amount of horizontal space on the page; for example, an *i* will take up less space than a *w*. In monospace fonts, on the other hand, every character takes up the same amount of horizontal space, kind of like on a typewriter.

continues on next page

NOTE:

Generic Font Families *continued*

The following chart shows some examples of the fonts that make up the generic font families:

Generic Font Families	
Family	**Examples**
Sans-serif	Arial, Verdana, Tahoma
Serif	Times New Roman, Garamond, Georgia
Fantasy	Critter, Cottonwood
Cursive	Adobe Poetica, Zapf-Chancery
Monospace	Courier New, Courier, Prestige

5 Save **ex0602.html**, switch to your browser, and reload **ex0602.html**.

Since I have all these fonts installed on my computer, in the illustration shown here, you'll notice the headings default to Verdana and the sidebar paragraph is in Courier New. This is also an excellent illustration of the proportional quality of serif fonts versus monospace fonts. Next you'll try one of the other generic font families.

6 Return to **ex0602.html** in your text or HTML editor. Modify the style sheet as follows:

```
h1, h2, h3, h4 {font-family: Verdana, Arial, Helvetica, sans-serif;}
#sidebar p {font-family: "Courier New", monospace;}
#content p {font-family: fantasy;}
```

7 Save **ex0602.html**, switch to your browser, and reload **ex0602.html**.

Depending on the number of fantasy fonts installed on your computer, you may get a very different-looking font for the content paragraph from the one shown here. You can't predict what font a browser will select when you specify only a generic font family. That's why it's generally recommended you leave the generic font family value at the end of your list of possible font values—it should really be a last resort.

8 Return to **ex0602.html** in your text or HTML editor. Modify the style sheet as follows:

```
h1, h2, h3, h4 {font-family: Verdana, Arial, Helvetica, sans-serif;}
#sidebar p {font-family: "Courier New", monospace;}
#content p {font-family: cursive;}
```

9 Save **ex0602.html**, switch to your browser, and reload **ex0602.html**.

Now here's a cursive font. Again, you probably will see a different cursive font displayed in your own browser. The main problem is no cursive fonts are common to all operating systems and all browsers. Sans-serif fonts, such as Verdana and Arial, are fairly widespread. You can find them on almost every computer. Serif fonts, such as Times and Times New Roman, are also common on Windows, Macs, and even Linux machines. But as far as cursive and fantasy fonts go, nothing is cross-platform. Why? Well, it's mostly because of historical reasons. When Microsoft created Web fonts for free distribution in the mid- to late-1990s, the fonts were all serif, sans-serif, and monospace. So those fonts were installed all over the place. Thanks to Microsoft, we have Verdana. But Microsoft did not include any cursive or fantasy fonts in that package. Thus, those fonts are rarely used in Web design to this day.

However, if the browser cannot find any font it can identify as cursive, it will fall back to a default. It's not as if you won't have any font at all; it just won't be cursive. But it can get even more interesting when you try to specify a font face.

10 Return to **ex0602.html** in your text or HTML editor. Modify the style sheet as follows:

```
h1, h2, h3, h4 {font-family: Verdana, Arial, Helvetica, sans-serif;}
#sidebar p {font-family: "Courier New", monospace;}
#content p {font-family: cursive; font-style: italic;}
```

11 Save **ex0602.html**, switch to your browser, and reload **ex0602.html**.

The way that CSS's font selection works is that for every character displayed, the browser looks for a cursive font that has an available italic face. If it can't find one, it "generates" them. So, first, it looks for the resources installed on the user's computer, and second, if it doesn't have the resources, it sees whether it can generate them on its own. Every browser might figure this out differently.

So, in the example shown here, Firefox might take the italic text you had and just add a slant, a little like a skew that you might find in Adobe Photoshop.

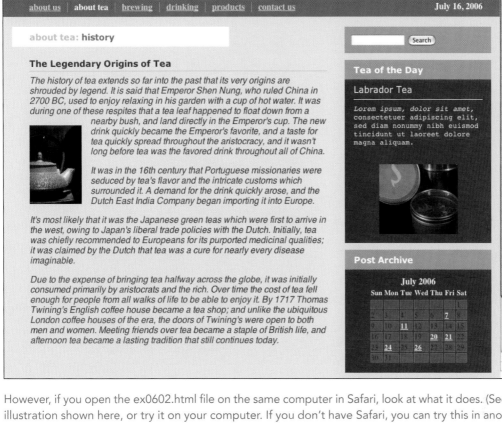

However, if you open the ex0602.html file on the same computer in Safari, look at what it does. (See the illustration shown here, or try it on your computer. If you don't have Safari, you can try this in another browser, such as Microsoft Internet Explorer.)

Safari knows it needs a cursive font family and an italic font face. Safari didn't find one. Rather than programmatically slanting the text, like Firefox did, it just stopped looking for cursive and looked for an available font with an italicized font face. Safari is not wrong for doing this—it's just not consistent with other browsers. For example, in the next step you'll try removing the italic **font-style** declaration.

---

12 Return to **ex0602.html** in your text or HTML editor. Modify the style sheet as follows:

```
h1, h2, h3, h4 {font-family: Verdana, Arial, Helvetica, sans-serif;}
#sidebar p {font-family: "Courier New", monospace;}
#content p {font-family: cursive;}
```

13 Save and close **ex0602.html**, switch to Firefox or your default browser, and reload **ex0602.html**.

---

14 Return to Safari or your other second browser, and reload **ex0602.html**.

> This is a serif font. Can you tell why?
>
> This is a sans-serif font. Can you tell why?

Here, you still have a cursive font effect, but it's not consistent with the display in Firefox. It would be nice if all browsers read documents the same way, but in the entire history of browsers, that has never happened. Even in the beginning, when there were only two contenders in the entire world, Netscape Navigator and Internet Explorer, they did not do the same things. Since then, we've actually come a long way—browsers today are more consistent than ever.

This is another reason why designers tend not to use cursive fonts. The way font selection works, it could cause major discrepancies in the way the page looks. It's the same with fantasy fonts. A browser may decide the only available fantasy font is Webdings and replace all the text with symbols. Yikes! Therefore, serif, sans-serif, and monospace are typically the only fonts you will see on the Web. Monospace is usually restricted to publishing code (or CSS, as the case may be). It is possible for even noncursive fonts to not have the face you're looking for, such as italic or bold. If the font displays strangely when you style it, it could simply be that the browser can't find the font face with the particular combination of effects in the font family you want to use, and it's falling back to a different font family. Therefore, it's always a good idea to specify a few extra font families you would be willing to fall back on so the browser isn't forced to make this choice for you.

In this exercise, you reviewed the basics of font families and font faces, practiced working with font selections, and reviewed discrepancies in font presentation in different browsers. In the next exercise, you will start to modify font styles and weights using CSS properties.

---

3 | Changing Font Styles and Weights

In this exercise, you'll look at three properties that affect font presentation. The first of these is `font-style`, and then you'll work with `font-weight` and `font-variant`.

1 In a browser, open **ex0603.html** from the **06_type** folder you copied to your desktop, as shown in the illustration here.

2 Open **ex0603.html** in your text or HTML editor. After the **<style>** start tag, type the following:

```
p {
font-style: italic;
}
```

3 Save **ex0603.html**, switch to your browser, and reload **ex0603.html**.

All the paragraph elements are now italic. This is a specific italic font face created for this font (Arial). **font-style** has one other value, which is **oblique**. Italic and oblique are ostensibly different. You'll view this in the next step.

---

4 Return to your text or HTML editor. Modify the **p** rule as follows:

```
p {
font-style: oblique;
}
```

5 Save **ex0603.html**, switch to your browser, and reload **ex0603.html**.

Well, there doesn't appear to be much of a difference, at least not in the browser in the illustration shown here. The oblique font is really just the regular font that is slanted. Italic is an actual font face; the letter forms are specifically drawn for the purposes of being displayed in italics. However, as it turns out, most browsers treat italic and oblique as equivalent. It might be that one or two browsers attempt to draw a distinction, but almost no Web designer uses `oblique` because of this reason.

The third value for `font-style`, by the way, is `normal`, but since this is the default value, you don't need to specify this in your style sheet. However, you have one more way to affect the appearance of your font, and that is using the property `font-weight`.

---

6 Return to your text or HTML editor. Modify the **p** rule as follows:

```
p {
font-style: italic;
font-weight: bold;
}
```

7 Save **ex0603.html**, switch to your browser, and reload **ex0603.html**.

Now you have bold and italic text. Bold-facing involves different faces than either italic or normal. If you were to dig into the guts of a font package on a computer, you would find a normal italic font face, a bold font face, and a bold italic font face, among others, as you reviewed in the previous exercise.

---

8 Return to your text or HTML editor. Modify the **p** rule as follows:

```
p {
font-style: italic;
font-weight: bolder;
}
```

9 Save **ex0603.html**, switch to your browser, and reload **ex0603.html**.

Changing the **font-weight** attribute to **bolder** tells the browser to "make the font of this element bolder than the parent element." However, it honestly doesn't have much of an impact in the browser shown in the illustration here, Firefox.

Another option for the **font-weight** attribute is setting a font weight as a numeric value (100–900, in increments of 100, effectively a choice of 9 weights), from a very light to very heavy font. Yet most browsers don't recognize these values, and the fonts that are available don't have the faces to support numeric values anyway. So, you will usually use a **font-weight** of **bold** or **normal** (the default).

You can affect font appearance in one more way—using the **font-variant** property. You'll review that in the next step.

---

10 Return to your text or HTML editor. Modify the style sheet as follows:

```
h1, h2, h3, h4 {
  font-variant: small-caps;
}
p {
font-style: italic;
font-weight: bolder;
}
```

Here you added another rule; this one has multiple selectors, headings 1–4. The **font-variant** property actually has only one other value besides its default, and that is what you specified here, **small-caps**. You'll next return to the browser and see how this impacts your Web page.

11 Save **ex0603.html**, switch to your browser, and reload **ex0603.html**.

You'll notice how the headings have changed to use **small caps**, or small capitals. In other words, capital letters are used throughout, but what would ordinarily be lowercase has small capitals (like a subscript), and those letters that would ordinarily use uppercase have normal capitals. So the word *tea* in "tea of the day" has a big capital *T* and a smaller capital *E* and *A*.

Again, because this property really has only two values, **normal** and **small-caps**, the only time you would ever use **font-variant** is when you want an element to have small caps. This has an interesting effect when applied to paragraphs, though, which you will do in the next step.

12 Return to your text or HTML editor. Modify the style sheet as follows:

```
h1, h2, h3, h4 {
  font-variant: small-caps;
}
p {
  font-variant: small-caps;
  font-style: italics;
  font-weight: bolder;
}
```

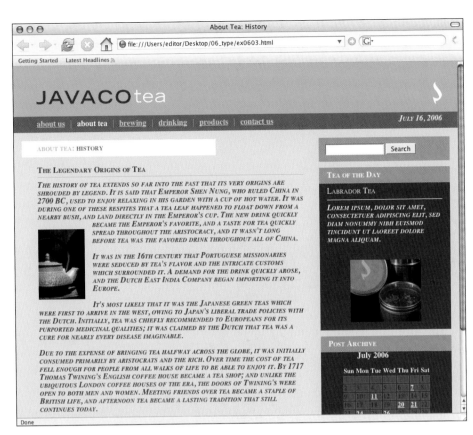

13 Save and close **ex0603.html**, switch to your browser, and reload **ex0603.html**.

As it turns out, the font you are using has the ability to have a bold, italic, small-caps font face. These are individual faces within the font. Note, not every font will allow you to combine these attributes, depending on the font faces available. Some fonts will not permit you to both bold and italicize them. This is rare, but it can happen.

I'll discuss font faces and the inner workings of fonts later in this chapter, but these are the main attributes used to affect font face. The main point to take away from this exercise is that you can use italic, use bold, and use small caps, and often you can combine them; however, occasionally, you may run into limitations because of the font you are using. With commonly used fonts, this is usually not an issue. In fact, you'll see in a later exercise how characters are assigned given font faces and what the implications can be.

In this exercise, you'll explore sizing fonts. This is a subject that could rightfully occupy its own book. I could spend entire chapters just discussing fonts and font sizing and all the ins and outs. However, the basics are really simple. You make an element have a font size that's either a specific length, such as 12 pixels, or a size related to its parent element, such as 1.5 em. In this exercise, I'll also discuss why you might want to choose one over another.

1 In a browser, open **ex0604.html** from the **06_type** folder you copied to your desktop, as shown in the illustration here.

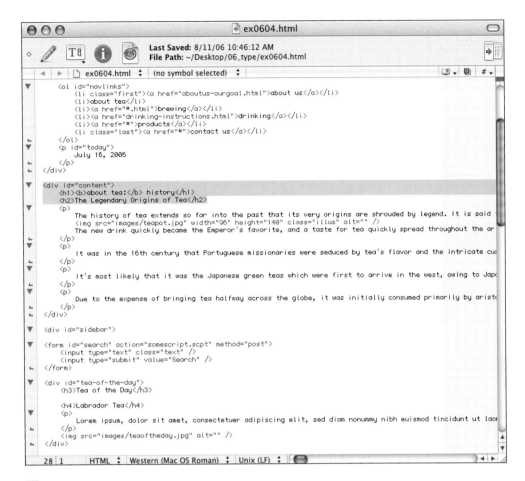

```
<ol id="navlinks">
    <li class="first"><a href="aboutus-ourgoal.html">about us</a></li>
    <li>about tea</li>
    <li><a href="#.html">brewing</a></li>
    <li><a href="drinking-instructions.html">drinking</a></li>
    <li><a href="#">products</a></li>
    <li class="last"><a href="#">contact us</a></li>
</ol>
<p id="today">
    July 16, 2006
</p>
</div>

<div id="content">
    <h1><b>about tea:</b> history</h1>
    <h2>The Legendary Origins of Tea</h2>
    <p>
        The history of tea extends so far into the past that its very origins are shrouded by legend. It is said 
        <img src="images/teapot.jpg" width="96" height="140" class="illus" alt="" />
        The new drink quickly became the Emperor's favorite, and a taste for tea quickly spread throughout the ar
    </p>
    <p>
        It was in the 16th century that Portuguese missionaries were seduced by tea's flavor and the intricate cus
    </p>
    <p>
        It's most likely that it was the Japanese green teas which were first to arrive in the west, owing to Japa
    </p>
    <p>
        Due to the expense of bringing tea halfway across the globe, it was initially consumed primarily by arist
    </p>
</div>

<div id="sidebar">

<form id="search" action="somescript.scpt" method="post">
    <input type="text" class="text" />
    <input type="submit" value="Search" />
</form>

<div id="tea-of-the-day">
    <h3>Tea of the Day</h3>

    <h4>Labrador Tea</h4>
    <p>
        Lorem ipsum, dolor sit amet, consectetuer adipiscing elit, sed diam nonummy nibh euismod tincidunt ut lao
    </p>
    <img src="images/teaoftheday.jpg" alt="" />
</div>
```

2   Open **ex0604.html** in your text or HTML editor. After the **<style>** start tag, type the following:

#content h1 {font-size: 200%;}

This rule instructs the browser to resize the font size of the first heading to 200 percent of the size of the parent element. If you scroll down in the markup, as shown in the illustration here, you can find the parent element of the **h1** element; it's actually the **div** element with the ID of **content**.

3 Save **ex0604.html**, switch to your browser, and reload **ex0604.html**.

There you go! The "about tea" header font size is now 200 percent, or twice the size, of the text in the parent element. In the style sheet, I could change the value to ems and have it be functionally equivalent. In fact, you can use three units of measurement with the **font-size** values. You'll see what they are in the next two steps.

---

4 Return to **ex0604.html** in your text or HTML editor. Modify the style sheet as follows:

```
#content h1 {font-size: 2em;}
#content h2 {font-size: 150%;}
```

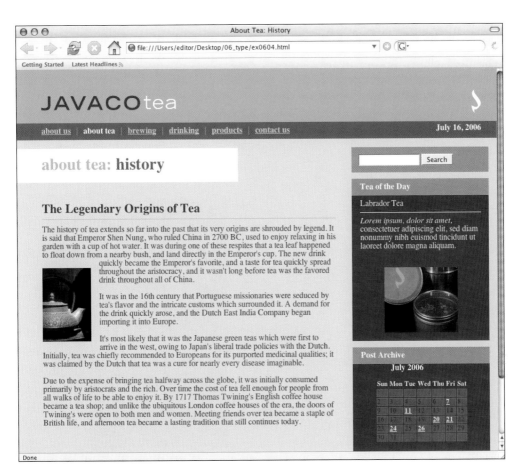

5 Save **ex0604.html**, switch to your browser, and reload **ex0604.html**.

And voila! The **h1** element did not change in size, because 2 ems is functionally equivalent in this case to 200 percent. The **h2** element was also increased in size to 150 percent, or 1.5 times the font size of the parent element. Now, you're not constrained to only ems and percentages; you'll now look at a third measurement you can use for font size.

---

6 Return to **ex0604.html** in your text or HTML editor. Modify the style sheet as follows:

```
#content h1 {font-size: 2em;}
#content h2 {font-size: 150%;}
p {font-size: smaller;}
```

7 Save **ex0604.html**, switch to your browser, and reload **ex0604.html**.

The font size of the paragraph element is now significantly smaller. How much smaller? Well, again, this is related to the font size of the parent element, the content **div**. The rule just states "make the font size of this element smaller than the parent element." It could be a tiny bit smaller; it could be a whole lot smaller. The CSS specification does not explicitly define the degree.

In practice, **smaller** usually comes out to be about 0.85 em. However, this is not always equivalent between browsers. I would love to be able to provide you with examples of situations in which there are differences, but the algorithms are not easily analyzable. Take it on faith that **font-size: smaller** is about 0.85 em. You might use this value when you are not too concerned about what size the paragraph element is—you just need it smaller. The same is true for the **font-size: larger** declaration. It just increases the font size of the element in relation to the font size of the parent element. Again, the CSS specification doesn't specify how much larger, but it's usually in the vicinity of 1.2 ems to 1.25 ems.

---

8 Return to **ex0604.html** in your text or HTML editor. Modify the style sheet as follows:

```
#content h1 {font-size: 2em;}
#content h2 {font-size: 150%;}
p {font-size: 85%;}
```

In this step, you're trying to see the difference between the **smaller** value and a stated value of 85 percent. Pay careful attention in the next step, particularly to the fourth and fifth lines of the first paragraph, after you hit Reload.

9 Save **ex0604.html**, switch to your browser, and reload **ex0604.html**.

See that? It's a tiny change. The fourth and fifth lines of the first paragraph seemed to get slightly smaller. That's what I mean about the algorithms; it's difficult to measure the change. You can use other keywords for font size, such as **plain**, **old small**.

10 Return to **ex0604.html** in your text or HTML editor. Modify the style sheet as follows:

```
#content h1 {font-size: 2em;}
#content h2 {font-size: 150%;}
body {font-size: small;}
```

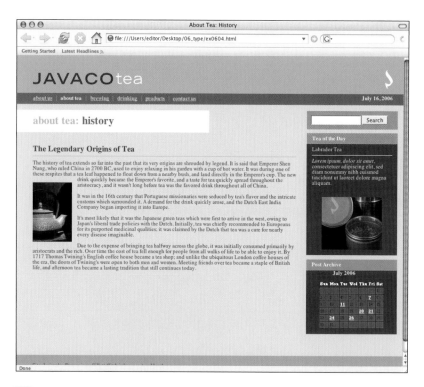

11 Save **ex0604.html**, switch to your browser, and reload **ex0604.html**.

You'll also notice everything scales in relationship to the **body {font-size...}** rule you just added because **body** is another parent element.

NOTE:

Font-Size Keywords

You can use seven keywords for the **font-size** value. These are listed in Appendix A, *"CSS 2 Properties,"* with the other attribute/value combinations, but it's useful to review them here.

Exactly what these values correspond to is up to each browser. The percentages listed here are only estimates. Every browser could translate **xx-large** as a completely different size, as long as in each browser, **xx-large** is larger than **x-large**, and so on. The default for CSS is always **medium**. This will always be the default in your browser.

Font-Size Keywords	
Keyword	**Estimated % of Original Font Size**
xx-small	60%
x-small	75%
small	85%
medium	100% (default value)
large	120–125%
x-large	150%
xx-large	200%

12 Return to **ex0604.html** in your text or HTML editor. Modify the style sheet as follows:

```
#content h1 {font-size: 2em;}
#content h2 {font-size: 150%;}
body {font-size: small;}
p {font-size: 85%}
```

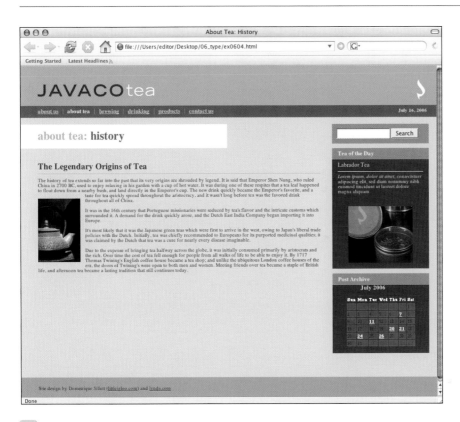

13 Save **ex0604.html**, switch to your browser, and reload **ex0604.html**.

Notice what happened here—it's something you should watch out for. The paragraphs have gotten even tinier. This is because, previously, you set the **body** element to a font size of **small** and its descendent elements all inherit this value. So here when you set the **p** element to 85 percent, it's translating this as 85 percent of **small**. In the next step, you'll do something potentially disastrous to reinforce this point.

14 Return to **ex0604.html** in your text or HTML editor. Modify the style sheet as follows:

```
#content {font-size: smaller;}
#content h1 {font-size: 2em;}
#content h2 {font-size: 150%;}
body {font-size: small;}
p {font-size: 85%}
```

15 Save and close **ex0604.html**, switch to your browser, and reload **ex0604.html**.

Yikes! The paragraph size is teeny, teeny, tiny now, basically unreadable, and I would never, ever, want to present this to the user. So, be careful when you're working with nested **font-size** declarations. Some browsers, such as Safari on the Mac, will enforce minimum font sizes, which will allow the user to ignore CSS statements. Others, such as Firefox, do not allow this. There's no particular fix for these kinds of mistakes, besides being careful.

You might think, why would I ever do this anyway? Well, what if you had a series of **nested lists**, lists within lists, in an outline like a course syllabus? You might say all unordered lists should have a font size of **smaller**, or unordered lists should have a font size of 85 percent. Whichever. Well, a third-level nested list would be 85 percent of 85 percent of 85 percent. Again, that basically would be unreadable. Check the tip shown here for a solution for font sizing with lists.

Sizing List Fonts

This is one tip I can share from my many, many years of font-sizing mistakes. Suppose you want your list to be smaller than the rest of the text of your page and all your nested lists under it to be the same size. First, you make your list font smaller, right?

```
ul {font-size: smaller}
```

This will indeed make your font size smaller, but unfortunately, your nested lists are just going to get smaller and smaller and smaller the further you nest. So here's the second rule you need to add:

```
ul ul {font-size: 1em;}
```

With descendent selectors, you assign a font size of 1 em. Remember, ems scale with changes to the font size of the parent element. So, 1 em means "keep this element's font size the same (100 percent) as the parent element's." This ensures the nested lists retain the same font size (**smaller**) as their parent element.

I hope you enjoyed this exercise. Again, the basics of font sizing are simple. It's just the combinations of nesting and relative sizing that can get complicated. Barring picking up a book just on font sizing, there's no substitution for practice and a willingness to make a few mistakes.

5 | Writing Font Shorthand Declarations

In this exercise, you'll learn how to bring together the various font-styling properties you've been working with throughout this chapter and write them as one shorthand declaration. This can be a great time-saver.

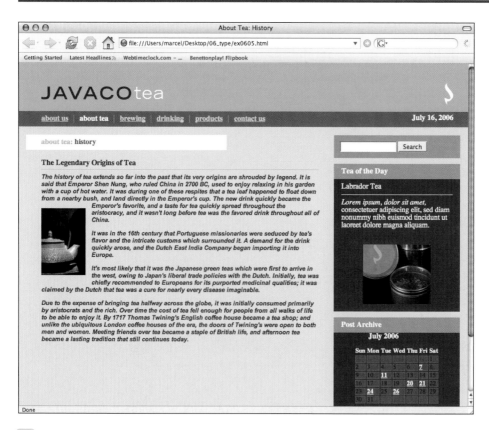

1 In a browser, open **ex0605.html** from the **06_type** folder you copied to your desktop, as shown in the illustration here.

As you'll notice, this particular design already contains some styling of the main paragraphs.

2 Open **ex0605.html** in your text or HTML editor. Find the following lines of code:

```
#content p {
    font-family: Arial, sans-serif;
    font-weight: bold;
    font-style: italic;
    font-size: smaller;
}
```

The styling effects you saw in the browser are accomplished by the declarations you see here. Wouldn't it be nice if you didn't have to say this all repetitively? In the next step, you'll write one shorthand declaration for this entire block.

3 In your text or HTML editor, modify the **#content** rule as follows:

```
#content p {
   font: bold italic smaller Arial, sans-serif;
}
```

4 Save **ex0605.html**, switch to your browser, and reload **ex0605.html**.

Nothing has changed stylistically, even though you dramatically shortened the declaration block. However, you'll notice you didn't put the shorthand declaration together in the same order in which the original declarations were written. You did this for a reason. Unlike other shorthand properties, with a font shorthand declaration, two things must be present, in a specific order and in a specific place. Those are the font size and the family. If you have a font declaration, the last two values must be size and then family, *in that order*. You can have multiple font families at the end of the declaration or many additional property values at the beginning—it doesn't matter, as long as the last two values are size and then the font family or families. The rest of the values can be in any order. You'll next add another value at random so you can see this again.

5 Return to your text or HTML editor. Modify the **#content** rule as follows:

```
#content p {
    font: bold italic small-caps smaller Arial, sans-serif;
}
```

Here you're adding **small-caps** as the third value, but you can also try adding it anywhere before the **size** value.

6 Save **ex0605.html**, switch to your browser, and reload **ex0605.html**.

There you go. All the styling is retained, plus the paragraphs are now in small caps.

7 Return to your text or HTML editor. Modify the **#content** rule as follows:

```
#content p {
    font-weight: bold;
    font-style: italic;
    font: smaller Arial, sans-serif;
}
```

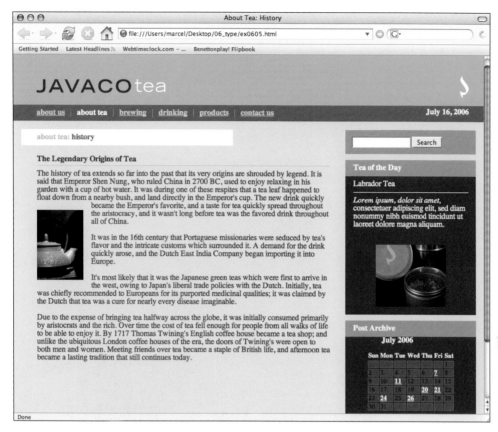

8 Save **ex0605.html**, switch to your browser, and reload **ex0605.html**.

You'll see the smaller Arial, but no bold and no italics. Here's the reason: With a shorthand property, if you leave out a given value, it gets reset to its default. It's as if you typed the following:

```
font: normal normal normal smaller Arial, sans-serif
```

The other property-value declarations are made redundant by the implicit defaults built into the **font** declaration. If you want to use shorthand declarations, you must include all the additional property values you want to include.

---

9 Return to your text or HTML editor. Modify the **#content** rule as follows:

```
#content p {
    font: bold italic smaller/1.5 Arial, sans-serif;
}
```

What's this 1.5 value? Well, as you probably remember from Exercise 1 in this chapter, it's the line height. This is the exception to the rule I mentioned previously: The last two values in your **font** shorthand declaration have to be the size and font family. You can stick the line height in as part of the font size.

10 Save **ex0605.html**, switch to your browser, and reload **ex0605.html**.

There you go. The lines in the paragraph get distributed at 1.5 times the font size. You could also write this as 1.5 ems; review Exercise 1 to understand the full implications of this. But you have one more task before you finish the exercise on font shorthand.

---

11 Return to your text or HTML editor. Modify the **#content** rule as follows:

```
#content p {
    font: bold italic smaller Arial, sans-serif;
    line-height: 1.5:
}
```

12 Save and close **ex0605.html**, switch to your browser, and reload **ex0605.html**.

There you are. The lines are still distributed according to the multiplier, even though you removed it from the font shorthand property. You actually can add declarations to the block, provided you type them *after* the shorthand. Otherwise, the values will be reset to **normal**, or whatever the browser's defaults are, because of the implicit values set in the shorthand.

In this exercise, you reviewed a CSS shortcut for one of the most common declarations—font property declarations. This should save you time and make your style sheets significantly smaller. Just remember to be careful; when you omit properties, they can be reset in ways you might not expect.

6 | Aligning Text Horizontally

In this exercise, you'll look at horizontal alignment text. This is a way to affect the presentation of text via its position on the page.

1 In a browser, open **ex0606.html** from the **06_type** folder you copied to your desktop, as shown in the illustration here.

2 Open **ex0606.html** in your text or HTML editor. After the leading **<style>** tag, type the following:

```
p {text-align: right;}
```

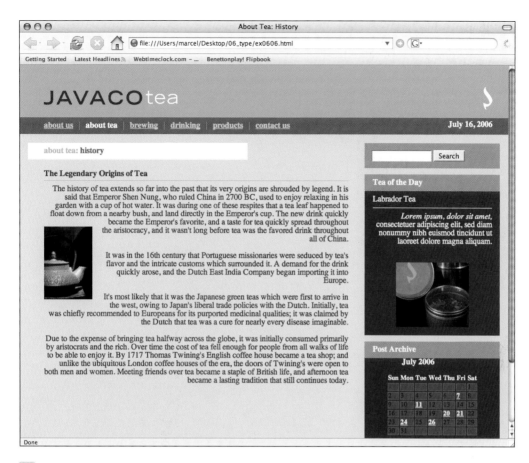

3 Save **ex0606.html**, switch to your browser, and reload **ex0606.html**.

The text is right aligned. Very simple, right? And it's very avant-garde—not necessarily the way those who are used to reading English or other Western languages might be used to reading text. Notice, within each paragraph box, each line of text is placed so that its right edge lines up with the right edge of its parent element. Actually, they're all lined up with the right edge of the content area of each paragraph. If there were any padding on the paragraph, the text would be right aligned with the left edge of the padding. I'll discuss padding in more depth in a later chapter.

---

4 Return to **ex0606.html** in your text or HTML editor. Modify the style sheet as follows:

```
p {text-align: center;}
```

5 Save **ex0606.html**, switch to your browser, and reload **ex0606.html**.

Each line is now centered in the middle of each paragraph box. Interesting to note, though, is that each of the lines between the image of the teakettle is centered in the space available to it. `text-align: center` respects the margins, borders, and so forth, of floated elements. This is probably what you expect, in keeping with the CSS specification, but I just wanted to bring it your attention.

6 Return to your text or HTML editor. Modify the style sheet as follows:

```
p {text-align: justify;}
```

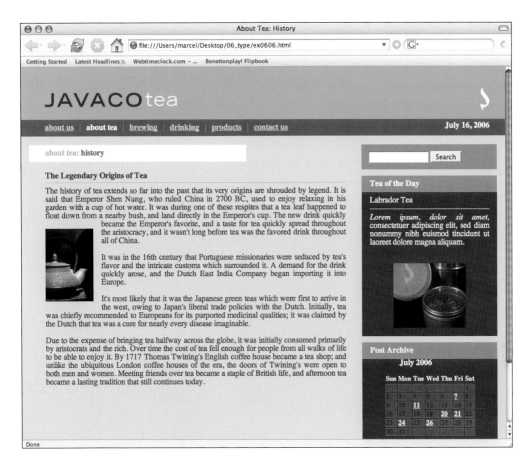

7 Save and close **ex0606.html**, switch to your browser, and reload **ex0606.html**.

`text-align: justify`, to put it simply, justifies text. Basically, it stretches lines of text so that the first and last characters of each line neatly align with the edges of the parent element (the paragraph boxes). Justified text is fairly common in print, and it can be tempting to use in Web design. However, it has some potential drawbacks.

The largest drawback is that since you can't necessarily control how the user might resize the page. Once you get really, really, narrow-sized paragraphs, the justified text spreads, and you can get these big gaps between words. In this illustration shown here, the lines "quickly spread" and "throughout the" really leap out at you. This isn't so much of a problem when you have a nice, wide browser window, but that's not something you as the designer can control. This is the main reason you won't see full-text justification, except in print, and you will get into print in Chapter 9, *"Styling for Print."*

This exercise was a short one, but I hope it was meaningful. You reviewed the alternatives to the standard left horizontal alignment of text, which can impact the overall design of your page in some interesting ways. In the next exercise, you will review vertical alignment.

7 | Aligning Text Vertically

In the previous exercise, you worked with aligning text horizontally, but you can also align text vertically. Actually, designers usually vertically align the elements within the text, as you will learn to do in this exercise.

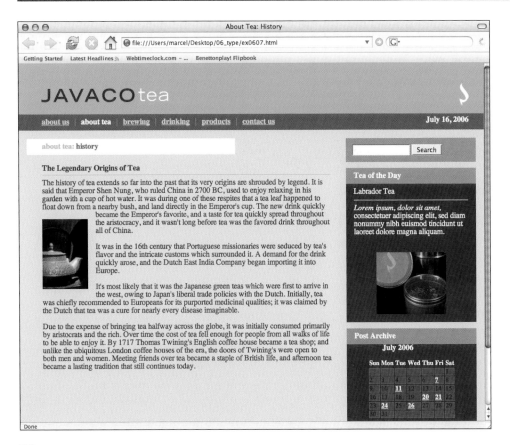

1 In a browser, open **ex0607.html** from the **06_type** folder you copied to your desktop, as shown in the illustration here.

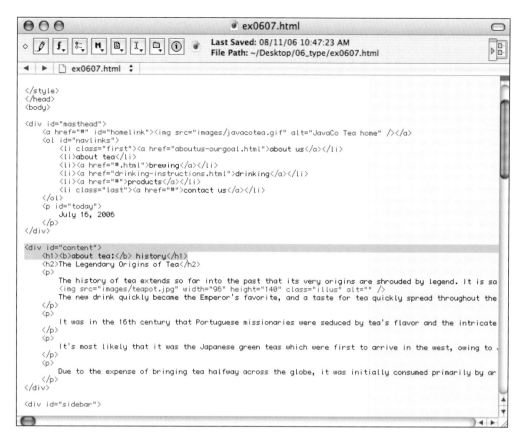

2   Open **ex0607.html** in your text or HTML editor. In the markup, find the following lines of code:

```
<div id="content">
<h1><b>about tea:</b> history<h1>
```

The **h1** element, "about tea: history," has a **b** element in it largely to change the color of the text halfway through the line. It's sort of used as a stylistic hook. You'll also use it as a hook to explore vertical alignment.

---

3   Scroll to the beginning of **ex0607.html**. After the leading **<style>** tag, type the following:

```
h1 b {vertical-align: sub;}
```

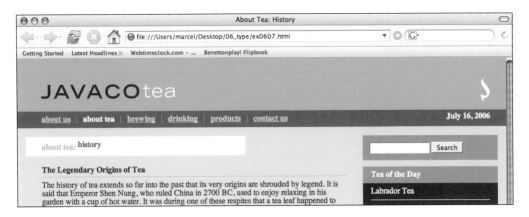

4 Save **ex0607.html**, switch to your browser, and reload **ex0607.html**.

The "about tea" portion of the header has shifted down. Obviously, it's the **sub** value in the declaration that comes into play here—like in *subscripting*. **vertical-align: sub** means "push this element down as though it were a subscript." Note, it doesn't say exactly how far that should be, and it doesn't change the font size, like subscripting in print might.

As you might have guessed, there is a corresponding value for pushing text up: **super**, as in *superscript*. You'll practice this next.

---

5 Return to **ex0607.html** in your text or HTML editor. Modify the style sheet as follows:

```
h1 b {vertical-align: super;}
```

---

6 Save **ex0607.html**, switch to your browser, and reload **ex0607.html**.

Now, "about tea" is lifted up slightly. The font size doesn't change and it doesn't have a specific offset, so different browsers might interpret this declaration differently, but that's superscript. It's fairly simple. You can use a variety of keywords such as **top**, **text-top**, and **text-bottom** for alignment, but these are rare and somewhat difficult to explain, so I recommend pursuing them after you've mastered the basics of vertical alignment. Another aspect of vertical alignment is using length measurements.

---

7 Return to **ex0607.html** in your text or HTML editor. Modify the style sheet as follows:

```
h1 b {vertical-align: 1em;}
```

8 Save **ex0607.html**, switch to your browser, and reload **ex0607.html**.

Now, "about tea" is lifted up higher than when you simply used the **super** value. Specifying a height allows a degree of control not possible with the **super** and **sub** values. You can use pixels or ems here. Note the background on the header, the white area, also got taller. Technically, "about tea: history" still comprises only one line of text, and the white bar you see is simply the background of the **h1** element containing that line. So, you can see how changes to vertical alignment can affect line height without ever specifying anything in your code. Even if you were to specify a line height of 1 em for this element, the vertical alignment would still force it to grow somewhat beyond that.

---

9 Return to **ex0607.html** in your text or HTML editor. Modify the style sheet as follows:

```
h1 b {vertical-align: baseline;}
```

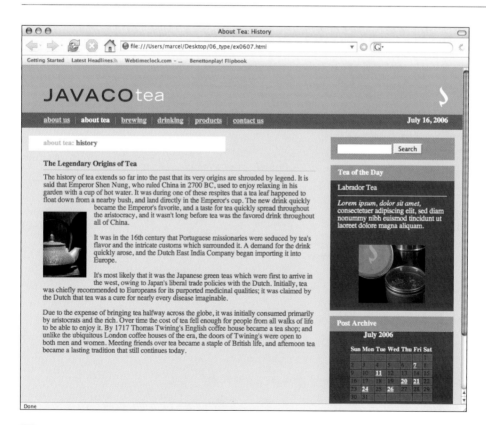

10 Save **ex0607.html**, switch to your browser, and reload **ex0607.html**.

This returns the "about tea" back to Earth, so to speak. `vertical-align: baseline` says "make this text align with all other text on this line." `baseline` is the default value for this property, by the way.

---

11 Return to **ex0607.html** in your text or HTML editor. Modify the style sheet as follows:

```
h1 b {vertical-align: -1em;}
```

---

12 Save **ex0607.html**, switch to your browser, and reload **ex0607.html**.

Negative vertical alignments affect the text in the same way as the **sub** value; the length measurement just gives you another degree of control over it. Notice the line's height has increased again to accommodate the change.

What if you wanted to create the appearance of a real subscript or superscript? Well, you can do that too.

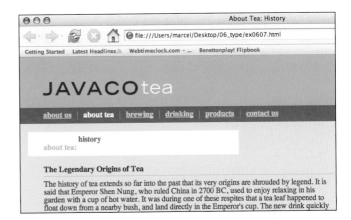

---

13 Return to **ex0607.html** in your text or HTML editor. Modify the style sheet as follows:

```
h1 b {vertical-align: .5em;
   font-size: .7em;}
```

---

14 Save and close **ex0607.html**, switch to your browser, and reload **ex0607.html**.

There you go. The "about tea" text now looks like a real superscript. I can't imagine why you'd want to use it in this context—making "about tea" a superscript doesn't add any meaning to the header here—but you may have occasion to use it in the future.

So, that's vertical text alignment in a nutshell. Again, I recommend you familiarize yourself with this subject before moving on to more advanced keywords. In the next exercise, you'll experiment with **text-transform**.

8 | Transforming Text

In this exercise, you'll use the property **text-transform**. The **text-transform** property is another font-related property, used for capitalization changes only. It is a great example of how CSS can be used to make changes within paragraph text, without having to touch your markup at all.

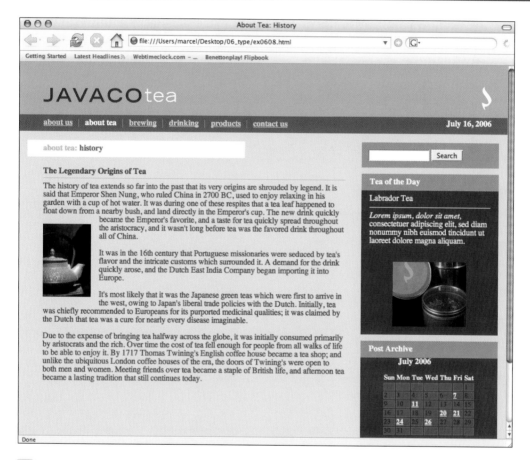

1 In a browser, open **ex0608.html** from the **06_type** folder you copied to your desktop, as shown in the illustration here.

You'll continue to concentrate on the text in the content area. As you can see, this is the same, unstyled text you've been working with throughout this chapter.

2 Open **ex0608.html** in your text or HTML editor. After the opening **`<style>`** tag, type the following:

```
#content h1 {
text-transform: uppercase;
}
```

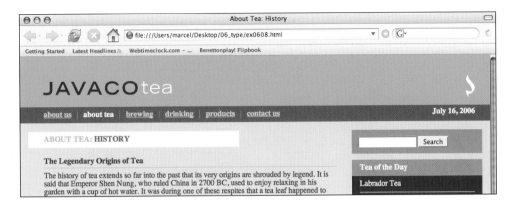

3 Save **ex0608.html**, switch to your browser, and reload **ex0608.html**.

Without touching the document source, you have changed the header text to uppercase. This is a purely stylistic change. If you were to return to the markup and find the **h1** element, you would see the text is all lowercase. As you'll notice in the sidebar, that text uses the capitalization still intrinsic to the document.

4 Return to your text or HTML editor. Modify the style sheet as follows:

```
#content h1 {
    text-transform: uppercase;
}
#sidebar h3 {
    text-transform: lowercase;
}
```

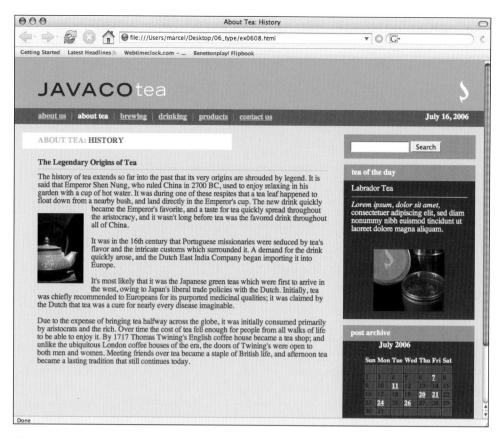

5 Save **ex0608.html**, switch to your browser, and reload **ex0608.html**.

Tada! Again, without touching the document source, you have changed the sidebar text to all lowercase, a purely stylistic change. Now you'll try something different.

6 Return to your text or HTML editor, and modify the style sheet as follows:

```
#content h1 {
    text-transform: uppercase;
}
#sidebar h3 {
    text-transform: lowercase;
}
#content p {
    text-transform: capitalize;
}
```

7 Save and close **ex0608.html**, switch to your browser, and reload **ex0608.html**.

Now, the first character of each word in the paragraphs is capitalized. Of course, you're relying on the browser to correctly interpret exactly what a "word" is. Firefox here does a pretty good job. It assumes every string of text that has a space before it is a word. Next you'll look at the results in another browser.

---

8 Open Safari, if you have it installed on your computer. If you don't have Safari, try this step with Internet Explorer or another browser, and look for the same sort of discrepancies.

---

9 In Safari or your alternate browser, choose **File > Open**, navigate to the **ch_06** folder on your desktop, select the **ex0608.html** file, and click **Open**.

As shown in the illustration here (or on your screen if you have Safari or your alternate browser open), the third paragraph opens with the line, "It'S Most Likely That It Was The Japanese Green Teas Which Were First To Arrive In The West, Owing To Japan'S…." The s in "It'S" as well as "Japan'S" is capitalized. This is because Safari's algorithm for determining what a word is assumes that an apostrophe (which could also be a single quotation mark, by the way) is the beginning of a word. This illustrates the problem in using these kinds of transformations. You are always at the mercy of the browser's creators.

CSS itself does not define what a word is. This is probably for the best—even linguists argue about this simple problem all the time. In fact, different languages have different ways of marking what a word is. In Latin-derived languages, such as Western European languages, words are usually separated by a non-breaking space. In certain other languages, such as Chinese and Japanese, no such distinction exists. So, the decision to use `text-transform: capitalize` is really up to you. My goal is to make sure you know about the implications of using this declaration so you can make an informed decision when you design your own pages using CSS.

In this exercise, you learned about the three values you can use with the `text-transform` property. You can use uppercase and lowercase with almost no recriminations, but exercise caution when using capitalization. In the next and final exercise in this chapter, you'll review text decorations.

In this exercise, as I mentioned, you will review text decorations. Now, these aren't the type of decorations you hang during the holidays. However, it is still a process of ornamentation, and you'll practice adding and removing decorations such as underlining, overlining, and strikethrough.

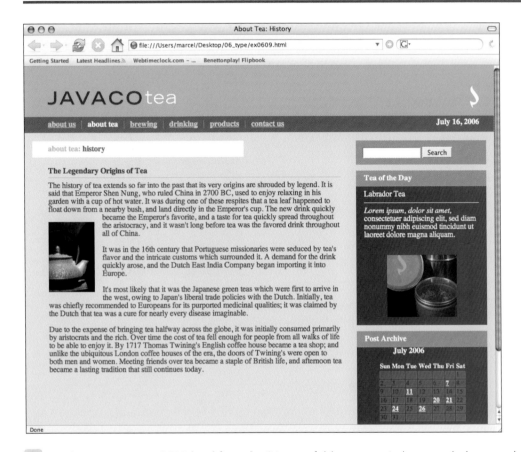

1 In a browser, open **ex0609.html** from the **06_type** folder you copied to your desktop, as shown in the illustration here.

As shown in the illustration here, you already have some text decoration that's coming straight from the browser's default styles. The links in the navigation bar—about us, brewing, and so on—are all underlined.

2 Open **ex0609.html** in your text or HTML editor. After the **<style>** start tag, type the following:

```
#navlinks a {
    text-decoration: none;
}
```

3 Save **ex0609.html**, switch to your browser, and reload **ex0609.html**.

Voila! You have removed the text decoration from those links. And, as you can probably imagine, the default value for text decoration is always **none**, the exception being hyperlinks, which are underlined as browser defaults.

---

4 Return to **ex0609.html** in your text or HTML editor. Modify the style sheet as follows:

```
#navlinks a {
    text-decoration: none;
}
h1 {
    text-decoration: underline;
}
```

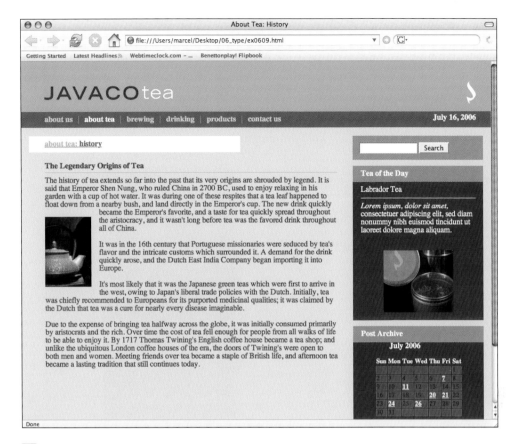

5 Save **ex0609.html**, switch to your browser, and reload **ex0609.html**.

There you go. The "about tea" header text is now underlined. Note, most users are used to underlined text acting as links. A user might try to click this header and become frustrated when nothing happens. Therefore, use underlining with discretion. Also, the underline color takes its color from the text color of the **h1** element. The "about tea" part, which you didn't actually assign an underline to, also has the blue line underneath it. Why? You'll get to that in a minute.

---

6 Return to **ex0609.html** in your text or HTML editor. Modify the style sheet as follows:

```
#navlinks a {
    text-decoration: none;
}
h1 {
    text-decoration: underline overline;
}
```

You can assign one of four values here: **none**, **underline**, **overline**, and **line-through**. Or you can assign any of the last three together, in any order. What does this resemble? Well, it resembles the font short-hand rule from Exercise 5. However, since these are all values for the same property, this is not technically a shorthand rule. It just looks like one.

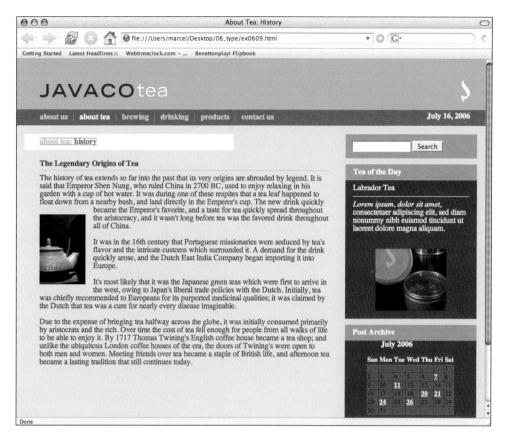

7 Save **ex0609.html**, switch to your browser, and reload **ex0609.html**.

Now the **b** element text, "about tea," and the regular header text, "history," are both now underlined and overlined in purple. This is how text decoration works. If you have a descendent element—for example, the **b** element inside the **h1** element—the descendent element inherits the properties of the parent element. You can't really remove decoration from the **b** element, because the parent values override it. But heck, you'll try anyway in the next step.

---

8 Return to **ex0609.html** in your text or HTML editor. Modify the style sheet as follows:

```
#navlinks a {
    text-decoration: none;
}
h1 {
    text-decoration: underline overline;
}
h1 b {
    text-decoration: none;}
```

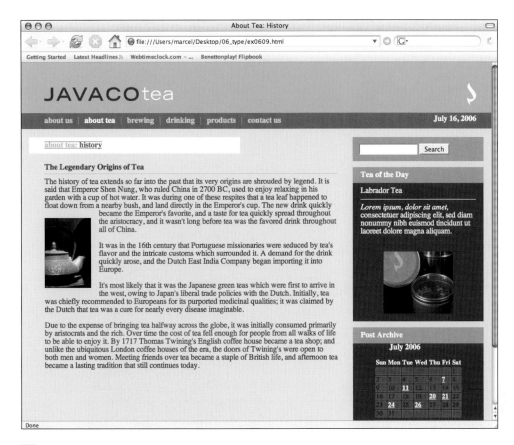

9 Save **ex0609.html**, switch to your browser, and reload **ex0609.html**.

And as they say, the proof is in the pudding. Nothing happens; you can't turn off the text decoration around that **b** element. The only way to do this is to, in effect, hide the entire element.

---

10 Return to **ex0609.html** in your text or HTML editor. Modify the style sheet as follows:

```
#navlinks a {
    text-decoration: none;
}
h1 {
    text-decoration: underline overline;
}
#content h1 b {
    text-decoration: underline overline;
    color: #FFF;
}
```

11 Save **ex0609.html**, switch to your browser, and reload **ex0609.html**.

So, by assigning a white color to the **b** element, you have made it disappear into the white background. In addition, its decorations are white, and they're drawn on top of the decorations on the **h1** element. That's why they seem to have disappeared. That's one way to get rid of the text decoration, but you got rid of the text as well. The next step will clarify this point.

12 Return to **ex0609.html** in your text or HTML editor. Modify the style sheet as follows:

```
#navlinks a {
    text-decoration: none;
}
h1 {
    text-decoration: underline overline;
}
#content h1 b {
    text-decoration: underline overline;
    vertical-align: .5em;
}
```

13 Save and close **ex0609.html**, switch to your browser, and reload **ex0609.html**.

This raises the **b** element slightly, and you can see now that it has its own green overline and underline; it was just obscured by the purple **h1** lines that were inherited by the inside element. This is the single caveat to text decoration: Descendent elements inherit the values, and you have no real way to override this.

In this exercise, you learned all about text decoration and also learned some easy ways to manipulate the look of page elements, such as hyperlinks.

A hearty congratulations on finishing this chapter! As I mentioned, entire books are dedicated just to typography, fonts, line heights, and other text properties, but this chapter provided a good overview. CSS has a limited but powerful number of property-value declarations you can use to achieve some interesting typographical effects. In the next chapter, you will learn more about margins, borders, and padding, which you were first introduced to in Chapter 4, *"Using CSS to Affect Page Layout."*

7

Using Margins and Borders to Create Whitespace and Separation

In the real world, Web page authors are often asked to reproduce a complicated visual, or **wireframe**, design prepared by a graphic designer. As the author/developer, your success is measured by how closely you can approximate the original design. So in this chapter, you'll examine the design composition provided by your "designer" and concentrate on using margins, borders, and padding to achieve the same look and feel. As you recall, these properties exist to separate elements on your page and control the amount of space between them. You already reviewed the basics of the CSS (**C**ascading **S**tyle **S**heets) box model properties in Chapter 4, *"Using CSS to Affect Page Layout,"* but now you'll work with these in specific ways to achieve calculated effects.

1 | Understanding Margins

In this exercise, you will work with margins. Remember that **margins** are the completely transparent space surrounding an element. You can use margins for spacing and also for centering, which you will do in this exercise using the automargin centering effect.

---

1 Copy the **07_whitespace** folder from the **CSS HOT CD-ROM** to your desktop.

2 Return to the **07_whitespace** folder. Double-click **javaco.jpg** to open it in your default picture viewer, as shown in the illustration here.

This is the design composition, or as it is more commonly referred to, the design comp, provided by the designer. It's a preliminary design for the web page that has met with the client's approval. Design comps are usually prepared in Adobe Photoshop, Macromedia Fireworks, or another graphic design program. The images, fonts, and color specifications should be provided separately.

3 Close **javaco.jpg** once you are finished examining it. In a browser, open **ex0701.html** from the **07_whitespace** folder you copied to your desktop, as shown in the illustration here.

---

4 Open **ex0701.html** with your text or HTML (**H**yper**T**ext **M**arkup **L**anguage) editor. After the **<style>** start tag, insert a break, and type the following:

```
#masthead {
    margin-bottom: 1.75em;
}
```

5 Save **ex0701.html**, switch to your browser, and reload **ex0701.html**.

In the previous step, you gave the masthead a bottom margin. This results in everything after the masthead "dropping" further down the page. Keep in mind when you have an em-based margin such as this, 1 em equals 1 times the font size for the element. In this case, the masthead **div** has a font size of 10 pixels, so the bottom margin is 1.75 times that, or 17.5 pixels high. Whether you want to use a length-based or em-based value for your margins will depend on the design. As you may recall from previous chapters, I prefer ems, but this is a matter of personal choice.

With CSS, you can also remove margins. From a CSS point of view, no elements have default margins. However, remember that browsers have intrinsic styles, which can include margin defaults for certain elements. For example, margins on paragraphs are built into the user agent style. Also, ordered and unordered lists may have margins and padding defaults in certain browsers. So, you may find yourself explicitly removing margins as opposed to adding them to combat these browser defaults.

6 Return to **ex0701.html** in your text or HTML editor. After the **#masthead** rule, insert a new line, and type the following:

```
#navlinks {
    margin: 0;
}
#navlinks li {
    margin-right: 0.5em;
}
```

Here you are first explicitly removing all the margins on the navigation bar and then adding a right margin to each of the list items, the ones containing navigation links, to spread them apart. The links are kind of squashed together right now, which makes them hard to distinguish from one another.

7 Save **ex0701.html**, switch to your browser, and reload **ex0701.html**.

There you go. The navigation bar is snug against the "Javaco tea" heading, and the list items are nicely spaced. You'll add some spacing in another exercise, but for now, these items are far enough apart to tell that each is a distinct item.

8 Return to **ex0701.html** in your text or HTML editor. Add the following rule, after the others, to your style sheet:

```
#homelink {
    margin: 1em 2em 1em 2em;
}
```

Remember, the margin value assignments start with the top and go in a clockwise order: top, right, bottom, left. A handy acronym to help you remember this is TRBL—as in to keep you out of "trouble."

Even handier—you don't have to type all four of these values. Instead, you could write this declaration like this: `margin: 1em 2em`.

The top and right values are actually copied down to the bottom and left margins. It's functionally equivalent to `margin: 1em 2em 1em 2em`. Again, as with so many other features of CSS, you have options. You can use the shortcut and have fewer characters, or you can type the complete set of values. Why would you type all the values? Well, it's a visual clue that the margins are set all around the element. By the way, if you don't want any bottom or left margin, you have to specify that. In this instance, you would need to write `margin: 1em 2em 0 0`. Otherwise, the top and right values will be automatically duplicated.

9 Save **ex0701.html**, switch to your browser, and reload **ex0701.html**.

Now, a space appears between the "Javaco tea" heading and the navigation bar, as you had at the beginning of the exercise, but now the margin is applied explicitly to the heading.

10 Return to **ex0701.html** in your text or HTML editor. Modify the `#homelink` rule as follows:

```
#homelink {
    margin: 1em 2em;
}
```

Now insert a new line directly after this rule, and type the following:

```
#content h1 {
    margin: 0 33% 1.25em 0;
}
```

11 Save **ex0701.html**, switch to your browser, and reload **ex0701.html**.

Notice the "about tea: history" heading just got significantly smaller. The space to the right of it, between the edge of the white background and the edge of the sidebar column, is the 33 percent margin. In other words, it's 33 percent of the total space that the **h1** contents were utilizing before you assigned the margin. The total space is determined by the area the element is restricted to by the content **div**.

12 Return to **ex0701.html** in your text or HTML editor. Insert a new line at the end of your style sheet, and add the following rule:

```
#content h2 {
    margin: 0.5em 0;
}
```

13 Save **ex0701.html**, switch to your browser, and reload **ex0701.html**.

Now the space between the "Legendary Origins of Tea" header and the first paragraph is slightly smaller. You can continue adding rules like this to the style sheet almost indefinitely. Some of the changes may seem subtle, and you might wonder whether you really have a reason to use them. In fact, you do—basically it's because that's what was shown in the comp. You may have to make many small changes like this to sync up your page with the designer's illustration.

14 Return to **ex0701.html** in your text or HTML editor. Add the following rule to the end of your style sheet:

```
#sidebar form {
    margin: 0;
}
#sidebar div {
    margin-top: 0.75em;
}
```

Sidebars are one of those elements that are assigned margins by default in most browsers. That is why you need to remove them here in the style sheet. Then, with the `#sidebar div` rule, you'll push the `div` elements in the sidebar apart from each other. `div` elements, by the way, do *not* have browser-assigned default margins in current browsers. They probably never will, either.

15 Save **ex0701.html**, switch to your browser, and reload **ex0701.html**.

Now, you see a precisely sized margin between the `div` elements.

---

16 Return to **ex0701.html** in your text or HTML editor. Add the following rule to the end of your style sheet:

```
#tea-of-the-day h4 {
    margin: 0 0 0.5em;
}
#post-archive table {
    margin: 1em auto 0;
}
```

Here you'll use the margin shorthand to make your life a little easier and trust that the browser will copy the right margin value over to the left and that the header will have neither right nor left margins. The second rules looks a little strange, but when you return to your browser, before reloading, notice that in the "post archive" element box the calendar aligns to the left.

---

17 Save **ex0701.html**, switch to your browser, and reload **ex0701.html**.

Terrific! The calendar is now neatly centered in the post archive **div**. What happens in CSS is that if you have an element such as a table with a limited width (which can be only as narrow as it can be and still display its content), or if you have an element with an explicit width and you give it automatic left and right margins, then the margins take the difference between the element's width and the total amount of width that it has, split it in two, and take it equally. That creates the centering. The left and right margins are set to be equal, within the boundaries of the parent element. What happens if you assign **auto** values to margins for elements with no explicit width? Next step, please!

18 Return to **ex0701.html** in your text or HTML editor. Modify the **#tea-of-the-day h4** rule as follows:

```
#tea-of-the-day h4 {
    margin: 0 auto 0.5em;
}
```

19 Save and close **ex0701.html**, switch to your browser, and reload **ex0701.html**.

This doesn't show any real change. The headings are technically centered, but visually, it's no different from what you saw previously. That's because if you don't assign an explicit width to something like a heading, a paragraph, or another **div** element, it will expand to fill all the available space. These elements take up the entire width of the **div** elements inside which they live, the content area. That's why right and left automargins aren't usually assigned, unless you are trying to center a table or another element with an explicit width.

Internet Explorer 5.5 and Auto Margins

Note that the **auto** value does have one possible issue, albeit an increasingly remote one. The centering effect does not work with Microsoft Internet Explorer 5.5 and earlier. However, you can work around this issue. First you need to center the text of the parent element of the element you would like to center using the **text-align:center** declaration. In the **ex0701.html** file you are working with, in the case of the **table** element, you add the following rule:

```
#post-archive {text-align: center;}
```

Next, you add a **text-align:left** declaration to the element you are trying to center:

```
#post-archive table {
    margin: 1em auto 0;
    text-align: left;
}
```

Why use **text-align**? Well, Internet Explorer 5.5 and earlier interpreted **text-align** also as **element-align**. The **text-align** property *is* intended for aligning text only; the CSS specification mentions nothing about centering or right justifying elements such as tables. But for whatever reason, the creators of Internet Explorer 5.5 and earlier thought it did, and they chose not to implement the auto margin centering. Luckily, using **text-align** and auto margins in conjunction will achieve the same effect.

Congratulations! This was a long exercise, but there was a lot of information about margins I wanted to share with you. In the next exercise, you'll get into some more advanced applications of borders.

In this exercise, you'll learn about borders and elements. **Borders** can provide more concrete separation between the pieces of the design. They are also the most clearly visible box model property and can create interesting decorative effects.

1 In a browser, open **ex0702.html** from the **07_whitespace** folder you copied to your desktop, as shown in the illustration here.

This is the Web page as it stands thus far. Next, you'll compare it to the mock-up provided by the designer.

2 Double-click **javaco.jpg** from the **07_whitespace** folder you copied to your desktop, as shown in the illustration here.

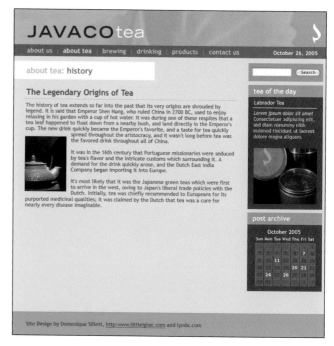

Among the other differences (changes you will make in later exercises and chapters), several borders here simply don't exist on your page. For example, underneath the "The Legendary Origins of Tea" heading, you'll see a green border; in addition, you'll see another border under "Labrador Tea" in the "tea of the day" sidebar.

You'll see one other set of borders in this design. It's the separators between the links in the navigation bar. You might see this and think, "oh, look, it's a vertical pipe character. I can just type that." Of course you can, if you're willing to type those characters in your document source. But you can do it just as easily, if not more so, in CSS by using borders. So, you'll now return to the document.

3 Open **ex0702.html** with your text or HTML editor. Scroll through your style sheet, and find the following rule:

```
#content h2 {
    margin: 0.5em 0;
}
```

Modify this as follows:

```
#content h2 {
    margin: 0.5em 0;
    border-bottom: 1px solid #B0D742;
}
```

This adds the border under the "The Legendary Origins of Tea" heading like you saw in the designer's comp. Most designers will also provide you, the programmer, with a list of color values to use in the markup, which is where you get the border color **#B0D742**.

4 Save **ex0702.html**, switch to your browser, and reload **ex0702.html**.

So, now you see that green border. It is a little closer to the text than what the designer had in mind, but don't worry. You'll fix that in a later exercise in this chapter with padding. Now you'll add the other borders.

---

5 Return to **ex0702.html** in your text or HTML editor. Scroll through your style sheet, and find the following rule:

```
#tea-of-the-day h4 {
    margin: 0 0 0.5em;
}
```

Modify this as follows:

```
#tea-of-the-day h4 {
    margin: 0 0 0.5em;
    border-bottom: 1px solid;
}
```

In this case, you can get away with not specifying a color for the border, because it should pick up the color of the text, matching the designer's comp. This works because borders are defined so that, if you don't explicitly give them a color, the color used for the element's foreground (e.g., the text) will be copied to the border.

---

6 Save **ex0702.html**, switch to your browser, and reload **ex0702.html**.

There you are. It's simple so far. Next, you'll work on the borders between the links in the navigation bar.

7 Return to **ex0702.html** in your text or HTML editor. In the markup, review the portion of the code containing the list of link items. Scroll to the style sheet, and find the following rule:

```
#navlinks li {
     margin-right: 0.5em;
}
```

Modify this rule as follows:

```
#navlinks li {
     margin-right: 0.5em;
     border-right: 1px solid #99C;
}
```

8 Save **ex0702.html**, switch to your browser, and reload **ex0702.html**.

The borders are starting to make an appearance. Now, this doesn't look exactly how it does in the comp, because you still have to add some padding, not only to the list items but also to the list in which they sit so you can expand the purple area of the navigation bar in turn. But it's a start. You already have vertical line separators between each of these links.

However, this has one more than you want. The extra border on the right side of "contact us" doesn't exist in the comp.

```
[window titlebar] ● ● ●                    ◉ ex0702.html                              ⬭

         𝄐  [toolbar icons]    ◉  Last Saved: 08/30/06 01:36:37 PM              ▶[icon]
                                  File Path: ~/Desktop/

         ◀ ▶ 🗋              ◆

<body>

<div id="masthead">
    <a href="#" id="homelink"><img src="images/javacotea.gif" alt="JavaCo Tea home" /></a>
    <ol id="navlinks">
        <li class="first"><a href="aboutus-ourgoal.html">about us</a></li>
        <li>about tea</li>
        <li><a href="#.html">brewing</a></li>
        <li><a href="drinking-instructions.html">drinking</a></li>
        <li><a href="#">products</a></li>
        <li class="last"><a href="#">contact us</a></li>
    </ol>
    <p id="today">
        July 16, 2006
    </p>
</div>
```

9 Return to **ex0702.html** in your text or HTML editor. In the markup, review the portion of the code containing the list of link items again, as shown in the illustration here.

Notice that the first item in the list has a class of **first** and the last item in the list has a class of **last**. In the next step, you'll use that to your advantage.

---

10 Scroll to the style sheet again, and after the **#navlinks li** rule, type the following:

```
#navlinks li.last {
    border-right: 0;
}
```

---

11 Save **ex0702.html**, switch to your browser, and reload **ex0702.html**.

Now the page doesn't have a border after the "contact us" link. You set the width of the right border for this element to 0. So, it's still technically present, just with a zero width. You could have also written this as **border-right: none**. The **none** value sets the style to, you guessed it, no border. You can use either value—just know one affects the width, and the other affects the style.

You can use other border styles besides **none** and **solid**, such as **dotted**, **dashed**, and **groove**. If you like, you can review these values in more detail in Appendix A, *"CSS 2 Properties."* However, you have one more border style to look at in this exercise—**double**.

---

12 Return to **ex0702.html** in your text or HTML editor. Scroll through the style sheet, and find the following rule:

```
#content h2 {
    margin: 0.5em 0;
    border-bottom: 1px solid #B0D742;
}
```

Modify this as follows:

```
#content h2 {
    margin: 0.5em 0;
    border-bottom: 3px double #B0D742;
}
```

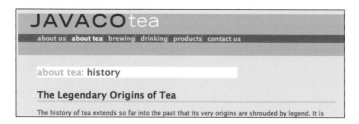

13 Save and close **ex0702.html**, switch to your browser, and reload **ex0702.html**.

The border underneath the **h2** element is now 3 pixels wide and "double." A gap appears between the two lines. The reason I wanted to discuss this style in particular is because it has one quirk. You can't control the ratio between the line widths and the width of the gap between them. For example, if you were to specify a 4 pixel wide double border, you would have no way to say whether the top line, the bottom line, or the gap should get 1 pixel wider. More to the point, you can't be sure it will be consistent across browsers. Odds are that it won't be.

Note: Another interesting point about double borders is that when assigning a 1 pixel double border, some browsers have been known to drop the gap. It would be pretty hard to see two .33 pixel lines anyway, but it is worth noting.

In this exercise, you reviewed applying borders to your elements according to a design spec. You added borders between list items, suppressed borders, and saw the different styles of available borders. Many more are available, and I encourage you to do some more research in Appendix A, *"CSS 2 Properties,"* if you are interested in using some different styles.

3 | Implementing Padding

In this exercise, you'll add padding to the page. **Padding**, which is the space between the content of an element and the border, will help you move this page closer to the designer's original design. Specifically, you'll add padding to expand the background elements on the page and to create space between the vertical separators and the links in the navigation bar.

1 In a browser, open **ex0703.html** from the **07_whitespace** folder you copied to your desktop, as shown in the illustration here.

Remember that padding is part of the background area, so the background element will extend or show through any padding you add. A good example of this is the purple navigation bar across the top of the page, which is actually the background for the link elements.

2 Open **ex0703.html** with your text or HTML editor. Scroll through your style sheet, and find the following rule:

```
#navlinks {
    margin: 0;
}
```

Modify this as follows:

```
#navlinks {
    margin: 0;
    padding: 0.5em 3em;
}
```

Here you are giving a top padding of .5 em and a right padding of 3 em. As you recall from the previous exercise, according to the CSS specification, if you omit the bottom and left values, .5 em and 3 em will be copied to the bottom and left sides, respectively.

3 Save **ex0703.html**, switch to your browser, and reload **ex0703.html**.

The navigation bar is now taller. The padding is at work pushing the page title and body elements away from the content, and you can see the background element showing through it here. The padding, as you may recall, is also what separates the content and the borders, and this is how you will push the links away from the vertical separators inside the navigation bar.

4 Return to **ex0703.html** in your text or HTML editor. Scroll through the style sheet, and find the following rule:

```
#navlinks li {
    margin-right: 0.5em;
    border-right: 1px solid #99C;
}
```

Modify this rule as follows:

```
#navlinks li {
    margin-right: 0.5em;
    border-right: 1px solid #99C;
    padding-right: 0.75em;
}
```

5 Save **ex0703.html**, switch to your browser, and reload **ex0703.html**.

There you go. The right padding pushes the right borders away from the text, and you get these nicely spaced vertical separators between the links. You might be asking why I used a right margin of .5 em and a padding of .75. Shouldn't they be equal? Good question. Let's return to the markup to find the answer.

6 Return to **ex0703.html** in your text or HTML editor. Scroll through the markup, and find the **div** section starting with **<div id="masthead">**, as shown in the illustration here.

Each of the line breaks between the list items in the document actually creates a little bit of space in the layout. It creates a little bit of a separation between the contents of the items. Experience has taught me that this tends to be about .25 em. So, the right margin of .5 em plus the .25 em of intrinsic whitespace handled by the list separation comes out to about .75 em, which is why the borders appear to be centered between the link text.

7 Scroll to the style sheet, and find the following rule:

```
#homelink {
    margin: 1em 2em 1em 2em;
}
```

Modify this rule as follows:

```
#homelink {
    margin: 1em 2em 1em 2em;
    padding: 2em 0 0.5em 1em;
}
```

8 Save **ex0703.html**, switch to your browser, and reload **ex0703.html**.

Suddenly, the masthead gets pushed out from the top of the page, and the background area also gets taller. Why? Well, do you notice the white curl icon in the upper-right corner of the screen? That's actually a background image on the `homelink` element. It was partially disguised in the previous step. You've used padding to make the hyperlink bigger so that the whole background image is visible. And padding of course extends the background area, making the masthead element larger. If you used margins instead of padding, the background area would be smaller, and the background image might get cut off even more—an even better reason to use padding in this case.

---

9 Return to the style sheet in your text or HTML editor, and find the following rules:

```
#content h1 {
    margin: 0 33% 1.25em 0;
}
#content h2 {
    margin: 0.5em 0;
    border-bottom: 1px solid #B0D742;
}
```

Modify these as follows:

```
#content h1 {
    margin: 0 33% 1.25em 0;
    padding: 0.5em 2em;
}
#content h2 {
    margin: 0.5em 0;
    border-bottom: 1px solid #B0D742;
    padding: 0.25em;
}
```

Here you're adding padding to the **h1** element, the "about tea: history" heading, and the **h2** element you added the bottom border to in a previous exercise.

---

10 Save **ex0703.html**, switch to your browser, and reload **ex0703.html**.

The white area around the **h1** element now expands while the **h2** header, along with everything below it, has dropped slightly on the page—these are the effects of that .25 em of top padding you added. This brings the page even closer in line with the designer's original vision.

Now, you'll add a little padding to the sidebar. If you look at the page again, the search bar form is constricted, as are the "tea of the day" and "post archive" headings. The contents of the "tea of the day" **div** are also compressed right up against the edge of the content box. For ease of reading, you would usually want a visual separation between the contents and the box, even if it weren't explicitly called for in the design comp.

---

11 Return to the style sheet in your text or HTML editor. Find the following rules:

```
#sidebar form {
    margin: 0;
}
#sidebar div {
    margin-top: 0.75em;
}
```

Modify these as follows:

```
#sidebar form {
    margin: 0;
    padding: 0.8em;
}
#sidebar div {
    margin-top: 0.75em;
    padding: 0 1em 1em;
}
```

12 Save **ex0703.html**, switch to your browser, and reload **ex0703.html**.

Now the form element is centered in a larger purple box. Why did you use 1.25 em here? Well, sometimes you just need to estimate by looking at the design comp. The nice feature of CSS is that you can always return to the style sheet and modify it later.

You'll also see more space on the bottom, left, and right sides of the sidebar contents. You didn't add a top margin to the sidebar because that would create a brown space above the headings. But wait a minute, the headings are still off. They're pushed in on both sides. Well, unfortunately, you can't apply padding to all contents of an element with the exception of one or two—not in CSS anyway. It's all or nothing. However, you can fake your way around it, which you will do in an upcoming exercise.

13 Return to the style sheet in your text or HTML editor. Find the `#sidebar div` rule from the previous step, insert a carriage return, and type the following:

```
#sidebar h3 {
    padding: 0.4em 0;
}
```

This padding will add a little extra space above and below the words in the **h3** headings, such as "tea of the day."

14 Save **ex0703.html**, switch to your browser, and reload **ex0703.html**.

There you go. You'll add two last padding details in the next step.

15 Return to the style sheet in your text or HTML editor. Find the following:

```
#tea-of-the-day h4 {
    margin: 0 0 0.5em;
    border-bottom: 1px solid;
}
```

Modify this as follows:

```
#tea-of-the-day h4 {
    margin: 0 0 0.5em;
    border-bottom: 1px solid;
    padding: 0.5em 0;
}
#footer {
    padding: 1.5em 3em;
}
```

Here you are adding padding to the **h4** headings as well as creating a new rule for the footer.

16 Save and close **ex0703.html**, switch to your browser, and reload **ex0703.html**.

Voila! The "Labrador Tea" heading is now generously spaced, and the footer has stretched taller. This is much closer to the design comp than when you started.

Congratulations on finishing this exercise! It was a long one, but here you were able to explore the effects of padding in more detail. You still have a few things to clean up—the "tea of the day" and "post archive" headings have extra padding you'll want to remove, and the "about tea: history" **h1** heading is not flush with the left side of the page, as requested by the designer. For that matter, extra space appears around the main body elements, such as the masthead and footer, which appear as flush with the edges of the page in the design comp. You'll address these discrepancies and more in the next exercise.

---

4 | Using Negative Margins

With the additions of margins, borders, and padding, you've come a long way in terms of what the designer requested. However, you still need to address some issues, such as the date in the navigation bar and the "about tea: history" heading. In this exercise, you'll use negative margins to align these elements.

1 In a browser, open **ex0704.html** from the **07_whitespace** folder you copied to your desktop, as shown in the illustration here.

This is the Javaco Web page as it stands thus far. Again, you'll notice the date is suspended below the navigation bar and the "about tea: history" heading is not against the left edge of the page. How are you going to fix these two elements? Well, you could take the "about tea: history" heading and move it out of its content columns so it's not pushed over along with that column. But that means rearranging the document structure just to create stylistic effects, and I usually try to avoid that if possible.

Similarly, trying to get the date up into the navigation bar could be tricky. You could try this with floats, but then you would have to move the date's paragraph element to another place in the markup. Again, that's structural hacking, which I dislike. So instead, you'll use a negative margin declaration to do a little trick.

2 Open **ex0704.html** with your text or HTML editor. Scroll through your style sheet, and find the following rule:

```
#today {
    padding: 0 2em 0 0;
}
```

Modify the rule as follows:

```
#today {
    margin-top: 0;
    padding: 0 2em 0 0;
}
```

You are starting by specifying a top margin of 0 to override the default value of 1 em.

3 Save **ex0704.html**, switch to your browser, and reload **ex0704.html**.

Closer! But it's not quite where it's supposed to be.

4 Return to your text or HTML editor. Modify the **#today** rule as follows:

```
#today {
    margin-top: -1.66em;
    padding: 0 2em 0 0;
}
```

5 Save **ex0704.html**, switch to your browser, and reload **ex0704.html**.

The date has actually been pulled upward into the navigation bar. It is contained in a paragraph element, so it's actually the paragraph that's moving up, thanks to this negative margin. Structurally nothing has changed, but visually, it's right where you want it. Or rather, it's where the designer wants it. And you didn't have to hack through the markup or create a two-cell table or anything like that. There's one teensy problem: In Internet Explorer, the results are much different (and much worse) than what's seen in the previous screenshot. That's due to layout bugs in Explorer which can cause all kinds of weirdness. Fortunately, there's an easy fix.

Return to your text or Web editor and find the following rule:

```
#masthead {
    margin-bottom: 1.75em; padding-top: 1px;
    background: #ABD240;
}
```

Modify it as follows:

```
#masthead {
    margin-bottom: 1.75em; padding-top: 1px;
    background: #ABD240;
    position: relative;
}
```

There's just something about relatively positioned elements (with no offsets, like we did here) that clears up lots of Explorer layout bugs. It's an essential tool in any CSS author's arsenal: if an element gets cut off, or grows way beyond where it should, try relatively positioning it or its parent element.

If you go back to the page in Explorer and reload, it should now match the previous **screenshot**. Since this will have no ill effect on the page's layout in any other browser, we don't have to worry ourselves any further. On to the about tea heading!

---

7 Return to your text or HTML editor. Find the following rule:

```
#content h1 {
    margin: 0 33% 1.25em 0;
    padding: 0.5em 2em;
}
```

Modify this as follows:

```
#content h1 {
    margin: 0 33% 1.25em -2em;
    padding: 0.5em 2em;
}
```

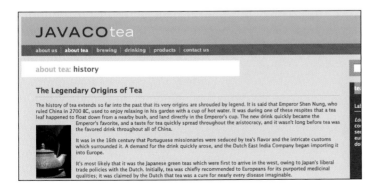

8 Save **ex0704.html**, switch to your browser, and reload **ex0704.html**.

This pulls the heading to the left. Now if you dig into the style sheet, it turns out the left margin of the content **div** is 3 em. The "about tea: history" heading is about 1.5 times the font size of the rest of the content **div**, so with a –2 em left margin, it gets pulled the same amount of space (3 em). Everything lines up nicely. Earlier, you added a right and left padding of 2 em, which happen to be equal to the distance of the negative margin, and that's why the a lines up nicely with the rest of the content area text. I didn't mention this when you assigned the padding in the previous exercise, but that was intentional. A good Web author always plans ahead. Now, you'll perform a similar action for the sidebar headings.

9 Return to your text or HTML editor. Find the following rule:

```
#sidebar div h3 {
    padding: 0.4em 0;
}
```

Modify this as follows:

```
#sidebar div h3 {
    margin: 0 -0.8em;
    padding: 0.4em 0;
}
```

10 Save **ex0704.html**, switch to your browser, and reload **ex0704.html**.

Again, the "tea of the day" and "post archive" headings have spread out nicely, in both the right and left directions. Why did you assign –0.8 em? Here's some math for you: It's because the **h3** elements have a font size of 1.25 em, and 1.25 times .8 equals 1. That equals the 1 em right and left padding of the sidebar **div**. However, as a result, the text on both these headings has been jammed over to the right side. You'll fix this in the next step.

---

11 Return to your text or HTML editor. Modify the **padding** property on your **#sidebar div h3** rule as follows:

```
padding: 0.4em 0.8em;
```

Here you are assigning right and left padding equal to the negative margin. This should move the text precisely that far from the left edge of the sidebar or, really, the left edge of the content area of the heading.

---

12 Save **ex0704.html**, switch to your browser, and reload **ex0704.html**.

You could continue to fiddle with the dimensions if you so choose, maybe making that 1 em padding, but this is the effect for which you've been going. It's looking great.

I want to point out the **body** element on this page. Can you see gutter space around the entirety of the design? You can see this most easily around the sides and top of the masthead, where a blank space is stuck between the design and the browser window. This is actually a browser Preferences default. Almost every browser that exists today inserts this space. Interestingly, this is typically implemented as a style on the **body** element, and it is usually done with margins. You could make the argument that this should be padding on the body, and some browsers do choose to implement this effect in this way. However, whatever the case, the designer does not show any extra space in the design comp. So, the safest way to override this default is to assign another rule to address both possibilities—margins or padding on the **body** element.

---

13 Return to your text or HTML editor. Insert a new line after the opening **<style>** tag, and type the following:

```
body {
    margin: 0;
    padding: 0;
}
```

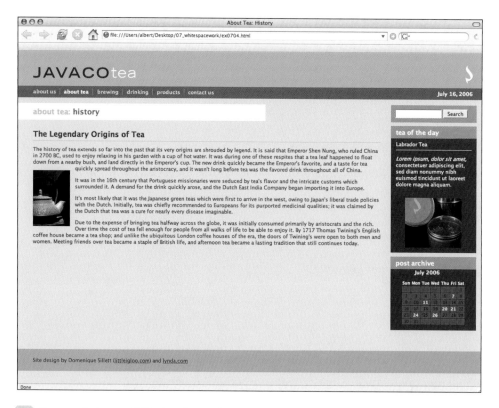

14 Save and close **ex0704.html**, switch to your browser, and reload **ex0704.html**.

Voila! You have overridden the browser's default settings and removed the padding and margins around the **body** element.

In this exercise, you used negative margins on several elements to achieve some special effects. I think the designer would be impressed. However, I have a few more points to touch on with margins, including margin collapsing, which you will work with in the next exercise.

5 | Collapsing Margins

In this exercise, I'll discuss margin collapsing. It might sound kind of boring or catastrophic, depending on your perspective, but it's really neither. **Margin collapsing** is just the process by which you combine margins to create some interesting layout techniques. Think about the "blank" space between paragraphs: This space isn't created by a carriage return; it is actually created by the margins on each paragraph. Margin collapsing is what happens when those paragraphs are laid on top of one another.

1 In a browser, open **ex0705.html** from the **07_whitespace** folder you copied to your desktop, as shown in the illustration here.

You'll first get rid of the margins on the paragraphs. I've removed the image in this exercise file to facilitate this.

2 Open **ex0705.html** with your text or HTML editor. Insert a new line after the opening **<style>** tag, and type the following:

```
p {margin: 0;}
```

3 Save **ex0705.html**, switch to your browser, and reload **ex0705.html**.

Pay special attention when you hit the Reload button. The paragraphs are squashed up against each other. The "blank line" inserted between paragraphs has actually nothing to do with paragraph breaks, line feeds, carriage returns, or anything like that. It's a margin effect. By default, paragraphs have 1 em of top and bottom margins. Well, what would happen if you added padding where those margins used to be?

---

4 Return to **ex0705.html** in your text or HTML editor. Add the following declaration to your **p** rule:

```
p {margin: 0;
    padding: 1em 0;
}
```

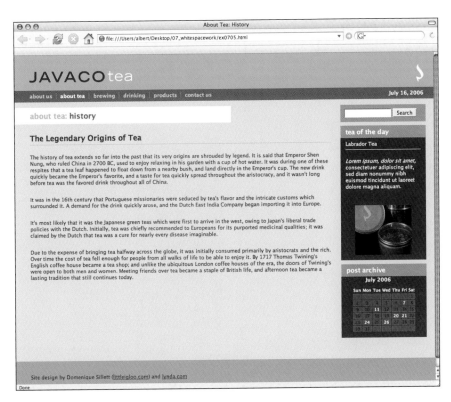

5 Save **ex0705.html**, switch to your browser, and reload **ex0705.html**.

Now, a lot of space is appearing where those margins used to be. It's more than before, in fact. What's happening is probably easiest to see with another example.

---

6 Return to **ex0705.html** in your text or HTML editor. Add the following declaration to your **p** rule:

```
p {margin: 0;
    padding: 1em 0;
    border-bottom: 1px dashed red;
}
```

7 Save **ex0705.html**, switch to your browser, and reload **ex0705.html**.

Here you added a really obvious border so you could see the difference between the two padding edges; 1 em of padding appears on each side of the border, meaning 2 ems of space appear between each paragraph. Let's revert to the 1 em margin to see the difference.

---

8 Return to **ex0705.html** in your text or HTML editor. Add the following declaration to your **p** rule:

```
p {margin: 1em 0;
    padding: 0;
    border-bottom: 1px dashed red;
}
```

9 Save **ex0705.html**, switch to your browser, and reload **ex0705.html**.

I wasn't kidding. The paragraphs really are closer together. A 1 em top margin is visible on each paragraph, but where's the bottom margin? Well, it's not that it has disappeared per se. This effect is due to margin collapsing.

When you have two vertically adjacent margins, as with the paragraphs here that are sitting right on top of each other, and the first element and second element have equal margins, they slide together until one margin touches the border of another element. Margin collapsing affects only top and bottom margins, not right and left margins. In addition, collapsing occurs only with margins, never with borders or padding.

Here's an analogy: The elements are like pieces of paper, and the margins are like thin strips of translucent plastic along the edges. As the elements move closer together, the translucent bits slide over each other until either one of them hits an edge of paper. And at that point, they stop. They don't get any closer. In effect, that's how margin collapsing works. But it may sometimes work in ways you don't expect, especially with nested elements. You'll see this in the next step.

---

10 Return to **ex0705.html** in your text or HTML editor. Insert a new line after your opening **<style>** tag, and type the following:

```
#masthead {
    padding-top: 0;
}
```

11 Save **ex0705.html**, switch to your browser, and reload **ex0705.html**.

Notice that at the top of the page, a blank space has appeared above the masthead. You can see the background color showing through. What happened? Well, by explicitly removing the padding from the masthead **div**, the margins of the masthead, the header element, and the body are now able to touch and are consequently collapsing into that 1 em "blank space."

Margin collapsing doesn't make much sense in this scenario, but the specification was written this way for a reason. It makes sense when you have a whole bunch of nested elements, such as lists. Without margin collapsing, lists could get very, very spacious.

Anyway, you now have a collapsed margin that looks like it's sticking out of this masthead. You can solve this in two ways. You can make sure no top or bottom margins appear in any of the nested elements. That's not always feasible. Alternatively, you can add either a border or padding to the **div** to prevent the margins from contacting and absorbing one another. You'll try that in the next step.

WARNING:

Margin Collapsing, the Exception to the Rule

The paper/plastic analogy with margins works pretty well, except when it comes to floated elements. Be forewarned—margins on floated elements will never collapse. You can use this to your advantage. If you are having a particularly difficult time with margin collapsing, you may want to float your element.

---

12 Return to **ex0705.html** in your text or HTML editor. Modify the **#masthead** rule as follows:

```
#masthead {
    padding-top: 1px;
}
```

In this case, it doesn't matter how much padding you assign; you just need some value here.

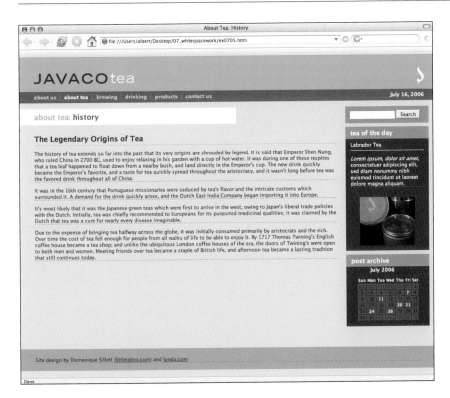

13 Save and close **ex0705.html**, switch to your browser, and reload **ex0705.html**.

There you go. That little bit of padding ensures the margin doesn't stick out of the **div**. You could have achieved the same effect with a top border. A 1 pixel solid border that was the same color as the background of the masthead element would have reined in the margin as well. The decision of which to use is up to you.

Those are the basics of margin collapsing, which exists for a reason—for lists, as I discussed, among other things. However, it can be a pain when you're working with nested elements. In this exercise, you learned a way to counteract that by adding a 1 pixel border or padding. In fact, 98 percent of the time, margin collapsing works to your advantage; the other 2 percent it does not. But knowing ways to work around it makes it even more beneficial.

And that's the end of this chapter! Congratulations. This chapter took a lot of the basic principles you learned in Chapter 3, *"Selectors and the Cascade,"* and had you apply those on a more advanced level. In the next chapter, you'll review tables—and be forewarned, they're not like anything you've seen in XHTML (e**X**tensible **HTML**). See you there!

8

Styling Tables

In this chapter, I'll talk about styling tables. I'm not talking about tables used for layout, such as backgrounds, but about tables that present data in rows and columns. Even though tables have gotten a bad rap in recent years, they aren't all that bad. They were just egregiously abused and forced to perform functions they were never intended to perform.

Basically, designers started to use tables to format page layouts. The tables ended up bloated and inefficient, which made documents difficult to manage. But don't hold it against them—legitimate uses for tables do exist. Whenever you're presenting tabular information, it makes sense to use a table. For example, a financial summary or a monthly calendar, such as the Javaco calendar, would make excellent tables. In a calendar, you have columns representing days of the week and rows representing weeks of the month—clearly that's a table.

A few diehard table haters claim it is possible to create a monthly calendar or a report without using any markup. You can check this out on the Web if you're really interested, but you don't have to do that. In this exercise, by accepting the wisdom of using a table, you will learn how to use CSS (**C**ascading **S**tyle **S**heets) to style the table contents. You'll learn about alignment and font sizing, special exceptions for the `caption` element, and how to add borders to the cells.

1 | Styling Tables and Captions

In this exercise, you'll learn about the basic elements of tables and then apply some simple styling properties, as you learned in previous chapters, to the entire table. Then you'll address the table caption.

1 Copy the **08_tables** folder from the **CSS HOT CD-ROM** to your desktop.

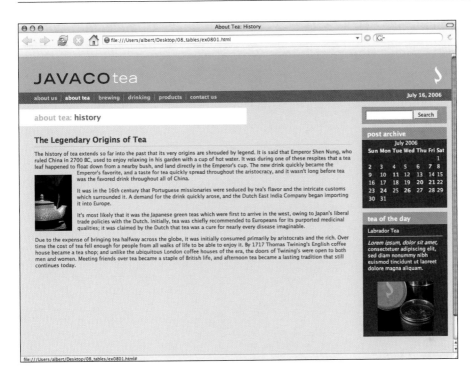

2 In a browser, open **ex0801.html** from the **08_tables** folder you copied to your desktop, as shown in the illustration here.

The **postarchive div** of course contains a table. The table includes everything after the "post archive" heading, including the "July 2006," the weekdays, and the numbers. (Also notice that I've moved the calendar up to the top of the sidebar for this chapter, since that makes it easier to see and work with.)

```
<table cellspacing="2">
<caption>July 2006</caption>
<thead>
<tr>
<th scope="col" class="sun">Sun</th>
<th scope="col" class="mon">Mon</th>
<th scope="col" class="tue">Tue</th>
<th scope="col" class="wed">Wed</th>
<th scope="col" class="thu">Thu</th>
<th scope="col" class="fri">Fri</th>
<th scope="col" class="sat">Sat</th>
</tr>
</thead>
<tbody>
<tr>
<td class="sun"></td>
<td class="mon"></td>
<td class="tue"></td>
<td class="wed"></td>
<td class="thu"></td>
<td class="fri"></td>
<td class="sat">1</td>
</tr>
<tr>
<td class="sun">2</td>
<td class="mon">3</td>
<td class="tue">4</td>
<td class="wed">5</td>
<td class="thu">6</td>
<td class="fri"><a href="#">7</a></td>
<td class="sat">8</td>
</tr>
<tr>
```

The window title bar reads: ex0801.html

Last Saved: 08/11/06 10:54:40 AM
File Path: ::Desktop:08_tables:ex0801.html

3 Open **ex0801.html** with your text or HTML editor. Scroll down to review the portion of the markup containing the **table** element, as shown in the illustration here.

Listed first is the table caption element, **caption**. The **caption** element is kind of like a header, except it's automatically associated with the table. The default browser style for captions is to center them above the table content area. After the caption, you can see the table head, **thead**, and then the table body, **tbody**. You may find one other element within tables that is not present here: a **tfoot** element, or table footer. One or more table rows (**tr** elements) and any number of table cells (**td** elements) reside in each of these table elements (with the exception of the caption).

In this example, each of the table cells has an additional **class**, indicating what day of the week it is, which you will explore in a later exercise. You can use any of the text-styling rules discussed in Chapter 6, *"Setting Typography,"* for the caption and for the contents of the table cells. This is all pretty obvious so far, but you can also use some special aspects to style the table caption, which you will get to later in this exercise. Now, you'll proceed to some simple styling of the cell contents.

4 Scroll to the style sheet. After the **<style>** start tag, insert a break, and type the following:

```
#post-archive table {
    font-size: smaller;
}
```

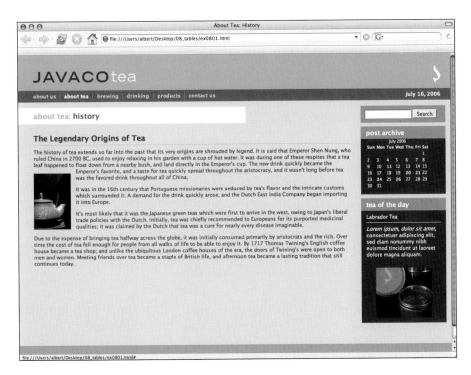

5 Save **ex0801.html**, switch to your browser, and reload **ex0801.html**.

There you go. The text of the entire table is now smaller. Because of this smaller font size, it might be nice to make the contents a bit more legible by adding a margin to push the table away from the column header and also to center it. You'll do that next.

---

6 Return to **ex0801.html** in your text or HTML editor. Modify the **#post-archive table** rule as follows:

```
#post-archive table {
    font-size: smaller;
    margin: 1em auto 0;
}
```

As you recall from the previous chapter, the right and left **auto** margins will center the table element inside the block box.

---

7 Save **ex0801.html**, switch to your browser, and reload **ex0801.html**.

Excellent. The contents of the **postarchive div** have dropped and are neatly centered…except for the caption. This is interesting—the margin opened up between the column headers and the caption. The caption *is* within the table, so it should have been included in the margin calculation, right? But that's not what happened here. So, you'll now try something different.

---

8 Return to **ex0801.html** in your text or HTML editor. Modify the #post-archive table rule as follows:

```
#post-archive table {
    font-size: smaller;
    margin: 0 auto;
}
```

Now insert a new line directly after this rule, and type the following:

```
#post-archive caption {
    margin-top: 1em;
}
```

---

9 Save **ex0801.html**, switch to your browser, and reload **ex0801.html**.

Very good. Now the caption is spaced properly, but it's still a little off center. You'll fix that next.

---

10 Return to **ex0801.html** in your text or HTML editor. Modify the #post-archive caption rule as follows:

```
#post-archive caption {
    margin: 1em auto 0;
}
```

---

11 Save **ex0801.html**, switch to your browser, and reload **ex0801.html**.

Now that's where you want the caption to be. Basically, you need to assign the same margins for the table and the caption, because in CSS, even though the caption functions more like a label than a true header, they are treated as two separate elements. This table/caption division is still somewhat controversial in CSS circles, but for cross-browser compatibility, this is the way it typically has been done. You'll next make one more change to this caption so it stands out in the calendar.

12 Return to **ex0801.html** in your text or HTML editor. Modify the **#post-archive caption** rule as follows:

```
#post-archive caption {
    font-size: larger;
    font-weight: bold;
    margin: 1em auto 0;
}
```

Most browsers will interpret this, in combination with the previous rule, as "make this one font size smaller and then go back one size larger." It should appear close to the same size as when you began the exercise.

---

13 Save and close **ex0801.html**, switch to your browser, and reload **ex0801.html**.

The month is bigger and bolder now. It stands out that much more.

And that wraps up this exercise. You could fiddle with the margins or padding again, but the lesson to take away from this exercise is that table captions are a great way to style your headings differently from the table cell contents, without having to add another header element or anything. Just make sure to include a caption within your XHTML (eXtensible **HTML**) markup.

In this exercise, you reviewed the basics of styling tables, in terms of font sizing and margins. In the next exercise, you'll dive into styling some of the child elements within the table.

---

2 | Styling Table Cells

In this exercise, you'll start styling the table cells. In the Javaco example, the days of the week are enclosed in their own cells. You can style these independently from your caption and sidebar elements so they are colored, spaced, and aligned differently.

1 In a browser, open **ex0802.html** from the **08_tables** folder you copied to your desktop, as shown in the illustration here.

2 Open **ex0802.html** with your text or HTML editor. After the **#post-archive caption** rule, insert a new line, and type the following:

```
#post-archive td {
    border: 1px solid #787A6B;
}
```

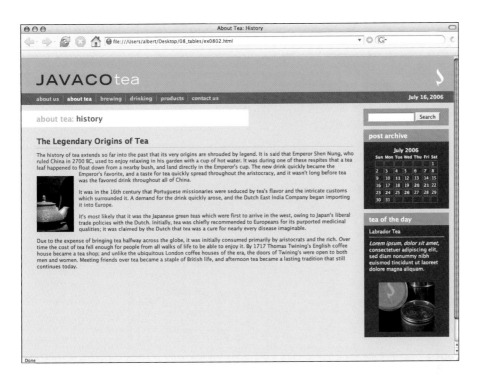

3 Save **ex0802.html**, switch to your browser, and reload **ex0802.html**.

The table border color comes from the designer's notes. The border goes on every single one of those table cells—including those cells before the 1st and after the 31st that don't even have dates in them. If you looked at the markup, you'd see that these table cells don't actually have any content at all.

This raises another important cross-browser discrepancy. In Microsoft Internet Explorer for Windows, when you don't have content, you don't get table borders. If you want the table borders, you have to put something in each of those cells, such as a nonbreaking space element, ** **. In other browsers, such as Firefox, cells are styled by default whether or not they have content. So if you want the empty cells to be styled in every browser, you have to type the nonbreaking spaces for Internet Explorer. If you don't— well, you'll see in the next step.

---

4 Return to **ex0802.html** in your text or HTML editor. Modify the **#post-archive td** rule as follows:

```
#post-archive td {
    border: 1px solid #787A6B;
    empty-cells: hide;
}
```

---

5 Save **ex0802.html**, switch to your browser, and reload **ex0802.html**.

If you are using a browser other than Internet Explorer, this should work as shown in the illustration here. The empty cells are no longer styled. Make sure you don't type *any* content in the cells you want to hide. Internet Explorer will not recognize this declaration, but then again, you don't really have to do anything because it will ignore empty cells by default.

Conversely, if you want your empty cells to show up in every browser, delete the **empty-cells: hide** declaration, and add a nonbreaking space to every one.

Next, you'll add some padding to the cells.

---

6 Return to **ex0802.html** in your text or HTML editor. Modify the **#post-archive td** rule as follows:

```
#post-archive td {
    border: 1px solid #787A6B;
    padding: 5px;
}
```

---

7 Save **ex0802.html**, switch to your browser, and reload **ex0802.html**.

The table cells are now physically larger, forcing the table to take up more of the available content area. They are taking up quite a bit of the sidebar. What would they look like if you removed all the padding?

---

8 Return to **ex0802.html** in your text or HTML editor. Modify the **#post-archive td** rule as follows:

```
#post-archive td {
    border: 1px solid #787A6B;
    padding: 0;
}
```

---

9 Save **ex0802.html**, switch to your browser, and reload **ex0802.html**.

Now the table cells are smaller, smaller than the browser default even. You don't get guaranteed consistency, but browsers usually have default table cell padding somewhere in the vicinity of 2 pixels.

So, what about the space between cells? Well, the cells themselves actually aren't allowed to have margins. The CSS specification states that internal table elements, such as table rows, table cells, table headers, and so on, don't get margins. A couple other CSS properties exist to enforce separation between table cells, but Internet Explorer does not support them. So instead, you would have to use the cell spacing attribute in your markup, in this case `<table cellspacing="2">`, as shown in the illustration here.

```
000                        ● ex0802.html                          ◯
 ┌─┬──┬──┬──┬──┬──┐       Last Saved: 09/15/06 05:36:07 PM
 │⚲│⋮ │🗎,│I,│🗋│ⓘ │       File Path:              :Desktop:08_tables:ex0802.html

<form id="search" action="somescript.scpt" method="post">
    <input type="text" class="text" />
    <input type="submit" value="Search" />
</form>

<div id="post-archive">
<h3>Post Archive</h3>

<table cellspacing="2">
<caption>July 2006</caption>
<thead>
<tr>
<th scope="col" class="sun">Sun</th>
<th scope="col" class="mon">Mon</th>
<th scope="col" class="tue">Tue</th>
<th scope="col" class="wed">Wed</th>
<th scope="col" class="thu">Thu</th>
<th scope="col" class="fri">Fri</th>
<th scope="col" class="sat">Sat</th>
</tr>
</thead>
<tbody>
<tr>
<td class="sun"></td>
<td class="mon"></td>
<td class="tue"></td>
<td class="wed"></td>
<td class="thu"></td>
<td class="fri"></td>
<td class="sat">1</td>
</tr>
```

If you wanted 1 pixel between neighboring cells, you would type that here. Of course, it is preferable to use CSS, but it's just not practical at the moment considering that, as of this writing, Internet Explorer accounts for 83 percent of the browsers used to surf the Web. The additional CSS cell spacing property, border spacing, is detailed in Appendix A, *"CSS 2 Properties,"* but I don't recommend using it.

---

10 Return to **ex0802.html** in your text or HTML editor. Modify the **#post-archive td** rule as follows:

```
#post-archive td {
    border: 1px solid #787A6B;
    padding: 0;
    background: #5B5D4E;
    color: #222;
}
```

---

11 Save **ex0802.html**, switch to your browser, and reload **ex0802.html**.

Voila! You just added a dark gray background to the contents of table cells and changed the font color for some of the numbers. The white numbers are hyperlinks, set elsewhere in the external style sheet. They have been present for quite some time, but now you can finally tell they're there!

Now, the next task you'll take care of in this exercise is to align the cell contents. Some of the characters seem to be offset, while the others, such as the two-digit dates, look OK. That's because, first, the dates are left aligned and because, second, some of the columns are wider than others. The column widths are dictated by the width of the headings. The "Wed" for Wednesday, for example, is wider than the "Fri" for Friday. (As you probably recall from Chapter 6, *"Setting Typography,"* this is because you are using a proportional font, not a monospace font, so the letters each take up different amounts of space.)

---

12 Return to **ex0802.html** in your text or HTML editor. Modify the **#post-archive td** rule as follows:

```
#post-archive td {
    border: 1px solid #787A6B;
    padding: 0;
    background: #5B5D4E;
    color: #222;
    text-align: center;
}
```

---

13 Save **ex0802.html**, switch to your browser, and reload **ex0802.html**.

Now, that just about evens up the dates. The dates are centered in their respective cells, and the centering is obscuring the fact that the columns are different widths. However, if this really bothers you, you can fix it.

---

14 Return to **ex0802.html** in your text or HTML editor. Modify the **#post-archive td** rule as follows:

```
#post-archive td {
    border: 1px solid #787A6B;
    padding: 0;
    background: #5B5D4E;
    color: #222;
    text-align: center;
    width: 15%;
}
```

---

15 Save **ex0802.html**, switch to your browser, and reload **ex0802.html**.

The columns may not be precisely equivalent now, but they are closer in size. The way table columns work is that they increase in size to fit their contents. You are actually widening the smaller columns rather than shrinking the larger columns.

Now, 15 times the number of columns, 7, is 105 percent. You might have a better result if you changed this to 14 percent so that the table reverts to 98 percent of its original size. You'll see what happens in the next step.

16 Return to **ex0802.html** in your text or HTML editor. Modify the **#post-archive td** rule as follows:

```
#post-archive td {
    border: 1px solid #787A6B;
    padding: 0;
    background: #5B5D4E;
    color: #222;
    text-align: center;
    width: 14%;
}
```

17 Save and close **ex0802.html**, switch to your browser, and reload **ex0802.html**.

Oddly enough, the table is now wider. That's because you can't always predict how a browser will interpret the table layout algorithms (so if you're using a different browser, you may have seen a different result). If you prefer having a more regular column width, feel free to define it in your style sheet, but be aware that it may not always work the same in every browser. Otherwise, use the **text-align:center** declaration, and you can rest assured that the cells will come out looking at least modestly even.

In this exercise, you modified the colors and alignment of the cell contents and indirectly impacted the width of the columns in your table. In the next exercise, you will work with the **class** attributes to style the columns directly.

3 | Styling Column Classes

In this exercise, you will review styling columns. It sounds easy, but if you look at the XHTML markup of tables, it's very row-centric. You have **tr** elements for table rows and **td** elements for table cells, but you don't have **tc** elements for table columns. You have a **col** element, but how that should relate to cells in the rows is actually an interesting question. How to style columns is currently still under debate, but in this exercise you'll learn one method using the **class** attributes.

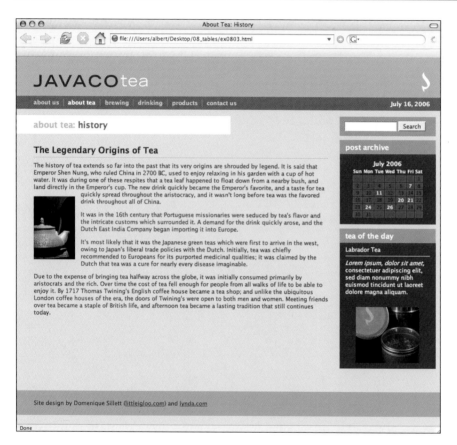

1 In a browser, open **ex0803.html** from the **08_tables** folder you copied to your desktop, as shown in the illustration here.

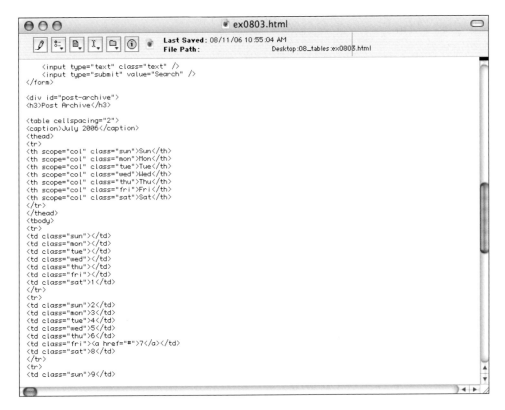

```
        <input type="text" class="text" />
        <input type="submit" value="Search" />
</form>

<div id="post-archive">
<h3>Post Archive</h3>

<table cellspacing="2">
<caption>July 2006</caption>
<thead>
<tr>
<th scope="col" class="sun">Sun</th>
<th scope="col" class="mon">Mon</th>
<th scope="col" class="tue">Tue</th>
<th scope="col" class="wed">Wed</th>
<th scope="col" class="thu">Thu</th>
<th scope="col" class="fri">Fri</th>
<th scope="col" class="sat">Sat</th>
</tr>
</thead>
<tbody>
<tr>
<td class="sun"></td>
<td class="mon"></td>
<td class="tue"></td>
<td class="wed"></td>
<td class="thu"></td>
<td class="fri"></td>
<td class="sat">1</td>
</tr>
<tr>
<td class="sun">2</td>
<td class="mon">3</td>
<td class="tue">4</td>
<td class="wed">5</td>
<td class="thu">6</td>
<td class="fri"><a href="#">7</a></td>
<td class="sat">8</td>
</tr>
<tr>
<td class="sun">9</td>
```

2 Open **ex0803.html** with your text or HTML editor. Scroll through the markup to review the table elements, as shown in the illustration here.

You'll notice each of the table cells (**td**) has a **class**. Mondays have a **class** equal to **mon**, Tuesdays have a **class** equal to **tues**, and so on. You have to specifically assign this in the markup, and some authors say it can lead to document bloat; however, when you're being discrete with your use of tables, it shouldn't impact your document too adversely to add these classes.

Now, say you want to highlight a particular day of the week, Thursdays. Thursdays are important days—maybe Javaco releases a new tea of the day every Thursday.

---

3 Scroll to the style sheet. Insert a new line before the closing **</style>** tag, and type the following:

```
#post-archive .thu {
    background: #686397;
    border: 1px solid;
}
```

Using Split View

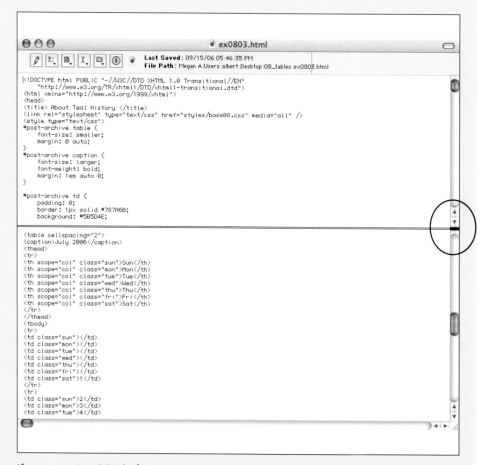

If you are using BBEdit from Bare Bones Software, there is a nice little feature called **split view** that allows you to scroll to separate areas of your document and view them both on the screen at the same time. This is great when you're working with CSS because you can use one view to look at your style sheet and the other view to examine your markup. Every text window and text pane in BBEdit has a **split bar**, the small black bar, as shown in the illustration here, directly above the scroll bar. To open split view, simply drag the split bar down and release. To collapse the views, drag the split bar to its original position.

4 Save **ex0803.html**, switch to your browser, and reload **ex0803.html**.

Here you have the result of your rule: All table cells with a class of **.thu** are assigned a background color and a 1 pixel solid border. By omitting a color, the borders pick up the foreground color of the table cells (in this case black). However, it does look a little strange. The table heading has one border color, and the table cells have another. In the interests of the design, you should probably assign an explicit value that's in keeping with the overall scheme.

The other reason to give an explicit border color is that, for one reason or another, Internet Explorer for Windows will automatically assign a table border color of white or another light color, if you don't assign it in the style sheet.

---

5 Return to **ex0803.html** in your text or HTML editor. Modify the **#post-archive .thu** rule as follows:

```
#post-archive .thu {
    background: #686397;
    border: 1px solid #686397;
}
```

You'll notice you are assigning a border color with the same value as the background, which will make the cell appear to grow by 1 pixel on each side.

---

6 Save **ex0803.html**, switch to your browser, and reload **ex0803.html**.

All the dates that fall on Thursdays are highlighted, and you've also highlighted the column header, since it also has a class of **thu**. With the extra border, that box seems to stick above the rest of the calendar and looks kind of awkward. So, you'll limit the rule here to just the **td** elements.

---

7 Return to **ex0803.html** in your text or HTML editor. Modify the **#post-archive .thu** rule as follows:

```
#post-archive td.thu {
    background: #686397;
    border: 1px solid #686397;
}
```

If you were to review the markup again, you'd notice that each of the **th** elements, or table headers, is identified as having a scope of **col**. The **col** scope is an accessibility feature meaning any table cells in the same column as this table header belong with the header. Applying the rule to **td** elements restricts the changes just to the dates, but because of the scope declarations in the markup, the elements still remain associated with the Thursday header.

---

8 Save **ex0803.html**, switch to your browser, and reload **ex0803.html**.

Ta-da! The "Thursday" column heading is no longer highlighted. You can stop there, or you might want to give the heading some distinction.

9 Return to **ex0803.html** in your text or HTML editor. Insert a new line after the **#post-archive .thu** rule, and type the following:

```
#post-archive th.thu {
    color: #686397;
}
```

10 Save **ex0803.html**, switch to your browser, and reload **ex0803.html**.

The "Thu" column heading now has the same foreground color as the background of the column cells. You should be starting to understand the implications of being able to use **th** and **td** to style your column headings and column cells separately from the entire table. You can identify these elements in the style sheet in one other way.

11 Return to **ex0803.html** in your text or HTML editor. Locate the following rules in your style sheet (the last two you have been working with):

```
#post-archive td.thu {
    background: #686397;
    border: 1px solid #686397;
}
#post-archive th.thu {
    color: #686397;
}
```

Modify these rules as follows:

```
#post-archive tbody .thu {
    background: #686397;
    border: 1px solid #686397;
}
#post-archive thead .thu {
    color: #686397;
}
```

12 Save and close **ex0803.html**, switch to your browser, and reload **ex0803.html**.

Nothing has changed. Really, these rules have the same effect on your page. This was just a different way of writing a selector to address the same portions of the document. Here, you told any element with a class of **thu** in the table body to apply this background and border. And you said, "any element with a class of **thu** in the table head, apply this foreground color." You merely identified the same elements by first going to the parent element and then drilling down by class. Neither statement is superior to the other, but as with so many features of CSS, you have plenty of options.

In this exercise, you reviewed column styling and addressed it in the most cross-browser friendly method possible. In the next exercise, you'll dig into styling the links residing in the cells. For example, if you wanted a certain date within your calendar to link to items on an event page, you would want those links to be clearly visible to your users. You'll learn how to do this next.

In this exercise, you'll learn about styling the links in table cells. You'll discover how to improve their static appearance and, hopefully, attract more users to navigate to different areas of your Web site as a result.

1 In a browser, open **ex0804.html** from the **08_tables** folder you copied to your desktop, as shown in the illustration here.

Notice the white, bold dates in the calendar. If you position your cursor on them, your cursor should change into a gloved hand, indicating these dates are in fact links. However, you might want to bump up the visual feedback to ensure your users know these are the interactive portions of the document.

2 Open **ex0804.html** with your text or HTML editor. Before the end **</style>** tag, insert a new line, and type the following:

```
#post-archive a:hover {
    background: #ABD240;
}
```

Here you are adding an effect so that when a user positions the cursor on an element, this new background color will appear.

Using :hover and Other Pseudo-Classes

Pseudo-classes are selectors used to refer to dynamic events or changes in a document that depend on a user's action. Pseudo-classes target a specific element that is designed to be interacted with, such as a form, a button, or a hyperlink, and they control how that element is styled depending on its current state. In CSS, pseudo-classes are always preceded by a colon. **:hover**, which you used in this exercise, is a pseudo-class. Many others exist, but they are not universally supported across browsers. Among the few common pseudo-classes are **:active**, which signifies an element the user is clicking, and **:link**, which signifies a link that has not yet been clicked.

The close relative of a pseudo-class is a **pseudo-element**, which indicates portions of the document that might be styled differently, not depending on a user's action but depending on whether the element is present.

For example, you might use the pseudo-element **:first letter** in a style sheet to make the first letter of the first paragraph bright green. As the text is modified—for example, on a journal page where a new paragraph might be inserted every day—the style skips to the first letter of the new paragraph.

Appendix A, *"CSS 2 Properties"* lists the pseudo-class and pseudo-element selectors.

---

3 Save **ex0804.html**, switch to your browser, and reload **ex0804.html**. Position your cursor on the white numbers to watch the background color change.

This effect is cutesy but it works. The only problem now is that the links are only as wide as their content. You'll notice, for example, that as you position your cursor on the cell containing 7, you must position your cursor exactly on the number. This is to be expected, but here it's not so great because it's such a small area. The user's cursor might be on the table cell, but if they click it and they're not actually on the hyperlink, nothing will happen. **Fitt's law** states if you have a hotspot, you should make the interactive area as large as possible without interfering with the other elements on the page. So in the next step, you'll convert the way these hyperlinks are drawn.

---

4 Return to **ex0804.html** in your text or HTML editor. Insert a new line after the **#post-archive a:hover** rule, and type the following:

```
#post-archive a {
    display: block;
}
```

This rule changes the links from displaying as inline elements to displaying as block boxes. You'll see what this means when you reload the page.

---

5 Save **ex0804.html**, switch to your browser, and reload **ex0804.html**. Position your cursor on the white numbers, and watch the background color change.

As you'll notice, the calendar hasn't changed visually in any way. However, if you position your cursor on any white date item, now the green background effect fills the entire cell. Your cursor should also change to the gloved hand, whether or not you're directly over the number. This is because the hyperlink has expanded to fill the entire area; it's now generating a block-level box as though it were a `div` or a paragraph inside this table cell.

6 Return to **ex0804.html** in your text or HTML editor. Scroll to the style sheet, and find the following rule:

```
#post-archive td {
    border: 1px solid #787A6B;
    padding: 0;
    background: #5B5D4E;
    color: #222;
    text-align: center;
}
```

Modify the rule as follows:

```
#post-archive td {
    border: 1px solid #787A6B;
    padding: 0;
    background: #5B5D4E;
    color: #222;
    text-align: center;
    width: 14%;
}
```

7 Save and close **ex0804.html**, switch to your browser, and reload **ex0804.html**.

The width of the entire table has expanded, as you saw in the previous exercise. If you position your cursor on any of the links, you'll notice that the clickable areas have also expanded to fill the wider cells. Again, this is because the **a** element is generating a block box and the box will expand to the edges of the available space.

So, you've come to the end of this exercise. I revealed one way to make the links in a table easier to interact with and a little bit better looking. Previously when you positioned your cursor on the links, you would get only a tiny green strip, and now the whole box is filled. Frankly, it looks much cleaner and more professional.

You've also come to the end of this chapter. I hope you found it useful. CSS offers many alternatives for styling tables and table contents, which could be achieved only in XHTML through heavy use of markup. This, in combination with a little prudence when it comes to using tables, should go a long way toward reducing the size and upkeep of your documents.

Styling for Print

In this chapter, I'll discuss styling for media other than the screen, the most common of which is styling for print. Print layout is an aspect of the user experience many Web page authors fail to consider during the design process. You might never have contemplated that a user could output a Web page in a medium other than a browser. But a Web page is really just an XHTML (e**X**tensible **HTML**) document with some styling, and neither XHTML nor CSS (**C**ascading **S**tyle **S**heets) is limited to presentation by a browser or on a monitor.

In fact, users often print these XHTML documents, so you'll want to conserve the user's resources. A badly designed printout can consume lots of printer toner and paper and lead to quite a bit of frustration. In this chapter, you'll learn how to modify your original design to make it "printer friendly." You'll also decide what information the user really wants to print so you can streamline the contents and present only the most relevant information on the final printout.

1 | Styling for Specific Mediums

In this exercise, you'll practice linking multiple style sheets to a document and learn how to restrict styles to certain media types. You will begin by associating an existing finished print style sheet, which you'll then build in future exercises in this chapter.

1 Copy the **09_print** folder from the **CSS HOT CD-ROM** to your desktop. Double-click the **09_print** folder to open it so you see the exercise files inside, as shown in the illustration here.

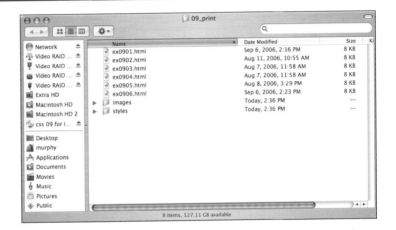

2 In Firefox or an alternative browser, open **ex0901.html** from the **09_print** folder you copied to your desktop, as shown in the illustration here.

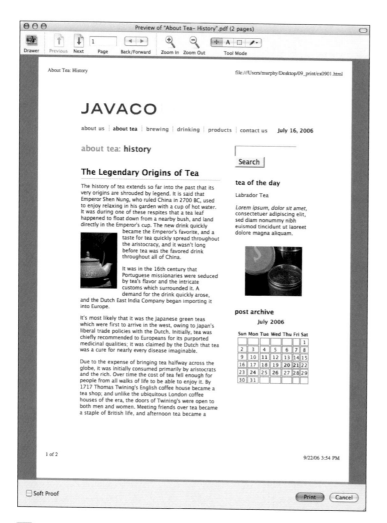

3 If you are using Firefox, Safari, or Internet Explorer on a Mac, choose **File > Print**. When the **Print** dialog box appears, click the **Preview** button. If you are working with any of these browsers using Windows, choose **File > Print Preview**.

As shown in the illustration here, Print Preview mode shows what the page will look like when you print it. The style sheet you have linked to will apply to the printout as well as to the screen—but with some differences. You can see some of the colors and the borders, but other parts of the page are missing, such as the backgrounds.

The user does not have to print backgrounds. In fact, almost every browser, as of this writing, is configured to not print backgrounds by default. You can probably imagine the reason for that. Let's say the browser was set up to print backgrounds by default and you published a Web page that featured white text on a black background. If the user decided to print it, that poor person would chew through a whole lot of toner cartridges before they were even done printing the first page.

This page looks like this now because the styles in the base.css style sheet you've linked are applying to all media. You'll now examine the document to find out where this code resides.

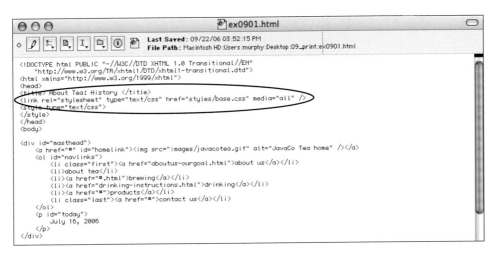

```
                                   ex0901.html
  Last Saved: 09/22/06 03:52:15 PM
  File Path: Macintosh HD:Users:murphy:Desktop:09_print:ex0901.html

<!DOCTYPE html PUBLIC "-//W3C//DTD XHTML 1.0 Transitional//EN"
    "http://www.w3.org/TR/xhtml1/DTD/xhtml1-transitional.dtd">
<html xmlns="http://www.w3.org/1999/xhtml">
<head>
<title> About Tea: History </title>
<link rel="stylesheet" type="text/css" href="styles/base.css" media="all" />
<style type="text/css">
</style>
</head>
<body>

<div id="masthead">
    <a href="#" id="homelink"><img src="images/javacotea.gif" alt="JavaCo Tea home" /></a>
    <ol id="navlinks">
        <li class="first"><a href="aboutus-ourgoal.html">about us</a></li>
        <li>about tea</li>
        <li><a href="#.html">brewing</a></li>
        <li><a href="drinking-instructions.html">drinking</a></li>
        <li><a href="#">products</a></li>
        <li class="last"><a href="#">contact us</a></li>
    </ol>
    <p id="today">
        July 16, 2006
    </p>
</div>
```

4 Close the **Print** (Mac) or **Print Preview** (Windows) dialog box. Open **ex0901.html** with your text or HTML (**H**yper**T**ext **M**arkup **L**anguage) editor. Near the beginning of the file, find the following block of code, as shown in the illustration here:

```
<link rel="stylesheet" type="text/css" href="styles/base.css" media="all" />
```

In this `link` element, `media="all"` means base.css should be applied to all media. This includes the screen medium, such as on a computer; the projection medium; the handheld medium; and so on. See the following chart for a description of all the media types. Note, these values are not case-sensitive, but I recommend using lowercase for consistency.

Media Types	
Value	**Applications**
all	All media types
braille	For tactical feedback devices for the visually impaired
embossed	For paged Braille printers
handheld	For handheld devices (Palm Pilots, some cell phones, and some pagers)
print	For print devices and documents viewed onscreen in **Print Preview** mode
projection	For projectors or for printing transparencies
screen	For a monitor or other screen device (such as a WebTV)
speech / aural	For speech synthesizers
tty	For media using a fixed-pitch character grid (such as Teletypes or terminals)
tv	For television

Again, as is, the base.css style will apply to all media on which the Javaco page is loaded. However, you can also restrict styles to certain media types.

5 Return to your text or HTML editor. Modify the previously mentioned block of code as follows:

```
<link rel="stylesheet" type="text/css" href="styles/base.css" media="screen" />
```

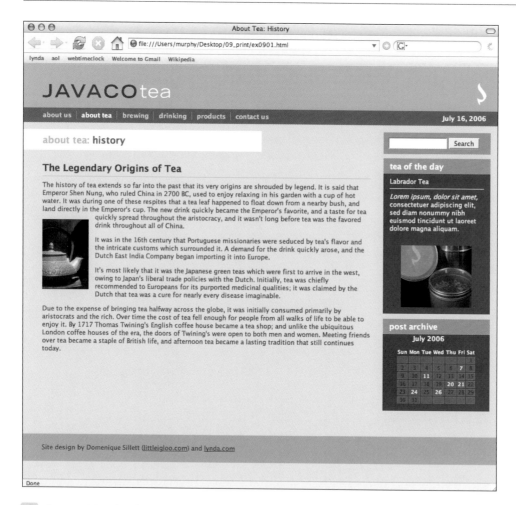

6 Save **ex0901.html**, switch to your browser, and reload **ex0901.html**.

Nothing appears to have changed, but then you are still viewing the page onscreen. The style sheet is currently being applied strictly to this medium.

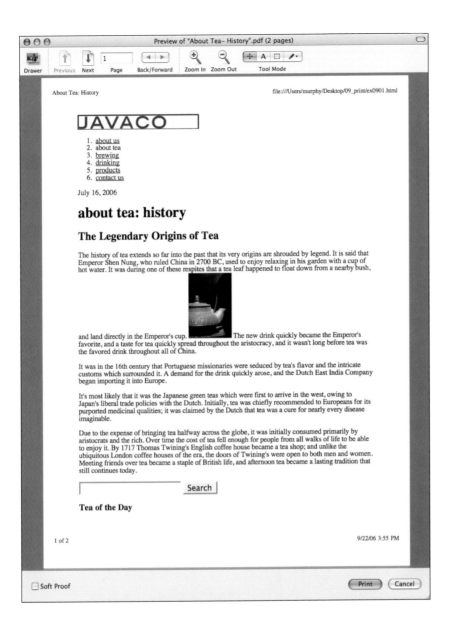

7 If you're on a Mac, in your browser, choose **File > Print**, and then click the **Preview** button in the **Print** dialog box. If you're using Windows, in your browser, choose **File > Print Preview**.

The print version of this page is now completely unstyled. Since you changed the media type, the style sheet no longer applies to print media—or any media other than the screen. However, the great feature of CSS is that you can add links to other style sheets ad infinitum. You could have a separate style sheet for every type of media if you wanted. But for now, you'll just include another for print.

Developing for Handheld Media

Practically speaking, the most common media types are screen and print. However, at the time of writing this book, handhelds are starting to make a fairly large upsurge in the United States. They're already quite popular overseas. Since mobile Web browsing is starting to become more and more common, so are mobile browsers that understand handheld style sheets. I won't cover handheld style sheets in this book, but the principles covered here apply to them as well. The way you set up a print style sheet is the same as you would set up a handheld style sheet. However, you should keep a couple of unique points about handheld media in mind.

First, horizontal scrolling is strongly discouraged in handheld Web design. Some handheld browsers, such as Opera's mobile browser, actually remove horizontal scrolling by default, unless you have fixed-width declarations in your style sheet. Second, though the Web-safe color palette has become slightly less relevant in recent years, because of advancements in displays and browser technology, it is still important when it comes to designing for handheld devices, which are still limited to 8-bit color displays. To find out more about the Web-safe palette, visit Lynda Weinman's great introduction at **www.lynda.com/hex.asp**. Lynda was the first author to identify and publish the colors in her book *Designing Web Graphics*. At her site, you can preview and print a handy visual index of the 216 colors and download a CLUT (**C**olor **L**ook-**U**p **T**able) file of the palette for free.

Another bit of advice: You shouldn't test your handheld style sheet in your browser unless it offers a "small devices" view, such as Opera does. Instead, several emulators are available so you can preview exactly how your page will appear to the user of a handheld device. **Emulators** are applications designed to mimic the functionality of another device or platform so you can run non-native software on your computer. The most difficult challenge when designing for handheld devices is correctly sizing the contents of your page, and using emulator software will help with that.

8 Return to **ex0901.html** in your text or HTML editor. Insert a new line after the existing **link** element, and type the following:

```
<link rel="stylesheet" type="text/css" href="styles/ex0901.css" media="print" />
```

9 Save **ex0901.html**, switch to your browser, and reload **ex0901.html**.

Again, nothing appears to have changed. You are still using the base.css external style sheet as the style sheet for the screen medium.

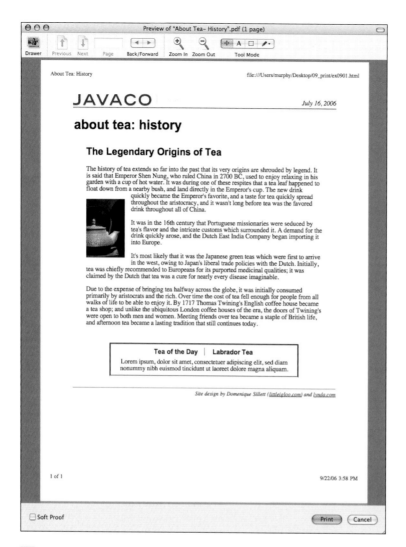

10 If you're on a Mac, in your browser, choose **File > Print**, and then click the **Preview** button in the **Print** dialog box. If you're using Windows, in your browser, choose **File > Print Preview**.

Ah-ha, the page looks different now. Associating the print style sheet and restricting the base.css styles to the screen medium finally bring the print styles into play. Again, they will apply only if you output the page to the print medium or view Print Preview mode in your browser.

11 When you are done reviewing the page, close the **Print** (Mac) or **Print Preview** (Windows) dialog box, the browser, and **ex0901.html**.

Those are the basics of associating a print style sheet! It's not too hard, is it? Feel free to actually print the document. I haven't included that step in the exercise because in the next exercise, I'll show you a shortcut that will save you time and quite a lot of paper. You'll also take a step back and walk through the process of creating the print style sheet that you just applied from scratch.

2 | Creating a Print Style Sheet

In this exercise, you'll set up and link to an external print style sheet and add some basic styling to the font and images, before moving on to more complicated effects in later exercises.

1 In a browser, open **ex0902.html** from the **09_print** folder you copied to your desktop, as shown in the illustration here.

This should look familiar! It's the same Javaco page you have been gradually building throughout this book.

2 Open **ex0902.html** with your text or HTML editor. Scroll through your style sheet, and find the following elements:

```
<link rel="stylesheet" type="text/css" href="styles/base.css" media="screen" />
<link rel="stylesheet" type="text/css" href="styles/ex0902.css" media="print" />
```

Here you have a link to the screen style sheet, base.css, and a link to the (currently blank) print style sheet, ex0902.css.

You can create a new print style sheet in two ways. One is to work on the print sheet more or less blind, getting far enough along until you can check your work against the browser—printing the page, checking your work, changing the style sheet, printing the page, over and over and over again.

Whew. If you have that kind of paper budget to burn, more power to you. I, on the other hand, prefer to do this: Instead of applying the screen styles, I pick a media type that would never possibly apply in order to temporarily invalidate it. You'll see what I mean in the next few steps.

---

3 Return to your text or HTML editor. Modify the first link element as follows:

```
<link rel="stylesheet" type="text/css" href="styles/base.css" media="tty" />
```

tty is a perfectly valid media type as far as CSS is concerned, but because almost no one ever works with Teletype displays anymore, it is practically obsolete. A browser is not a Teletype device, and neither is a printer. By changing the media type of the basic style sheet to **tty**, it will not apply to this page. You are sort of relegating it to the background for the moment.

Why? Well, now you can focus on the print style sheet. If you change the media type of the print style sheet to **screen**, you will get a handy preview right in the browser—without having to waste all that paper.

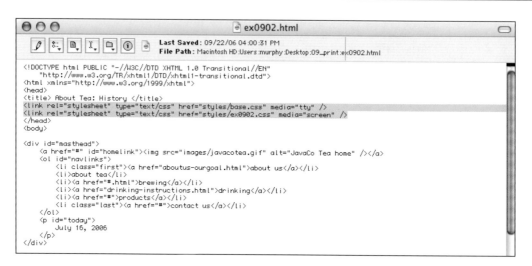

4 You should still be in your text or HTML editor. Modify the second link element as follows, as shown in the illustration here:

```
<link rel="stylesheet" type="text/css" href="styles/ex0902.css" media="screen" />
```

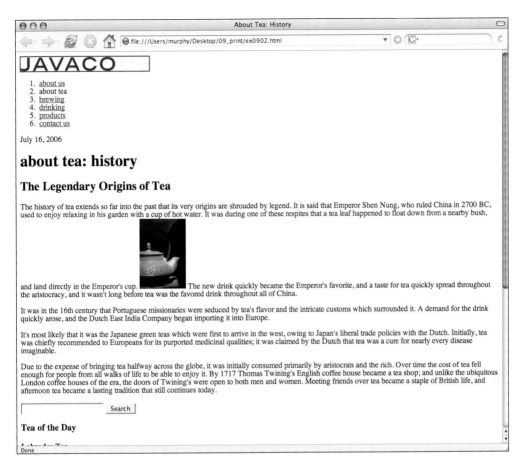

5 Save **ex0902.html**, switch to your browser, and reload **ex0902.html**.

The styles are gone! Of course, you haven't added any rules to the print style sheet yet, so this makes sense.

You may have noticed that up until this point, except for a few instances in Chapter 2, you've been doing all the styling using embedded style sheets. Embedded style sheets are easier to learn from because you have the rest of the markup there to reference. But since print style sheets are invariably external style sheets, you'll practice working with them in this exercise and throughout the rest of this chapter. Toggling between the XHTML and CSS documents is a little more complicated, but managing multiple files should be second nature to you if you have experience working with XHTML.

---

6 Return to your text or HTML editor. Choose **File > Open**, and navigate to the **09_print** folder you copied to your desktop in Exercise 1. Open the **styles** folder, and open **ex0902.css**.

When you click Open, the style sheet opens as completely blank. Again, this should be no surprise, because you haven't added anything yet. You'll start by selecting a font family that is appropriate for print.

```
body {
   font-family: "Times New Roman", TimesNR, Times, serif;
}
```

Some debate exists about whether a serif or sans-serif font is easier to read and whether any one family is easier to read onscreen or in print. I can't claim to know the answers; you can use your own best judgment. Here, you'll go with serif by typing the four fonts in this step, because, as you may recall from the exercises in Chapter 6, *"Setting Typography,"* this will allow for instances in which certain fonts might not be available on the user's computer.

8 Save **ex0902.css**, switch to your browser, and reload **ex0902.html**.

The font styling has a slight effect, since the browser was probably previously defaulted to Times or something similar. Now, it should display the text in Times New Roman, your first selection, because this is a fairly common font.

9 Return to **ex0902.css** in your text or HTML editor. Modify the first rule in the style sheet as follows:

```
body {
    font: 12pt "Times New Roman", TimesNR, Times, serif;
}
```

In this step, you'll use the font shorthand property to specify a font family and a font size. This is where things can get interesting....

Best practices state you should avoid using point sizes in Web design. It's true; using point sizes in screen styles is a horrible, horrible idea for a variety of reasons that would take too long to explain here. The most pertinent reason is that the accurate presentation of point measures depends on your display knowing how many pixels exist per inch. Unfortunately, your display almost never knows that. Displays aren't built to be that smart.

Printers, on the other hand, *do* know how many pixels (or rather, **dots**) exist per inch. Printer software first converts your output, whether it's a photo, a document, or a Web page, to an image and then calculates how many dots per inch exist in the image. You may have heard of this terminology—dpi (**d**ots **p**er **i**nch). **dpi** is the method of measuring print resolution. It is different from ppi (**p**ixels **p**er **i**nch). **ppi** is intended for computer display, and ppi resolutions can differ from one computer display to another; dpi is a fixed feature of the printer. It is always recommended that you purchase a printer that has a dpi resolution equal to or better than the ppi of the images you want to print so you can retain the quality in the resulting printouts.

Basically, printers know exactly how many dots they need to make 12-point text. Therefore, you might think about using point measurements in your print design. Some critics point out that if you specify a point measurement, in some browsers the user is completely unable to restyle the font size before printing. However, I have not seen that many other drawbacks. Of course, if you deploy a style sheet with a font size like this and receive complaints from your users, you can easily edit the style sheet.

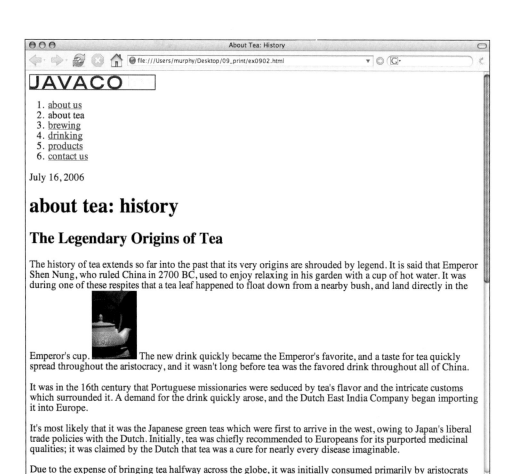

10 Save **ex0902.css**, switch to your browser, and reload **ex0902.html**.

Voila! The font size is now larger, appearing as it should if you printed the document. Next, you'll reproduce a style from the screen style sheet—removing the borders from around any images inside hyperlinks.

---

11 Return to **ex0902.css** in your text or HTML editor. Insert a new line after the first rule in the style sheet, and type the following:

```
a img {
    border: 0;
}
```

12 Save **ex0902.css**, switch to your browser, and reload **ex0902.html**.

You can see the thick blue border around the "Javaco tea" image is no longer visible when you reload the page. These borders around images are actually a browser default from the Mosaic days.

Now, one of the other images in the page, the teapot, is suspended between the paragraphs, as it was before you floated it in Chapter 4, *"Using CSS to Affect Page Layout."* This is a foreground image, so unlike a background image, it will print; however, you want it to match the screen style as closely as possible.

13 Return to **ex0902.css** in your text or HTML editor. Insert a new line after the **a img** rule in the style sheet, and type the following:

```
#content img.illus {
    float: left;
    margin: 1em 1em 1em 0;
}
```

These are, in fact, the same declarations in your screen style sheet. Almost every rule will work the same for print media as for screen media.

14 Save and close **ex0902.css**, switch to your browser, and reload **ex0902.html**.

Excellent! The basic page styling is all there.

In this exercise, you styled the font, removed some of the borders, and floated an illustration image, effectively reproducing a lot of the effects in your screen style sheet in print. This is a great foundation for the next exercise, where you'll "switch off" some aspects of the page that don't really need to be printed.

3 | Hiding Elements for Print

In this exercise, now that you have some basic print styles, you need to think about what you actually want to print. For example, do you want to print the "Javaco tea" image? "Javaco" displays nicely, but "tea" is quite faint, because it's basically white text on a white background. You'll make some decisions and some changes in this exercise.

1 In a browser, open **ex0903.html** from the **09_print** folder you copied to your desktop, as shown in the illustration here.

You can see the image I was referring to quite plainly at the top of the screen. The "tea" in "Javaco tea" is almost completely consumed by the white background. Now, you could add a colored background to the masthead, but you have no guarantee that it would print. Actually, it's almost certain it wouldn't. In print design, designers rarely, if ever, set background colors unless the document can print properly without them.

A more relevant example is the navigation links. They are completely unstyled here so they comprise an ordered list of links. The second item is plain, unlinked text because that's the page at which you're looking. The question remains, do you really need to print the links at all? You can stab your finger at a link on a printout all you want, and nothing will ever happen (not in 2006, at least!). In other words, the interactive aspect is totally lost in print. It's the same story with the sidebar elements. Do you really need them? Does the tea of the day need to appear on the page? Or the search box? In every page you design, you need to make similar types of decisions and consider what the user is really going to want to print.

It will be up to you as the author to make the ultimate decision about what needs to be included on the final printed page, but the following are the items traditionally excluded: navigation items (buttons, links, and so on), animated images, scripting, advertising, and nonessential images.

---

2 Open **ex0903.css** with your text or HTML editor. Insert a new line after the **body** rule, and type the following:

```
#navlinks {
    display: none;
}
```

---

3 Save **ex0903.css**, switch to your browser, and reload **ex0903.html**.

The navigation links have disappeared. Once you are done and switch this style sheet from screen to print media, the links will reappear on the Web page but not on the printed page. This is good. Again, why chew up printer toner—or paper, for that matter—by making the page longer than necessary with content that is irrelevant in the print medium? I would say that the search box, however useful on the Web, also falls into the "irrelevant in print" category, as does the Post Archive calendar.

4 Return to **ex0903.css** in your text or HTML editor. Modify the **#navlinks** rule as follows:

```
#navlinks, #search, #post-archive {
    display: none;
}
```

Here you are starting to build a grouped selector, adding both the search bar and the `post-archive div` to the list of nondisplayed items. The post-archive content might be relevant the day the page was printed, but six days or six months from now...not so much.

5 Save **ex0903.css**, switch to your browser, and reload **ex0903.html**.

There you are. Now the masthead, the date, the main content, the tea of the day, and the footer remain. You may decide that although the teapot image should stay, the "tea of the day" image isn't especially important. It's enough that you're going to include the text.

Setting Page Breaks and Orientation

At the start of this exercise, if you had printed the page, you would have noticed that the contents spilled over on to two or even three pages, depending on your printer settings. However, you have a few ways in CSS to enforce how a document actually prints on paper. Namely, you can enforce page breaks and landscape or portrait print orientation.

Earlier versions of CSS had no way to specify this. CSS 2 introduced the page model, similar to the box model when it comes to the screen. It is the means to specify print layouts including page tiling, one- or two-sided printing, page orientation, and even output trays on the printer. The page model involves some advanced concepts that are beyond the scope of this book, but I'll mention a few features, in case you want to explore this more on your own.

The page model contains two areas, the content area and the margins. The CSS page model doesn't include any borders or padding. The selector **@page** is used for some page box rules. The most commonly used properties are **size**, which dictates the page size (which does not necessarily correspond to the sheet on which it will be translated) and the orientation (**auto**, **portrait**, or **landscape**), and **page-break-before** (also **page-break-after** and **page-break-inside**), which obviously inserts page breaks in the document. For a list of properties and values you can use with the **@page** selector, please see Appendix A, *"CSS 2 Properties."* To learn more about the CSS page model, check out some of the resources in Appendix C, *"CSS Resources."*

6 Return to **ex0903.css** in your text or HTML editor. Modify the **#navlinks** rule as follows:

```
#navlinks, #search, #post-archive, #tea-of-the-day img {
    display: none;
}
```

7 Save and close **ex0903.css**, switch to your browser, and reload **ex0903.html**.

You have removed the "tea of the day" image. The rest of the content you see here will remain on the printout. That's probably sufficient. But again, whether the tea of the day should be printed is an interesting question. It largely depends on your client's needs, or if you are your own client, it depends on your personal preference. One of the most important questions to ask is, will this be relevant for the expected life of this printout? For how long do you expect your users to retain this printout?

In this example, imagine your client has said, "Yes, include this content." You may not need the picture, but the text is a reminder that they have interesting teas and that this section is updated on a daily or weekly basis.

In this exercise, you used the display property to "switch off" areas of content you do not want to include on the printout. In the next exercise, you'll start styling the content so it looks more like a professional printout.

4 | Styling for Print

In this exercise, you'll improve the way the print style looks so you (or your client) have something you would want to hold in your hands as a printout.

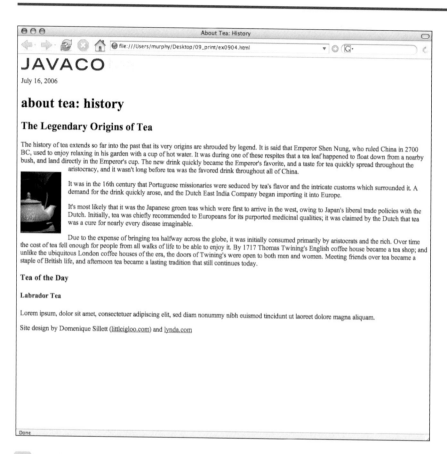

1 In a browser, open **ex0904.html** from the **09_print** folder you copied to your desktop, as shown in the illustration here.

You'll start by adding some simple improvements. For example, you'll add a bottom border to the masthead. In the screen styles, you had a background color for the masthead to set it apart from the rest of the page. Yet, as I mentioned previously, you cannot expect background colors to show up in print.

2 Open **ex0904.css** from the **09_print/styles** folder with your text or HTML editor. Insert a new line after the **a img** rule, and type the following:

```
#masthead {
    border-bottom: 1px solid #000;
}
```

Now the foreground colors, as you've assigned to the masthead border here, should show up, assuming the user has a color printer.

3   Save **ex0904.css**, switch to your browser, and reload **ex0904.html**.

The border adds a nice visual separation, even without the background color. Again, you can specify colors in print styles, but don't rely on that color being there. For example, say you need to draw attention to something so you assign a red color to that content, and then you instruct the user to "look for the red text." The user may not have a color printer, they might not have replaced their empty color cartridge, and so on. They might have a perfectly legible black-and-white printout but still feel a little lost. Therefore, never rely on color for visual cues, especially in print, because you have no way to know whether the user will end up with a color printout.

So, what else can you do to distinguish the headings from the rest of the document, besides using color? Maybe you could change the font. Next step, please!

4 Return to **ex0904.css** in your text or HTML editor. Insert a new line after the **a img** rule, and type the following:

```
h1, h2, h3, h4 {
    font-family: Arial, Verdana, Helvetica, sans-serif;
}
```

5 Save **ex0904.css**, switch to your browser, and reload **ex0904.html**.

The headings should now all be in some sort of sans-serif font, depending on what's available on your computer. As shown in the illustration here, they are styled in Arial, because that's what was installed on this computer. Either way, it gives the heading some extra impact. Then again, you might decide that mixing serif and sans-serif fonts on a single page isn't your cup of tea. (Little joke there!) With CSS, you can always decide to change it later.

Now you have to address the date. It's sitting smack between the header and the border. It would be nice to move it to the right side to match the screen style and also to italicize it.

6 Return to **ex0904.css** in your text or HTML editor. Insert a new line after the **#masthead** rule, and type the following:

```
#today {
    text-align: right;
    font-style: italic;
    margin: -1em 0 0;
}
```

Here you are also assigning no side or bottom margins but adding a negative top margin, which, as you may recall from Chapter 7, *"Using Margins and Borders to Create Whitespace and Separation,"* should move the date up into the masthead.

7 Save **ex0904.css**, switch to your browser, and reload **ex0904.html**.

It's quite a nice effect overall. However, it does bring the date rather close to that bottom border you added. You can fix that with just a little bit of bottom margin on the #**today** element.

8 Return to **ex0904.css** in your text or HTML editor. Modify the **#today** rule as follows:

```
#today {
    text-align: right;
    font-style: italic;
    margin: -1em 0 0.25em;
}
```

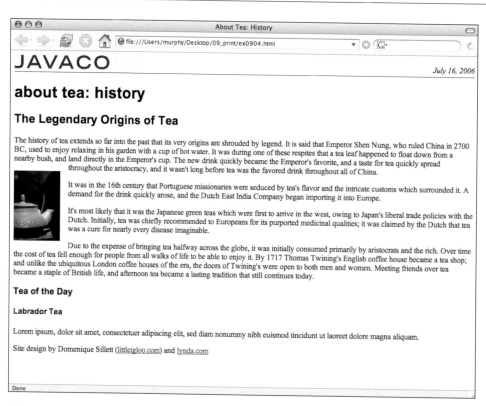

9 Save **ex0904.css**, switch to your browser, and reload **ex0904.html**.

The extra margin pushes the border element down just enough to create a well-defined visual separation.

10 Return to **ex0904.css** in your text or HTML editor. Insert a new line after the **#today** rule, and type the following:

```
#content {
    margin: 0 5%;
}
```

11 Save **ex0904.css**, switch to your browser, and reload **ex0904.html**.

The main contents have shifted to the right. The reason you added 5 percent is because the content looks better in proportion to the widespread aspect of the masthead, and eventually a footer will do the same. This formatting is a little more sophisticated, more like a magazine layout. It does reduce the amount of print area available for the content and could increase the page count, but with the rather short document here, that's not much of an issue. You could, however, reposition the "about tea: history" header just to make it a little more conspicuous.

12 Return to **ex0904.css** in your text or HTML editor. Insert a new line after the **#content** rule, and type the following:

```
#content h1 {
    margin-left: -5%;
}
```

This –5 percent should counteract the 5 percent left margin you applied to the entire content **div**.

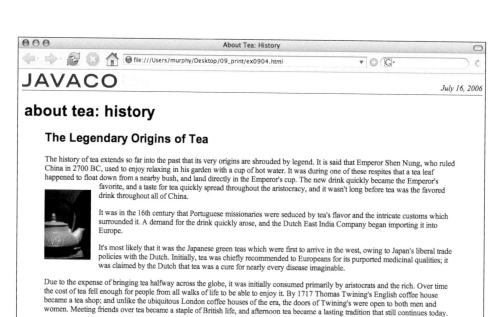

13 Save and close **ex0904.css**, switch to your browser, and reload **ex0904.html**.

The "about tea: history" heading now starts on the left. Nice job!

You definitely improved the look and feel of this printout. You used some of the same CSS properties you learned about in previous chapters while working with certain factors unique to print. In the next exercise, you will address the "Tea of the Day" section and the currently nondescript footer.

5 | Applying Complex Styling for Print

At this point in your print styling, you need to deal with the "Tea of the Day" sidebar. If you read the headers again, certainly both sections are about tea, but "The Legendary Origins of Tea" section is a historical perspective, whereas "Tea of the Day" is about, well, today. The sidebar contents are an aside—they don't make sense within the current flow of the document. On the actual Web page, the sections are separated into columns, but this isn't so in the print style. In this exercise, you'll learn how to segment the contents.

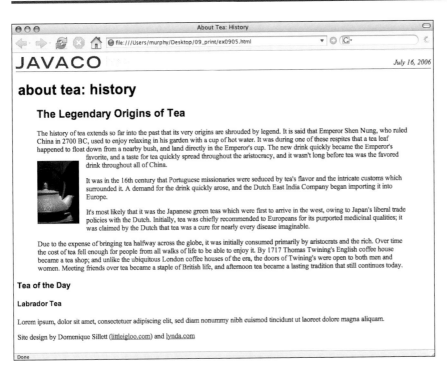

1 In a browser, open **ex0905.html** from the **09_print** folder you copied to your desktop, as shown in the illustration here.

2 Open **ex0905.css** from the **09_print/styles** folder with your text or HTML editor. Insert a new line after the **#content img.illus** rule, and type the following:

```
#tea-of-the-day {
    border: 3px double;
    text-align: center;
    padding: 0.5em;
}
```

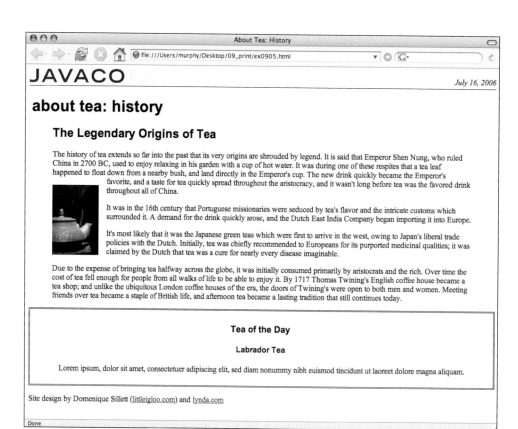

3 Save **ex0905.css**, switch to your browser, and reload **ex0905.html**.

Wow. What a difference a rule makes. However, this section is taking up an awful lot of space. It's extending from one side of the page to the other, even though the contents are not that wide in the original design. So next, you'll make this section narrower.

4 Return to **ex0905.css** in your text or HTML editor. Modify the **#tea-of-the-day** rule as follows:

```
#tea-of-the-day {
    border: 3px double;
    text-align: center;
    padding: 0.5em;
    margin: 0 10%;
}
```

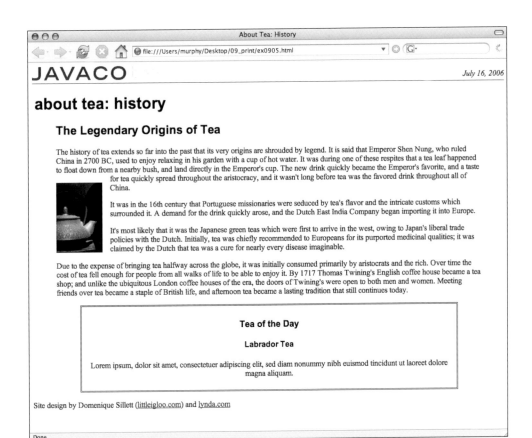

5 Save **ex0905.css**, switch to your browser, and reload **ex0905.html**.

Earlier, you assigned 5 percent margins to the main content area. Now you have 10 percent side margins on the sidebar. It's a good width, but at this point you might want to find a way to reduce the height. You'll start with the two headings, because they sort of compete with the "The Legendary Origins of Tea" and "about tea: history" headings at the top of the page.

---

6 Return to **ex0905.html** in your text or HTML editor. Insert a new line after the **#tea-of-the-day** rule, and type the following:

```
#tea-of-the-day h3, #tea-of-the-day h4 {
    margin: 0;
    display: inline;
    font-size: 1em;
}
```

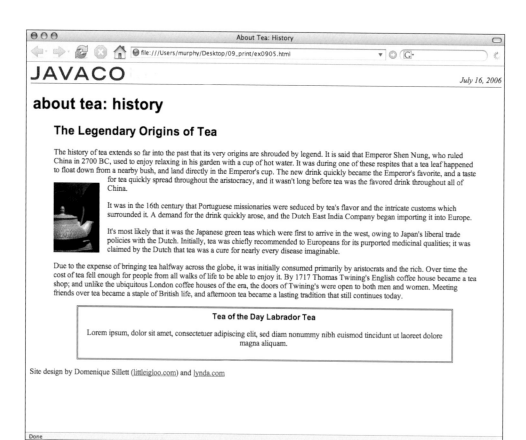

7 Save **ex0905.css**, switch to your browser, and reload **ex0905.html**.

Because you changed them from generating black boxes to display as if they were inline elements, the headings are now perched on one line together. However, the text appears to run together. That's no good.

---

8 Return to **ex0905.css** in your text or HTML editor. Insert a new line after the **#tea-of-the-day h3…h4** rule, and type the following:

```
#tea-of-the-day h3 {
    border-right: 2px solid;
    margin-right: 1em;
    padding-right: 1em;
    color: gray;
}
```

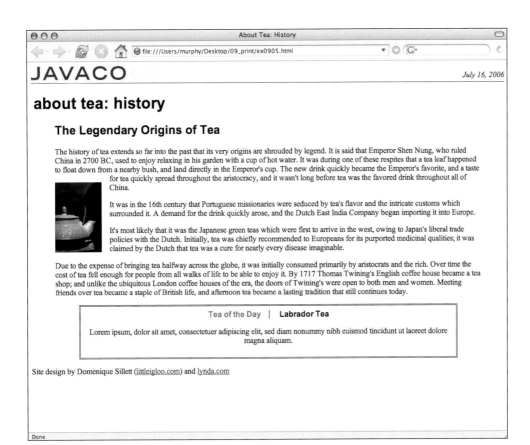

9 Save **ex0905.css**, switch to your browser, and reload **ex0905.html**.

Now "Tea of the Day" is visually deemphasized. And because of the right border, you have a concrete separation between the two headings. However, a little too much space is still appearing above and below the paragraph element.

10 Return to **ex0905.css** in your text or HTML editor. Insert a new line after the **#tea-of-the-day h3** rule, and type the following:

```
#tea-of-the-day p {
    margin: 0.5em 0 0;
}
```

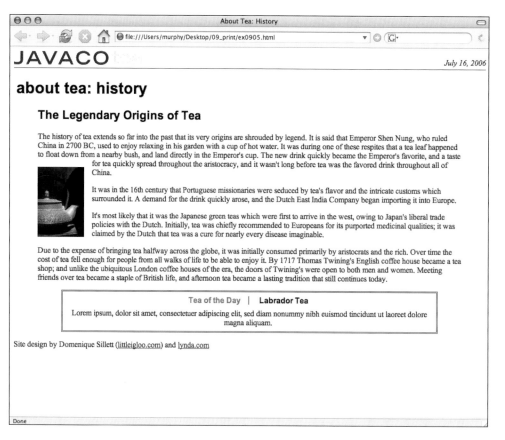

11 Save and close **ex0905.css**, switch to your browser, and reload **ex0905.html**.

Excellent. Now your sidebar paragraph is taking up less space, and it's not distracting from the main content as much. The visual separation alerts the user that, hey, this is a different subject matter. Jumping from the origins of tea to today's tea is not quite as abrupt now.

In this exercise, you worked with some more advanced styling techniques that you learned in previous chapters and applied these to the print medium. To complete this print layout, you'll want to update the footer, change the link elements so this style sheet is confined to print media, and restore the base style sheet to the Web page. You'll do all that in the next exercise.

6 | Creating a Footer

You're coming to the end of the chapter on print styling! In this exercise, somewhat appropriately, you'll tackle the footer element. As it stands, it's styled differently than the other elements and doesn't mimic the placement of the footer text on the screen.

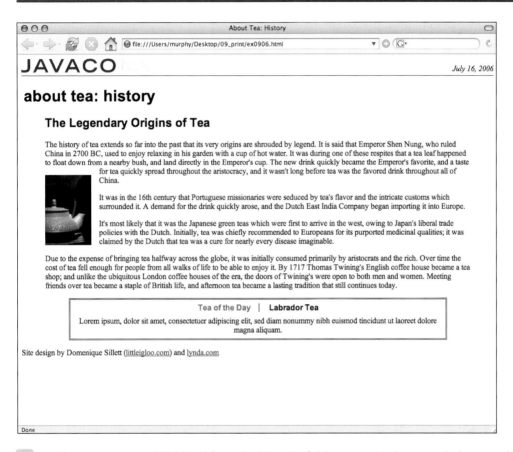

1 In a browser, open **ex0906.html** from the **09_print** folder you copied to your desktop, as shown in the illustration here.

You'll notice the footer at the bottom of the page appears in plain text. In the next step, you'll spruce that up a little bit. You'll change the style so the footer's appearance visually echoes the masthead elements. Specifically, you'll italicize and align the text to the left like today's date and add a solid border to separate it from the rest of the document.

2 Open **ex0906.css** from the **09_print/styles** folder with your text or HTML editor. Insert a new line after the **#tea-of-the-day p** rule, and type the following:

```
#footer {
    border-top: 1px solid #000;
    margin-top: 2em;
    font-style: italic;
    font-size: smaller;
    text-align: right;
}
```

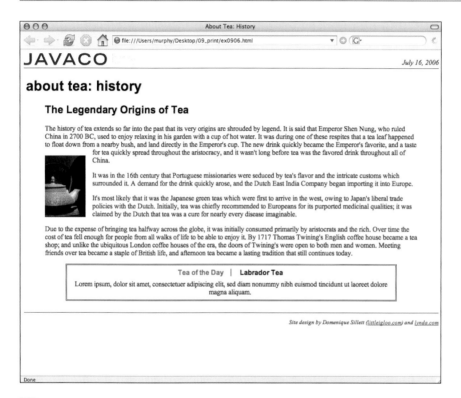

3 Save **ex0906.css**, switch to your browser, and reload **ex0906.html**.

The footer text now aligns with the right side of the page and is italic, mimicking the masthead elements. Because this text is a paragraph element, the browser automatically applies top and bottom margins to it. If you wanted to remove the margins, you would have to create a rule to explicitly do so.

4 Return to **ex0906.css** in your text or HTML editor. Insert a new line after the **#footer** rule, and type the following:

```
#footer p {
    margin: 0;
}
```

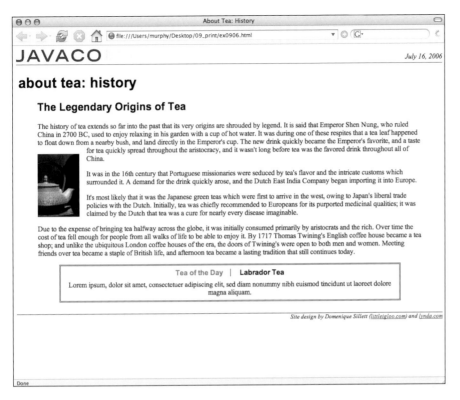

5 Save **ex0906.css**, switch to your browser, and reload **ex0906.html**.

The footer text is dramatically close—spitting distance, for sure—from that top border. Maybe that's a little too close for comfort.

6 Return to **ex0906.css** in your text or HTML editor. Modify the **#footer** rule as follows:

```
#footer {
    border-top: 1px solid;
    margin-top: 2em;
    padding-top: 0.25em;
    font-style: italic;
    font-size: smaller;
    text-align: right;
    color: gray;
}
```

While you're at it, deemphasize the footer's contents a little by changing the font color to gray to match the other secondary elements, such as the "Tea of the Day" heading.

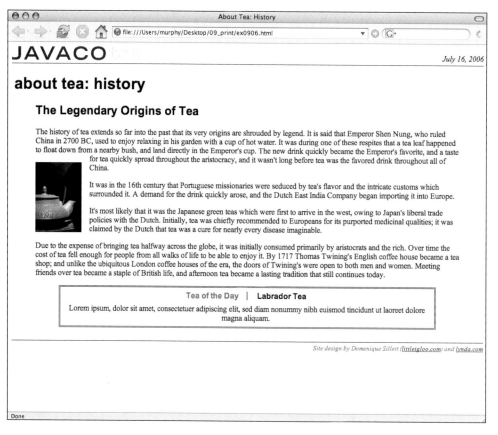

7 Save **ex0906.css**, switch to your browser, and reload **ex0906.html**.

There you are. The text turns gray, and the border goes with it because, as you may recall, you didn't specify a color for the top border; therefore, it is inherited from the parent element.

This is a great example of why you might not want to explicitly define a border color—it creates a dynamic relationship between the paragraph text and the border. You need to change only one to change the other. The exceptions, as stated in the previous chapter, are table cells in Microsoft Internet Explorer because Internet Explorer automatically assigns white or another light color to table cell borders unless you explicitly define a color.

You could also define a color to apply to the link text in the footer, but this way, the URLs (**U**niform **R**esource **L**ocators) will be there in the printout for the user to type in a browser; also, the underlining attracts the eye and says, "Hey, these are Web addresses."

You have to perform one more task to create the print style sheet. You have to redefine the link elements in the HTML document so the style sheets apply to the intended media.

8 Return to **ex0906.css** in your text or HTML editor. Close the file (not the application). Choose **File > Open**, navigate to the **09_print** folder on your desktop, and select **ex0906.html**.

9 Find the following element in your markup, as shown in the illustration here:

```
<link rel="stylesheet" type="text/css" href="styles/base.css" media="tty" />
<link rel="stylesheet" type="text/css" href="styles/ex0906.css" media="screen" />
```

Modify this code as follows:

```
<link rel="stylesheet" type="text/css" href="styles/base.css" media="screen" />
<link rel="stylesheet" type="text/css" href="styles/ex0906.css" media="print" />
```

Here, you are returning the style sheets to their original purposes. Instead of using the value **tty**, base.css will now apply to screen media and ex0906.css will apply to print media.

10 Save and close **ex0906.html**, switch to your browser, and reload **ex0906.html**.

Bingo! You can now see all the original screen styles. Basically, you just shoved them out of the way while you were actively working on the print style sheet, and now they're back. Nice trick! Next, you'll see the print style sheet in action.

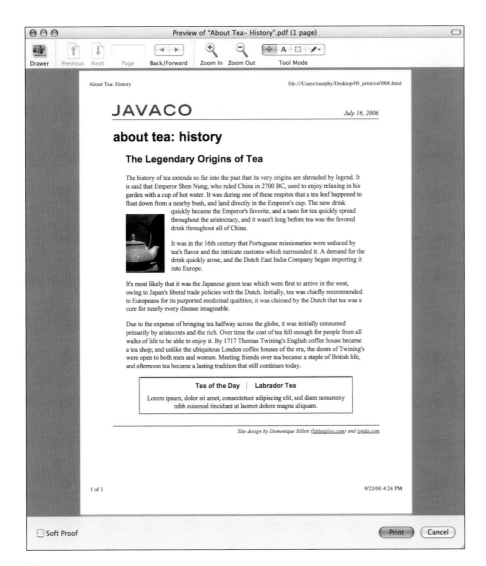

11 If you're on a Mac, in your browser, choose **File > Print**, and then click the **Preview** button in the **Print** dialog box. If you're using Windows, in your browser, choose **File > Print Preview**.

As shown in the illustration here, this is what the actual printout will look like. It's extremely close to what you previewed in the browser. It looks more professional, although a true graphic designer would probably have a dozen additional suggestions. The important lesson to keep in mind from this chapter is that you can have style sheets for a variety of media; in addition, when creating a print sheet, you should consider both why your user is printing the page and what elements are most important to display to them. Usability is the key concept here.

This exercise closes the chapter on print styling. If you are interested in more aspects of print design, check out some of the resources listed in Appendix C, *"CSS Resources."* In the next and final chapter, you bring together everything you've learned from the exercises in the previous chapters to create a single .css file for the Javaco Web site.

10

Bringing It All Together

In this chapter, you'll assemble all the pieces of the document you've worked on in previous chapters and turn it into the final design. You'll apply the foreground and background colors, update the font faces, modify the page layout using the box model properties and effects such as floats, and style the table and other aspects of the sidebar. This chapter is mostly review, but it will reiterate just how efficient CSS (Cascading Style Sheets) is once you're familiar with it. I know it has been a long, hard road to this point, but by the end of this chapter, you'll have a single style sheet, no longer than three pages, containing every presentational change for your document. Nothing in your XHTML (eXtensible Markup Language) markup will be referring to color, font size, or any other aspects of the presentation layer. My hope is that after you've finished with this review, you can take the lessons you've learned here and apply them to your own documents, resulting in ultimately more rich and more powerful designs.

Working with Text Fragments

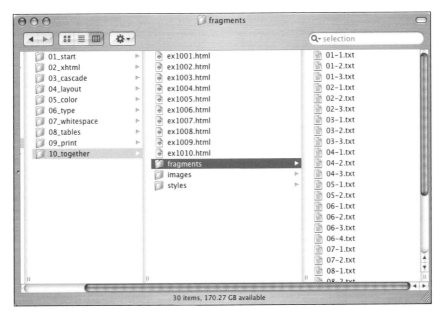

In this chapter, you'll take a slightly different approach to working with your text documents than you have in previous chapters. If you open the **exercise files** folder on the **CSS HOT CD-ROM** and navigate to the **10_together** folder, you'll see your HTML (Hyper**T**ext **M**arkup **L**anguage) files as usual. Then in the **styles** folder, you'll see several CSS files.

As in the previous chapter, you'll continue to work with external style sheets. However, if you open those CSS files—such as **ex1001.css**, for example—you'll notice it's completely blank. This is because another folder, **fragments**, contains plain-text files with the portions of the style sheet you'll be using in each exercise. If you prefer, you can simply type the code in the style sheet, but I've prepared an easier method for users of BBEdit from Bare Bones Software. Simply click and drag the **.txt** file icons into your open CSS file to paste the contents there. If you have a different editor that supports this method, please feel free to take advantage of it.

VIDEO: **working_with_fragments.mov**

To learn more about working with text fragments and CSS files, check out **working_with_fragments.mov** in the **videos** folder on the **CSS HOT CD-ROM**.

1 | Setting Global Styles

In this exercise, you'll start with a blank CSS file. The first step is to set the generic, or global, styles in the style sheet. **Global styles** are styles that apply to all the elements in the document.

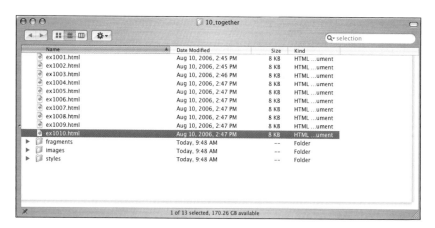

1 Copy the **10_together** folder from the **CSS HOT CD-ROM** to your desktop. Double-click the **10_together** folder to open it so you see the exercise files inside, as shown in the illustration here.

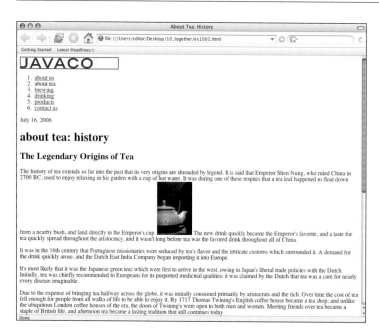

2 In a browser, open **ex1001.html**, as shown in the illustration here.

3 Return to the **10_together** folder, and double-click **javaco.jpg** to preview it.

This is the wireframe design provided by the designer. So, how are you going to get from ex1001.html to this? It may seem like a daunting task, but trust me, you have all the tools you'll need.

---

4 Close **javaco.jpg** when you are finished looking at it. Return to the **10_together** folder, and open the **styles** folder. Open **ex1001.css** with your text or HTML editor.

The document is blank. Again, in this chapter, you'll be building your style sheet from scratch. Don't be intimidated! I'm here to walk through it with you.

---

5 Drag fragment file **01-1.txt** in from the **fragments** folder, or type the following:

```
/* ————— "generic" styles */
body {
    margin: 0; padding: 0;
    background: #E3EDC2; color: #333;
    font: small "Lucida Grande", Arial, sans-serif;
}
```

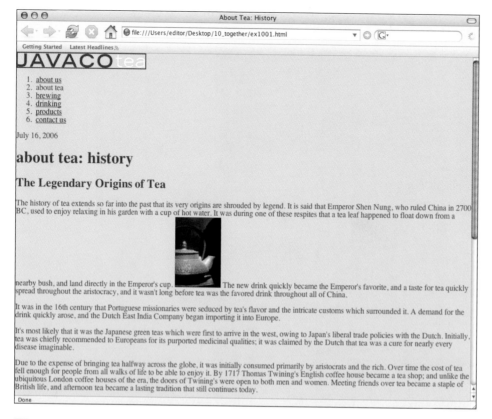

6 Save **ex1001.css**, switch to your browser, and reload **ex1001.html**.

You're already on the way. Notice that the font changed a bit, the background colors reappeared, and the extra spaces around the edges of the design disappeared.

---

7 Return to **ex1001.css** in your text or HTML editor, insert a new line after the last rule, and either drag **01-2.txt** in from the **fragments** folder or type the following:

```
a {
    text-decoration: none;
}
a img {
    border: 0;
}
```

The point of this fragment is to remove the text decoration from **a** elements, which include both hyperlinks *and* nonhyperlinked **a** elements (that are possible to have but not common). As a result of the first rule, the navbar links will no longer be underlined. The second rule addresses the fact that in some browsers, Firefox among them, any image inside an **a** element gets a border by default. This is built into the browser styles. So, you're saying any image descended from an **a** element, or inside an **a** element, should have a border width of 0, essentially none.

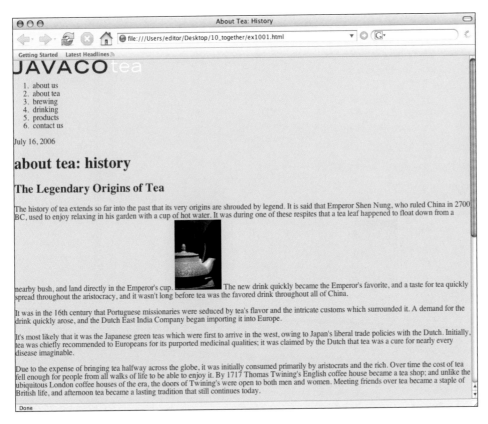

8 Save **ex1001.css**, switch to your browser, and reload **ex1001.html**.

The underlining on the links and the borders on the images have disappeared. And thanks to CSS, these changes will apply throughout the document. Should you choose to add more links to the navbar or different images to the page, these styles will apply to those new elements as well.

---

9 Return to **ex1001.css** in your text or HTML editor, insert a new line after the last rule, and either drag **01-3.txt** in from the **fragments** folder or type the following:

```
p {
    margin: 0 0 1em;
}
```

Now you'll change the way margins are calculated on paragraphs. Because of the way margin collapsing works, as discussed in Chapter 7, "Using Margins and Borders to Create Whitespace and Separation," you don't actually need to have margins both on the top and bottom of paragraphs. You could just have margins on the bottom of the paragraph, and the space between the paragraphs would be the same.

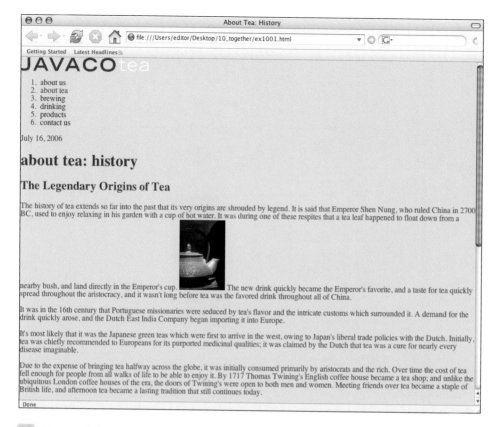

10 Save and close **ex1001.css**, switch to your browser, and reload **ex1001.html**.

You won't see any obvious change, but the advantage here comes when you have a paragraph following a heading, such as with the heading "The Legendary Origins of Tea." Suppose you wanted the paragraph to come up right against the heading, without any space between them. Since you've explicitly removed the top margin from the paragraph, all you need to do to complete the effect is remove the bottom margin from the headings. Then you get this nice nestled effect. I mention this because it is oftentimes an effect a designer will request, and it is difficult to achieve with ordinary XHTML. But with CSS, it's a snap.

So, you've set up your global, or generic, styles. In the next exercise, you'll dive into the individual document elements and start styling the masthead.

2 | Defining Masthead and Navbar Colors

In this exercise, you'll continue adding styles to the current state of the Javaco page, starting with the masthead.

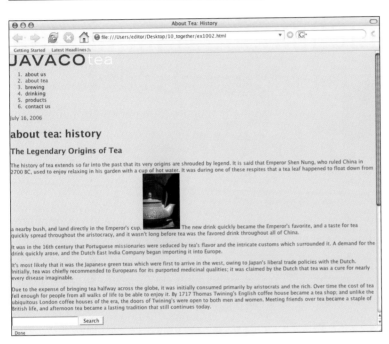

1 In a browser, double-click **ex1002.html** to open it, as shown in the illustration here.

2 Return to the **10_together** folder, and open the **styles** folder. Open **ex1002.css** with your text or HTML editor.

3 Drag fragment file **02-1.txt** in from the **fragments** folder, or type the following:

```
/* ———— masthead styles */
#masthead {
    margin-bottom: 1.75em; padding-top: 1px;
    background: #ABD240; position: relative;
}
```

In this step, you are adding a background color and a little bit of a bottom margin to the masthead elements. The top padding, if you recall, is to contain the margins of any elements within the masthead that might stick out from the content area. There's also a **position: relative** declaration to overcome layout bugs in Internet Explorer, as discussed in Chapter 7.

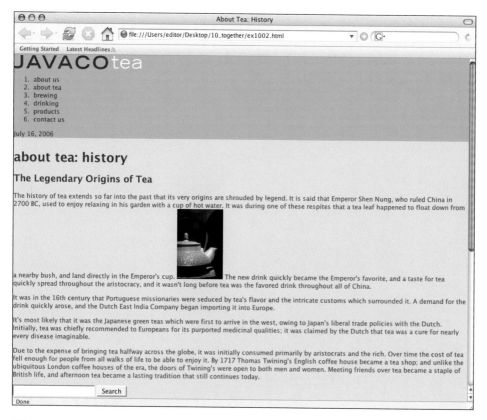

4 Save **ex1002.css**, switch to your browser, and reload **ex1002.html**.

Ah. A little bit of color makes all the difference. Again, you're building an external style sheet from scratch to bring your page up to where you left it in Chapter 9, *"Styling for Print."* The masthead color and margins are just one piece of that.

---

5 Return to **ex1002.css** in your text or HTML editor, insert a new line after the previous rule, and either drag fragment file **02-2.txt** in from the **fragments** folder or type the following:

```
#homelink {
    display: block;
    margin: 1em 2em 1em; padding: 2em 0 0.5em 1em;
    background: url(…/images/curl.gif) 100% 100% no-repeat;
}
```

Here you are styling the **a** element that links to the home page of the Javaco site. That's the area surrounding the "Javaco tea" image in the masthead. However, you want the entire masthead to be a link to the homepage, so set this to display as a block box, as though it were a **div**, and the entire space will become clickable. The padding will also increase the clickable area by increasing the size of the masthead. Lastly, you are adding a background image, a little white curl, to the hyperlink. It will appear in the bottom-right corner of the masthead and not repeat.

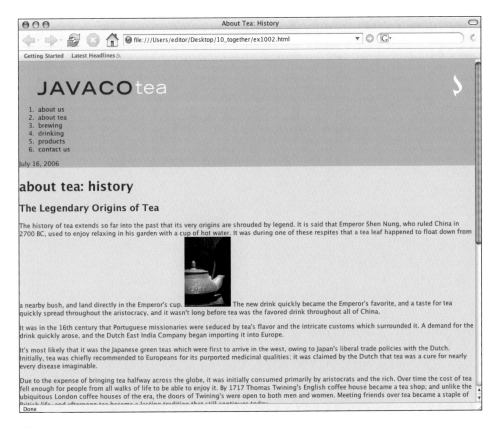

6 Save **ex1002.css**, switch to your browser, and reload **ex1002.html**.

Awesome. The white curl is in place. Also, if you position your cursor on the slightly larger masthead area, you'll notice the cursor changes to that little white glove of magic, indicating a link element. You now need to complete the masthead styles by styling the list items.

---

7 Return to **ex1002.css** in your text or HTML editor, insert a new line after the previous rule, and either drag fragment file **02-3.txt** in from the **fragments** folder or type the following:

```
#navlinks {
    margin: 0; padding: 0.5em 3em;
    background: #68697; color: #FFF;
}
```

The navigation links are in an ordered list. Ordered lists by default have margins and padding that help indent the list items, among other things. What you are doing is removing the margin and constraining the padding to only .5 em of top and bottom padding and 3 em of left and right padding. This will control where the line wraps. You shouldn't run into that problem on your page, but it will prevent the problem if your list grows someday. This step also includes color declarations for the background and foreground elements.

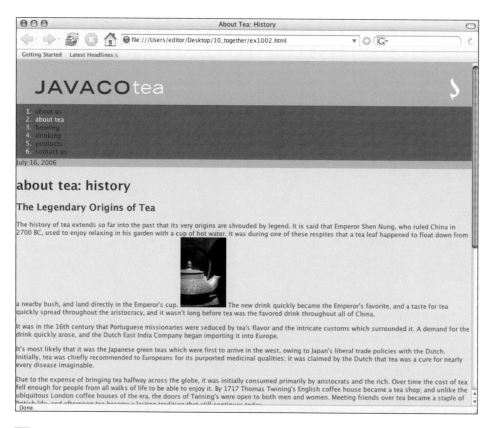

8 Save and close **ex1002.css**, switch to your browser, and reload **ex1002.html**.

So there you have it. At the close of this exercise, you have a green masthead with slightly different dimensions than when you started. You also have an ordered list of navigation links with a purple background and a white foreground, represented by the color of the plain text. The links, of course, stay blue because they are links and the browser default settings are still kicking in here. Last but not least, underneath the list, but still in the masthead, is today's date.

In the next exercise, you will address the remaining issues with the masthead elements: pulling the date up into the navigation bar and styling and modifying the display order of the list items.

3 | Laying Out the Navbar

In this exercise, you'll finish styling the navbar by adding the borders and separation between the links and by styling the date element.

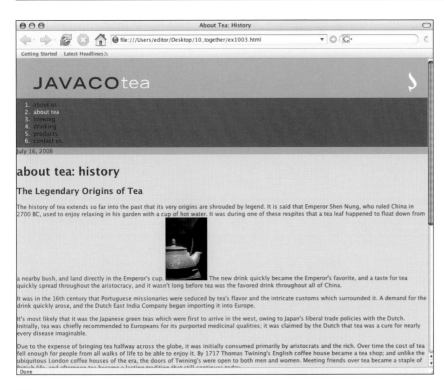

1 In a browser, open **ex1003.html** from the **10_together** folder, as shown in the illustration here.

2 Return to the **10_together** folder, and open the **styles** folder. Open **ex1003.css** with your text or HTML editor.

3 After the last rule on the page, **#navlinks**, insert a new line, and either drag fragment file **03-1.txt** in from the **fragments** folder or type the following:

```
#navlinks li {
    display: inline;
    margin-right: 0.5em; padding-right: 0.75em;
    border-right: 1px solid #99C;
    font-weight: bold;
}
```

In this rule, first you are changing the display of the list items from block box to inline. Then, the right margin, right padding, and right border will set up the vertical separators you first worked on in Chapter 7, *"Using Margins and Borders to Create Whitespace and Separation."* If you recall, the breaks between the list items in the markup actually generate a margin of about .25 em, which makes up for the difference between the margin and padding values in this rule.

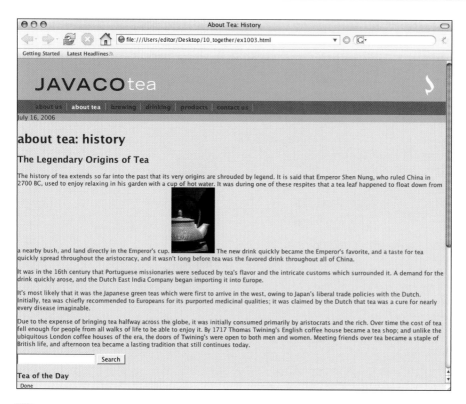

4 Save **ex1003.css**, switch to your browser, and reload **ex1003.html**.

Surprise! Well, not really, since this is just a review. However, this is quite a dramatic change and an equally dramatic visual improvement, if I dare say so myself. The reason why the list items, starting with "about us," are pushed to the left is because of that 3 em of padding you assigned to the parent element, **navlinks**, in the previous exercise.

5 Return to **ex1003.css** in your text or HTML editor, insert a new line after the previous rule, and either drag fragment file **03-2.txt** in from the **fragments** folder or type the following:

```
#navlinks li.last {
    border-right: 0;
}
#navlinks a {
    color: #D4EC84;
}
```

The first rule removes the extra border from the last list item, "contact us," and the second rule overrides the browser default and changes the color of the text of the links.

6   Save **ex1003.css**, switch to your browser, and reload **ex1003.html**.

As expected, the link items change color and the last border is removed. The next step in this exercise is to target the date that's skirting below the general masthead area, bring it back up into the navbar, and then align it to the right of the page.

7   Return to **ex1003.css** in your text or HTML editor, insert a new line after the previous rule, and either drag fragment file **03-3.txt** in from the **fragments** folder or type the following:

```
#today {
    margin-top: -1.66em; padding: 0 2em 0 0;
    color: #FFF;
    font-weight: bold;
    text-align: right;
    line-height: 1;
}
```

So, you are styling the text itself, aligning it to the right, and making it white and bold. Now, the line height of 1 makes sure certain rounding problems don't occur when the browser tries to calculate the line height. Of course, the secret to the success of this rule is the negative top margin, which will actually lift the date up into the navbar. I arrived at the exact figure, −1.66 em, through some calculation and a tiny bit of experimentation.

8 Save and close **ex1003.css**, switch to your browser, and reload **ex1003.html**.

Feeling better about the design now? This brings this exercise to a close. In the next, you will address the main content area, creating the side-by-side columns you initially might have struggled with in Chapter 4, *"Using CSS to Affect Page Layout."* I have a feeling that, if you completed the previous exercises in the book, you should be more confident working with floats now.

4 | Using Columns

You've taken care of the masthead and the navigation links, so it's time to turn your attention to the main area of the page. In this exercise, you'll style the main content elements using floats to replicate the two-column layout shown in the designer's comp.

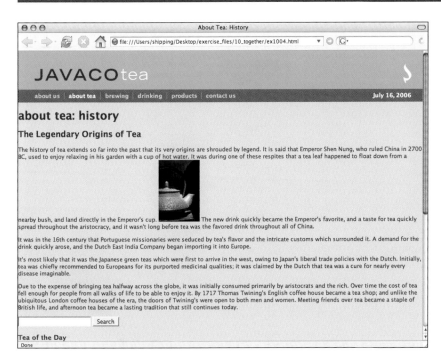

1 In a browser, open **ex1004.html** from the **10_together** folder, as shown in the illustration here.

2 Return to the **10_together** folder, and open the **styles** folder. Open **ex1004.css** with your text or HTML editor.

3 After the last rule on the page, **#today**, insert a new line, and either drag fragment file **04-1.txt** in from the **fragments** folder or type the following:

```
/* ———- main column styles */
#content {
    float: left;
    padding: 0 20em 4em 3em;
}
```

This rule, in effect, floats the content **div** left and adds padding around the column.

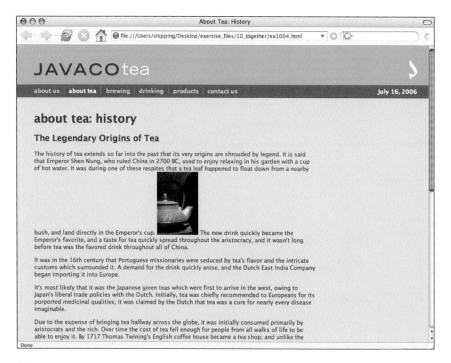

4 Save **ex1004.css**, switch to your browser, and reload **ex1004.html**.

There it is. If you scroll down, you can see that the rest of the elements eventually going into the sidebar have dropped to the bottom of the page. Nevertheless, you've set up the content column with the basic rules. Next, you will style the child elements within the content column.

---

5 Return to **ex1004.css** in your text or HTML editor, insert a new line after the previous rule, and either drag fragment file **04-2.txt** in from the **fragments** folder or type the following:

```
#content h1 {
    margin: 0 33% 1.25em -2em; padding: 0.5em 2em;
    background: #FFF; color: #686397;
    font-size: 1.5em;
}
```

This rule addresses the "about tea: history" heading. This increases the font size to 1.5 times the size of the main content text, basically the text of the paragraph elements. You also are adding a white background, a different foreground color (which will primarily impact the text color), and some margins and padding. Notice how you used scaling factors for all the measurements, either ems or percentages. The 33 percent right margin will make the background element smaller by 33 percent, as you saw in the design comp. The negative left margin will pull the entire element over to the left, offsetting it from the paragraph text, and the 2 em of right padding will push the text only to the right. When you hit Reload in the next step, the position of the text in the heading should not appear to have changed at all!

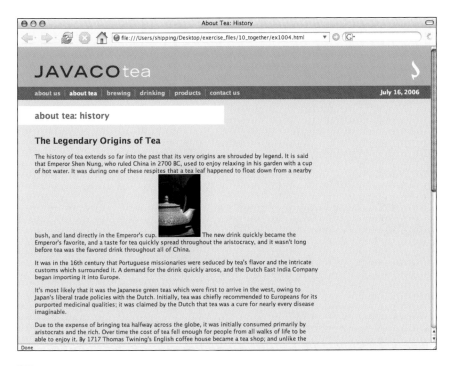

6 Save **ex1004.css**, switch to your browser, and reload **ex1004.html**.

Actually, the text didn't move horizontally but it did vertically, because of the top and bottom padding and the bottom margins you added in the previous step. The white background is kissing the edge of the content column but stops short a little more than halfway across the page—actually 33 percent of the way from the right edge of the content column.

This is all being retrofitted according to the designer's wishes. In the next step, you'll address something else the designer has requested—that the text color of the heading changes partway through the text.

---

7 Return to **ex1004.css** in your text or HTML editor, insert a new line after the previous rule, and either drag fragment file **04-3.txt** in from the **fragments** folder or type the following:

```
#content h1 b {
    color: #B0D742;
}
```

Here, you are utilizing the separate **b** element within the **h1** element to assign a different color to that part of the text. Why use **b**? Isn't that just a presentational element? Exactly. Changing text color is purely a presentational change, and you don't have any real structural reason to add another **h** element. Of course, you add this knowing that in a non-CSS browser, in an older browser that doesn't recognize CSS, or in a completely unstyled state, the **b** portions of the text might appear stronger. However, it doesn't seem like the risk outweighs the usefulness of this tag here. This is a case where using a presentational element such as **b** for presentational purposes is justified.

NOTE:

Presentational Versus Structural Markup

Throughout this chapter, you may see me refer to code changes as either presentational or structural. The roots of this terminology lie in HTML. Originally, HTML was intended for creating only basic document structures. Elements such as **p**, **h1**, and `table` are structural elements. However, interest in the Web increased and so did the complexity of web pages and other tags, such as **i** and **b**, were added to allow HTML authors to also control the look of their page.

Unfortunately, this led to several problems, including document bloat and indexing problems, not to mention accessibility issues. Users with speech synthesizer devices were left to wander in the mire that was an HTML document bloated with presentational tags, with no ability to skip around and no sense of what was important on the pages.

Finally, with HTML 4.0 and XHTML 1.0, many of the presentational tags were deprecated, and CSS was introduced to take their place. However, you can still use presentational elements on occasion, such as you did in this exercise, when you're called upon to make a purely presentational change.

8 Save and close **ex1004.css**, switch to your browser, and reload **ex1004.html**.

There you are. The "about tea:" text is a greenish hue, and "history" remains the original purplish color you assigned in Step 5. Now, if your designer requested that the "history" portion be emphasized, then you would have to mark "history" with an **em** element for emphasis. Basically, you would reverse the style sheet. You would assign the **h1** element the greenish color to start, and then you would add the purplish color to the **em** element. These are the sorts of structural decisions you will always have to make, and there is not always one right answer.

In the next exercise, you'll finish up styling the elements in the content column, such as the poor teakettle image adrift in the middle of the page, before moving on to the rest of the document.

5 | Setting Content Styles

In this exercise, you'll perform a little bit of cleanup in the main content column. This includes spiffing up the paragraph heading and pushing the teakettle image to the side so the rest of the text can flow around it.

1 In a browser, open **ex1005.html** from the **10_together** folder, as shown in the illustration here.

2 Return to the **10_together** folder, and open the **styles** folder. Open **ex1005.css** with your text or HTML editor.

3 After the last rule on the page, #**content h1 b**, insert a new line, and either drag fragment file **05-1.txt** in from the **fragments** folder or type the following:

```
#content h2 {
    margin: 0.5em 0; padding-bottom: 0.25em;
    border-bottom: 1px solid #B0D742;
    font-size: 1.5em;
}
```

This rule addresses the heading "The Legendary Origins of Tea," which you fiddled with originally in Chapter 6, "Setting Typography."

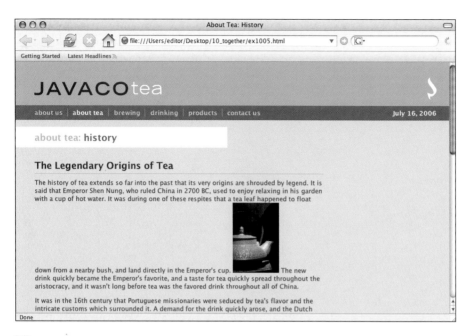

4 Save **ex1005.css**, switch to your browser, and reload **ex1005.html**.

Here are the changes: a bottom, greenish border; a top and bottom margin; some padding; and a slightly larger font size. Actually, this is the same size as the "about tea: history" **h1** heading, but it might appear a little different because the text is mixed case, whereas "about tea: history" is all lowercase.

---

5 Return to **ex1005.css** in your text or HTML editor, insert a new line after the previous rule, and either drag fragment file **05-2.txt** in from the **fragments** folder or type the following:

```
#content img illus {
    float: left;
    margin: 1em 1em 1em 0;
}
```

Here you are floating the teakettle image to the left and assigning some margins so the paragraph text doesn't crowd it.

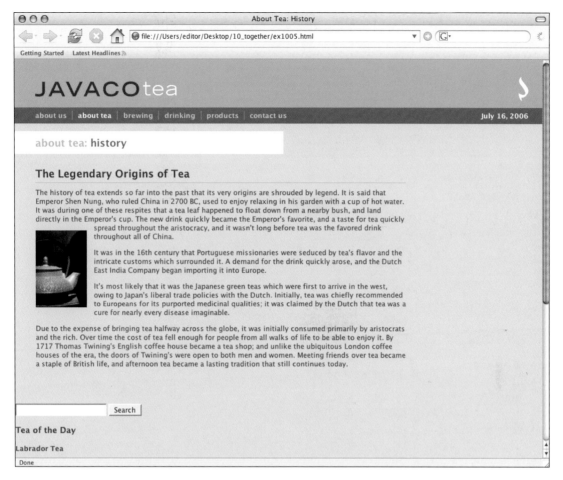

6 Save and close **ex1005.css**, switch to your browser, and reload **ex1005.html**.

Excellent! The image is placed correctly, and the text is flowing around it. This is the best example for using a float that there could be.

So now, having taken care of the issues in the content column, you'll move on in the next exercise to styling the sidebar. This is a more interesting and somewhat more complicated challenge that will occupy you for the next few exercises.

Starting the Sidebar

At this point, you've styled roughly half the design. Now it's time to style the sidebar. It's invisible at this point, but if you scroll down the page, you could see that all the elements have been dumped at the bottom of the page. Why? Column drop happens when two floated columns can't fit in the width of the browser window. You need to fix this before moving on to the sidebar contents.

1 In a browser, open **ex1006.html** from the **10_together** folder, as shown in the illustration here.

2 Return to the **10_together** folder, and open the **styles** folder. Open **ex1006.css** with your text or HTML editor.

3 After the last rule on the page, **#content img.illus**, insert a new line and either drag fragment file **06-1.txt** in from the **fragments** folder or type the following:

```
/* ————- sidebar styles */
#sidebar {
    float: left;
    width: 17em;
    margin: 0 0 4em -18em;
}
```

You are first floating the entire column to the left. Then, you are using the negative margin trick you first worked with in Chapter 4, *"Using CSS to Affect Page Layout,"* to negate the column drop effect. To summarize, you are assigning an explicit width and then assigning a negative margin greater than the width to fool the browser into thinking that the sidebar is small enough to fit next to the content column. Note, you can assign any negative value to the margin, provided it is equal to or greater than the width of your column. The goal is to have the layout width of the sidebar be zero or less.

4 Save **ex1006.css**, switch to your browser, and reload **ex1006.html**.

Ta-da! The sidebar is now fitting in the 20-em right-padding allowance you assigned to the content **div** in the previous exercise. Handy, isn't it? The next step is to fill in the background colors.

5 Return to **ex1006.css** in your text or HTML editor, and after the previous rule #**sidebar**, insert a new line, and either drag fragment file **06-2.txt** in from the **fragments** folder or type the following:

```
#sidebar form, #sidebar div h3 {
    background: #9B96CA;
}
```

The search form and all the **h3** elements in the sidebar actually have the same background color, so you're using a grouped selector here to apply the same color to all of these elements with a single rule. This is much more efficient than creating multiple duplicate rules, don't you think?

6 Save **ex1006.css**, switch to your browser, and reload **ex1006.html**.

The search form and the "Tea of the Day" and "Post Archive" headings now all share the same background, a variation on the hue you've used for the navbar and some of the text elements. In the next step, you'll address the kind of funky layout of the search form. The background color looks like it is practically shrink-wrapped around the form.

7 Return to **ex1006.css** in your text or HTML editor, and after the previous rule **#sidebar from...**, insert a new line, and drag fragment file **06-3.txt** in from the **fragments** folder or type the following:

```
#sidebar form {
    margin: 0; padding: 0.8em;
}
```

Now, the reason that the background is tight all around the form is that form elements, by default, do not have any padding. They do, however, have margins. This code effectively removes the default margins and adds a small amount of padding around all the sides.

---

8 Save **ex1006.css**, switch to your browser, and reload **ex1006.html**.

As you can see, the padding not only centers the form, but it also provides more separation between the form and the other sidebar elements, pushing the **tea of the day** and **post archive div** elements further down the page. By removing the margins, you don't need to worry about those margins creating strange effects elsewhere. For example, it might push the tea of the day too far away, or indeed the entire sidebar column, if you had the top margin sticking out of the floated sidebar column. This is an effect, of course, of margin collapsing, as discussed in Chapter 7, *"Using Margins and Borders to Create Whitespace and Separation."*

Now you have the text input box and the search button sitting on two separate lines. By default, the text input box expands so that the search button has to wrap to the next line. You'll take a look at this in the markup.

```
                    <img src="images/teapot.jpg" width="96" height="140" class="i
                    The new drink quickly became the Emperor's favorite, and a ta
        </p>
        <p>
                    It was in the 16th century that Portuguese missionaries were
        </p>
        <p>
                    It's most likely that it was the Japanese green teas which we
        </p>
        <p>
                    Due to the expense of bringing tea halfway across the globe,
        </p>
</div>

<div id="sidebar">

<form id="search" action="somescript.scpt" method="post">
        <input type="text" class="text" />
        <input type="submit" value="Search" />
</form>

<div id="tea-of-the-day">
        <h3>Tea of the Day</h3>

        <h4>Labrador Tea</h4>
        <p>
                Lorem ipsum, dolor sit amet, consectetuer adipiscing elit, se
        </p>
        <img src="images/teaoftheday.jpg" alt="" />
</div>

<div id="post-archive">
<h3>Post Archive</h3>

<table cellspacing="2">
<caption>July 2006</caption>
```

9 In your browser, choose **View > PageSource** (Firefox/Safari) or **View > Source** (Microsoft Internet Explorer). Find the following code, as shown in the illustration here:

```
<form id="search" action="somescript.scpt" method="post">
    <input type="text" class="text" />
    <input type="submit" value="Search" />
</form>
```

The input has a **type** of text, but it also has a **class** of text. I added this because I knew we were probably going to have to style this form in some way. CSS offers a way to style text inputs without affecting other types of inputs such as, for example, the submit button. But unfortunately, Internet Explorer for Windows does not currently support this particular bit of CSS. It's called an **attribute selector**, and I haven't covered it in this book because of the cross-browser support problems. Instead, for form elements, whatever **type** they are, make sure to assign the same **class**. Ideally this wouldn't be required, but if you ever have to style text inputs or just check boxes, you'll need the **class** selector in order for your styling to take effect in Internet Explorer. If you're like me, a good portion of the users visiting your site will be using Internet Explorer. At any rate, in the next step you'll use this **class** attribute to your advantage to style the form elements.

---

10 Close the source. Return to **ex1006.css** in your text or HTML editor, and after the previous rule **#sidebar form**, insert a new line, and either drag fragment file **06-4.txt** in from the **fragments** folder or type the following:

```
#sidebar form .text {
    width: 9em;
}
```

11 Save and close **ex1006.css**, switch to your browser, and reload **ex1006.html**.

The text input box and the submit button now fit on the same line. You defined an explicit width for the input box, and now the page has room for the button to sit next to it!

The whole subject of form elements and styling is a complicated and abstract one. Styling form elements is an inexact science, in part because though there are certain things you can do to form elements, there are more things you can't. On top of everything else, various browsers may or may not recognize certain styles. For example, as of this writing, the search button on the Javaco page cannot be styled in Safari. Generally, if you can avoid styling a form element, you want to do so. If you have no way around it and you have to add a margin or set a width, do it through the **class** route.

In the next exercise, you'll work on styling the block boxes and headings in the sidebar.

7 | Creating the Sidebar Boxes

In this exercise, now that you have the sidebar in the correct location, it's time to add the boxes you need.

1 In a browser, open **ex1007.html** from the **10_together** folder, as shown in the illustration here.

2 Return to the **10_together** folder, and open the **styles** folder. Open **ex1007.css** with your text or HTML editor.

3 After the last rule on the page, **#sidebar form .text**, insert a new line, and either drag fragment file **07-1.txt** in from the **fragments** folder or type the following:

```
#sidebar div {
    background: #343C2D; color: #FFF;
    padding: 0 1em 1em;
    margin-top: 0.75em;
}
```

Now, if you were to examine the markup, you would notice that each of the sidebar elements is enclosed in a div. This makes sense because div stands for *division*—these are divisions of content in the sidebar. Putting the content into boxes not only creates a visual separation, but it also implies a structural separation.

So for each div element, you'll assign dark backgrounds and white foregrounds as well as add a little bit of padding to push the contents away from the edges of the box. You don't want to assign any top padding because that would push the headings away from the top of each div. Finally, you'll give each div a top margin, because this gives two div elements in a row, as on this page, a little bit of separating space.

4 Save **ex1007.css**, switch to your browser, and reload **ex1007.html**.

The space between the search form and the **tea of the day div** and the space between the "Tea of the Day" and the "post archive" box are because of the top margin. The contents of each box are now inset because of the 1 em padding along the right, left, and bottom sides of the div. Unfortunately, this also pushed the headings in along the right and left sides. You'll fix this in the next step.

5 Return to **ex1007.css** in your text or HTML editor, and after the last rule on the page, `#sidebar div`, insert a new line, and either drag fragment file **07-2.txt** in from the **fragments** folder or type the following:

```
#sidebar div h3 {
    font-size: 1.25em;
    margin: 0 -0.8em;
    padding: 0.4em 0.8em;
    text-transform: lowercase;
}
```

You're tampering a bit with the text, changing the font size and the case, but most importantly, you're adding –0.8 em right and left margins to the headings. The reason for that number is that –0.8 em times the font size, 1.25 em, equals –1. That's equivalent to the 1 em of padding you added around the `divs`, plural in Step 3 of this exercise. The negative margins counteract the effects of the first rule, which squeezed the headings inward. Lastly, although the purple backgrounds will extend to the edges of the `div`, the 0.8 em padding will push the heading text back in.

6 Save and close **ex1007.css**, switch to your browser, and reload **ex1007.html**.

There you have it. The contents of each box are still centered, but the headings are spread out to the edges of each `div` element.

That's it for this exercise. It was a short one, but you made some dramatic visual changes. In the next exercise, you'll deal with the contents of the two `div` elements individually.

8 | Completing the Sidebar

In this exercise, you'll clean up the "tea of the day" sidebar a bit, bringing it into line with the designer's comp. There's not a lot to do, but as they say, the devil is in the details.

1 In a browser, open **ex1008.html** from the **10_together** folder, as shown in the illustration here.

2 Return to the **10_together** folder, and open the **styles** folder. Open **ex1008.css** with your text or HTML editor.

3 After the last rule on the page, **#sidebar div h3**, insert a new line, and either drag fragment file **08-1.txt** in from the **fragments** folder or type the following:

```
#tea-of-the-day h4 {
    margin: 0 0 0 0.5em; padding: 0.5em 0;
    border-bottom: 1px solid #FFF;
    font-weight: normal;
}
```

Here you're addressing the **h4** headings in just the **tea of the day div**, specifically the "Labrador Tea" bit. You're removing most of the margins and padding, adding a bottom border to mimic the **h2** subheading in the main content area, and lastly, specifying a font weight of **normal** to remove any bold that might be inherited from the browser styles.

4 Save **ex1008.css**, switch to your browser, and reload **ex1008.html**.

Removing the margins has caused the **h4** heading to move closer to the **h3** heading, but the top and bottom padding ensure it doesn't get too crowded in there.

5 Return to **ex1008.css** in your text or HTML editor, and after the last rule, #**tea-of-the-day h4**, insert a new line, and either drag fragment file **08-2.txt** in from the **fragments** folder or type the following:

```
#tea-of-the-day p:first line {
    font-style: italic;
}
```

This is a treat for making it to this exercise: a pseudo-element selector! You are setting the font style of the first line of the paragraph text to italic. This is purely a presentational change, which you could implement the same way by adding **i** tags in the markup, but you're doing it structurally here by using this pseudo-element selector.

6 Save **ex1008.css**, switch to your browser, and reload **ex1008.html**.

When you hit Reload, you should see the first line of text, "Lorem ipsum, dolor sit amet," change to italic. Press Cmd+plus/minus (Mac) or Ctrl+plus/minus (Windows) to increase or decrease the font size of the text, and watch as the number of words on the first line of the paragraph changes. The nice feature of pseudo-element selectors is that they have a dynamic relationship to the contents on the page. You could have also used a first-letter pseudo-element selector here, but that would style only the first character of the paragraph.

7 Return to **ex1008.css** in your text or HTML editor, and after the last rule, **#tea-of-the-day p:first line**, insert a new line, and either drag fragment file **08-3.txt** in from the **fragments** folder or type the following:

```
#tea-of-the-day img {
    display: block;
    margin: 2em auto 0;
}
```

Here, to center the image, you are changing the element to display as a block box element. As you may recall from previous chapters, any block box with some sort of width, either intrinsic or explicitly defined automatic right and left margins (as you've assigned here) will work to center that element.

8 Save and close **ex1008.css**, switch to your browser, and reload **ex1008.html**.

Reload, and the image is centered! That's pretty straightforward. The other way to center the image would be to make the **tea of the day div** text aligned center and then individually set the **tea of the day h4** and the **tea of the day p** elements to be text aligned left. In that case, you wouldn't have to set the block-level display on the image; it would have been centered automatically. But setting center alignment on the container element and then overriding it for the descendent elements that you don't want to center is kind of clumsy, and this **display: block** solution works quite well in all recent browsers. So, you don't have any real reason not to use it.

In this exercise, you styled the contents of the sidebar a bit more and, in the process, had the chance to work with a pseudo-element selector. In the next exercise, you'll take care of the calendar.

9 | Styling the Table

You have just one more feature to take care of in the sidebar: the "post archive" calendar. You'll want to make the calendar a little bit smaller and make the caption a little larger.

1 In a browser, open **ex1009.html** from the **10_together** folder. Scroll down to make sure you are viewing the calendar, as shown in the illustration here.

2 Return to the **10_together** folder, and open the **styles** folder. Open **ex1009.css** with your text or HTML editor.

3 After the last rule on the page, **#tea-of-the-day img**, insert a new line, and either drag fragment file **09-1.txt** in from the **fragments** folder or type the following:

```
#post-archive table {
    margin: 0 auto;
    font-size: smaller;
}
```

Tables, like images, have intrinsic widths. So by setting the auto right and left margins, you will be able to center the contents.

---

4 Save **ex1009.css**, switch to your browser, and reload **ex1009.html**.

As expected, the table is centered, and the font, including the font of the caption, is smaller.

---

5 Return to **ex1009.css** in your text or HTML editor, and after the last rule, **#post-archive table**, insert a new line, and either drag fragment file **09-2.txt** in from the **fragments** folder or type the following:

```
#post-archive caption {
    margin: 1em auto 0;
    font-size: larger;
    font-weight: bold;
}
```

Now you're addressing the caption element separately, centering it using the right and left auto margins in addition to adding a 1-em top margin that distances it slightly from the "post archive" heading. Then, to give it the feel of a real heading, you're increasing the font size and adding bold.

---

6 Save **ex1009.css**, switch to your browser, and reload **ex1009.html**.

The table contents are starting to shape up nicely. Next you'll take on the table cells, adding borders so they form a clear grid.

---

7 Return to **ex1009.css** in your text or HTML editor, and after the last rule, **#post-archive caption**, insert a new line, and either drag fragment file **09-3.txt** in from the **fragments** folder or type the following:

```
#post-archive td {
    padding: 0;
    border: 1px solid #787A6B;
    background: #585D4E; color: #222;
    text-align: center;
}
```

---

8 Save **ex1009.css**, switch to your browser, and reload **ex1009.html**.

Quite elegant. The text in each individual cell is centered. You've also added a darkish background color and a darker foreground color, even darker than the background of the **div** surrounding the table, along with a contrasting border. If you recall, the off-colored numbers are the link items. They are blue because the browser defaults are still applied. The next step is to style these according to the designer's request.

---

9 Return to **ex1009.css** in your text or HTML editor, and after the last rule, **#post-archive td**, insert a new line, and either drag fragment file **09-4.txt** in from the **fragments** folder or type the following:

```
#post-archive table a {
    display: block;
    font-weight: bold;
    color: #FFF;
}
#post-archive table a:hover {
    background: #ABD240;
}
```

The first rule makes any links in the table white and bold. It also makes the links display as block boxes, filling the entire area of the cells in which they rest. From the user's point of view, this makes the whole cell clickable. However, that's not entirely true. Remember it's the **a** element that's the active link; it just happens to be filling the cell.

The second rule adds a greenish background that appears when users position their cursors on the (now expanded) **a** elements.

10 Save and close **ex1009.css**, switch to your browser, and reload **ex1009.html**.

Everything seems to have worked out as planned. The links are white, and if you position your cursor on them, the entire cell gets a greenish background. This is a clear signal to the user that this is an interactive area.

Congratulations! This exercise was a review of the principles you learned in Chapter 8, *"Creating Tables,"* but at a much faster pace. In the next exercise in this chapter, the exercise that concludes this book, you'll add the finishing touches to this page.

This is the last exercise! The page looks good, until you scroll to the bottom and realize the footer needs a little bit of work. In this exercise, you'll use the `clear` property to push the footer below the two floated columns, you'll add a background and padding, and you'll style the text.

1 In a browser, open **ex1010.html** from the **10_together** folder. Scroll down to make sure you are viewing the footer, as shown in the illustration here.

2 Return to the **10_together** folder, and open the **styles** folder. Open **ex1010.css** with your text or HTML editor.

3 After the last rule on the page, **#post-archive table a:hover**, insert a new line, and either drag fragment file **10.1.txt** in from the **fragments** folder or type the following:

```
/* ——————— footer styles */
#footer {
    clear: both;
    padding: 1.5em 3em;
    background: #A0C63A;
}
```

In this step, you're clearing the footer below the floated columns. In theory, you don't really need to do this because the footer already comes after the rest of the content, but just to be safe, you should always clear the footer. You're also adding padding and a background color with this rule.

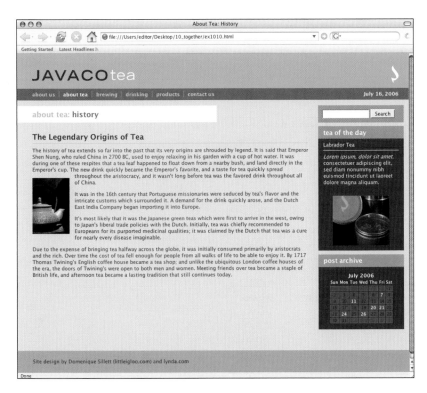

4 Save **ex1010.css**, switch to your browser, and reload **ex1010.html**.

Excellent job! This looks pretty close to a finished page. You might notice that some space appears between the bottom of the sidebar and the top of the footer. That's because in the style sheet, the first sidebar rule contains a 4-em bottom margin. At this point, since the sidebar is the tallest float, the 4-em margin is taking effect. If you were to resize the contents so the main column was forced to get taller, then no gap would appear between the footer and the main content area. At any rate, this gap appears in the design comp, so you'll leave it.

Also, even though you assigned an equal amount of top and bottom padding, the footer text is still not vertically centered within the background element. That's because the footer has a bottom 1-em margin. So in the next step, you'll remove the margins.

5 Return to **ex1010.css** in your text or HTML editor, and after the last rule, **#footer**, insert a new line, and either drag fragment file **10-2.txt** in from the **fragments** folder or type the following:

```
#footer p {
    margin: 0;
}
```

6 Save **ex1010.css**, switch to your browser, and reload **ex1010.html**.

When you remove the bottom margin, the space above and below the text balances out. Next, you'll style the links in the footer.

---

7 Return to **ex1010.css** in your text or HTML editor, and after the last rule, **#footer p**, insert a new line, and either drag fragment file **10-3.txt** in from the **fragments** folder or type the following:

```
#footer a {
    color: #333;
    text-decoration: underline;
}
```

This rule overrides the purple-and-blue browser default colors while maintaining the underline effect.

8 Save and close **ex1010.css**, switch to your browser, and reload **ex1010.html**.

Now the links are a nice dark gray in keeping with the designer's color palette. The underlining still alerts the user that these are interactive elements.

In this exercise, you used the `clear` declaration and added some text decoration effects. That takes care of the footer, which is, somewhat fittingly, the last element to be styled in this design.

I hope you found this chapter useful. You took this page from an unfinished to a finished product, which is an excellent note on which to close the book. This shows you how easy it can be, once you're up to speed, to style your own pages using CSS. The advantages of separating the structure of your document from the presentation are manifold. In short, CSS makes your Web pages easier to maintain, makes them easier to scale up and out, improves their accessibility, and last but not least, results in richer styling options for you, the author. Sadly, this also brings us to the end of our time together, but I recommend revisiting chapters as frequently as you need. Please also check out some of the materials listed in Appendix C, *"CSS Resources,"* to continue your learning. CSS is a complex, evolving language—but give it a little time and a little effort, and you can make it your own.

CSS 2 Properties

This appendix lists the major CSS 2 properties and their common values and pseudo-class and pseudo-element selectors. Where appropriate, I have included properties and selectors from the level 3 specification, as these are starting to be adopted in the CSS community and recognized by some browsers (most notably, Mozilla's Firefox). That said, this appendix does include some properties that are not fully supported across all browsers. Exercise discretion when using these, especially those that have not been discussed in this book.

The following chart lists the major CSS 2 properties:

Properties

background

Description	Shorthand property that combines `background-color`, `background-image`, `background-repeat`, `background-attachment`, and `background-position`
Example	`body {background: green 0% 0% url('images/javaco.jpg') no-repeat;}`
Values	See individual properties
Default	See individual properties
Inherited?	No
Applies to	All elements
Cross-browser?	Yes

background-attachment

Description	Sets whether a background image moves along the page as the user scrolls horizontally or vertically (when scroll bars are activated)
Example	`body {background-attachment: scroll;}`
Values	**scroll**: Image will scroll with viewport **fixed**: Image will be fixed in specified position
Default	`scroll`
Inherited?	No
Applies to	All elements (generally used for **body** only)
Cross-browser?	Yes

background-color

Description	Sets the background color for an element
Example	`body {background-color: green;}`
Values	**<color>**: Keywords, RGB (**R**ed, **G**reen, **B**lue) values, or short/long hexadecimal values **transparent**: Background is transparent

continues on next page

Properties (continued)

background-color (continued)

Default	`transparent`
Inherited?	No
Applies to	All elements
Cross-browser?	Yes

background-image

Description	Sets a background image for an element. The image resource must be stored at a relative or absolute URL (**U**niform **R**esource **L**ocator).
Example	`body {background-image: url(images/javaco.jpg);}`
Values	`<url>` `none`
Default	`none`
Inherited?	No
Applies to	All elements
Cross-browser?	Yes

background-position

Description	Sets the position of the background image on the page. Both vertical and horizontal positions must be specified.
Example	`body {background-image: url(images/javaco.jpg); background-position: 100px 200px;}`
Values	`<percentage>` (such as **20% 20%**) `<length>` (such as **5em 2em**) `top/center/bottom`, `left/center/right` (such as **bottom, left**)
Default	`0%, 0%`
Inherited?	No

continues on next page

Properties (continued)

background-position (continued)

Applies to	All elements
Cross-browser?	Yes

background-repeat

Description	Sets how a background image tiles across the page
Example	`body {background-img: url(images/javaco.jpg); background-position: 100px 200px; background-repeat: repeat;}`
Values	**repeat**: Image is tiled horizontally and vertically
	repeat-x: Image is tiled horizontally only
	repeat-y: Image is tiled vertically only
	no-repeat: Image is not tiled
Default	**repeat**
Inherited?	No
Applies to	All elements
Cross-browser?	Yes

border

Description	Shorthand property that combines **border-width**, **border-style**, and **color**
Example	`h3 {border: 3px green double;}`
Values	See individual properties
Default	N/A
Inherited?	No
Applies to	All elements
Cross-browser?	Yes

continues on next page

Properties (continued)

border-bottom, border-top, border-right, border-left

Description	Shorthand property that combines **border-width**, **border-style**, and **border-color** for the bottom, top, right, or left border of an element
Example	`h3 {border-bottom: 1px green solid;}`
Values	See individual properties
Default	N/A
Inherited?	No
Applies to	All elements
Cross-browser?	Yes

border-bottom-width, border-top-width, border-right-width, border-left-width

Description	Sets the width of the bottom, top, right, or left border of an element
Example	`h3 {border-bottom-width: thick;}`
Values	`thin`, `medium`, `thick` `<length>`: Any unit of measurement
Default	`medium`
Inherited?	No
Applies to	All elements
Cross-browser?	Yes

border-color

Description	Sets the color of the border of an element. If a border color is not specified, the border will inherit the foreground color of the parent element.
Example	`#sidebar {border-color: gray;}`
Values	`<color>`: Keywords, RGB values, or short/long hexadecimal values
Default	Foreground color of the parent element
Inherited?	No

continues on next page

border-color (continued)

Applies to	All elements
Cross-browser?	Yes

border-spacing

Description	Sets the distance between the borders of adjacent cells in a table.
Example	`#post-archive table {border-spacing: 10px;}`
Values	`<length>`: When one value is specified, it is used for both the horizontal and vertical spacing measurement.
Default	N/A
Inherited?	Yes
Applies to	Table and inline table elements
Cross-browser?	No – not supported by Internet Explorer

border-style

Description	Sets the style of the border of an element
Example	`#sidebar {border-style: double;}`
Values	`none`: No border; lowest specificity
	`hidden`: No border; highest specificity
	`dotted`, `dashed`, `solid`: Border is dashed, dotted, or lined
	`double`: Double border with space in the middle. Border width may be calculated unevenly.
	`groove`, `ridge`: Border appears to be embossed or engraved
	`inset`, `outset`: Border appears to be embedded or transposed
Default	`none`
Inherited?	No
Applies to	All elements
Cross-browser?	Yes

continues on next page

Properties (continued)

border-width

Description	Sets the width for a border of an element
Example	`#sidebar {border-width: 2em;}`
Values	`thin`, `medium`, `thick` `<length>`
Default	N/A
Inherited?	No
Applies to	All elements
Cross-browser?	Yes

clear

Description	Defines the side or sides of an element on which no floating element may be placed. This has the effect of pushing the selected element below the floated element. Elements that are to be cleared must appear below floated elements in the document source.
Example	`#footer {clear: right;}`
Values	`none`: Element is not cleared `left`: Element is cleared so that the top border is below the outer edge of any left-floated element `right`: Element is cleared so that the top border is below the outer edge of any right-floated element `both`: Element is cleared below any floated elements
Default	`none`
Inherited?	No
Applies to	Block level elements
Cross-browser?	Yes

continues on next page

Properties (continued)

clip

Description	Sets which portion of an element is visible by defining a clipping region
Example	`img {clip: rect (5px, 15px, 5px, 15px);}`
Values	**<shape>**: `rect` **<top><right><bottom><left>** is the only valid CSS 2 value, where **<top>**, and so on, are **<length>** values. `auto`: Inherits size/shape of the specified element
Default	`auto`
Inherited?	No
Applies to	Absolutely positioned elements
Cross-browser?	Yes

color

Description	Sets the foreground color for an element
Example	`body {color: #FCA53A;}`
Values	`<color>`
Default	Browser-defined
Inherited?	Yes
Applies to	All elements
Cross-browser?	Yes

cursor

Description	Sets the appearance of the cursor on the user's monitor as it passes over the element. The appearance will differ from computer to computer depending on the cursor files installed on the user's computer.
Example	`h3 {cursor: crosshair; border: 1px solid #FFF;}` or `h3 {cursor: url('crosshair.ani');}`

continues on next page

cursor (continued)

Values	
	\<url\>: The cursor displays as resource from specified URL.
	auto: The cursor display is determined by the browser default.
	crosshair: The cursor displays as a crosshair resembling a plus (+) sign.
	default: The cursor display is determined by the platform and usually displays as an arrow.
	pointer: The cursor displays as a pointer (arrow) and indicates a link.
	move: The cursor displays as a crosshair with arrows, indicating something is to be moved.
	e-resize / ne-resize / nw-resize / n-resize / se-resize / sw-resize / s-resize / w-resize: The cursor displays as a double-sided arrow that points in various directions and indicates something can be resized.
	text: The cursor indicates text is to be selected. This is usually rendered as an I-beam.
	wait: The cursor displays as a progress indicator, usually an hourglass.
	help: The cursor displays arrow with a question mark or balloon, indicating a help menu is available.
	progress: The cursor displays as a progress indicator but signifies user may still interact with the page while waiting. Usually this displays as an arrow with an hourglass.
Default	**auto**
Inherited?	Yes
Applies to	All elements
Cross-browser?	No; only partially supported by Firefox 1.7, Opera 7.5, and Safari 1.2

display

Description	Determines how an element will display on the page
Example	`li {display: inline;}`
Values	**block**: Element will generate a block box
	inline: Element will generate an inline box
	list-item: Element will display as a list item
	none

continues on next page

display (continued)

Default	`block`
Inherited?	No
Applies to	All elements
Cross-browser?	Yes

empty-cells

Description	Determines whether empty table cells will display. This property is not supported in Internet Explorer, where empty cells are hidden by default.
Example	`#post-archive table {empty-cells: hide;}`

Values	`show`
	`hide`
	`inherit`

Default	Browser dependent
Inherited?	Yes
Applies to	`td` elements
Cross-browser?	No; not supported in Internet Explorer

float

Description	Sets the float direction for an element
Example	`#sidebar {float: right;}`
Values	`left, right, none`
Default	`none`
Inherited?	No
Applies to	All elements (where `display` and `position` declarations do not conflict)
Cross-browser?	Yes

continues on next page

font

Description	Shorthand property that combines `font-style`, `font-variant`, `font-weight`, `font-size`, `line-height`, and `font-family`. `font-size` and `font-family` are required values.
Example	`h3 {font: 12px gray bold Arial;}`
Values	See individual properties
Default	N/A
Inherited?	Yes
Applies to	All elements
Cross-browser?	Yes

font-family

Description	Sets the font family for an element
Example	`p {font-family: Arial, serif;}`
Values	`<family-name>` `<generic-family>`
Default	Browser-defined
Inherited?	Yes
Applies to	All elements
Cross-browser?	Yes

font-size

Description	Sets the size of the font of a text element
Example	`p {font-size: 1.2em;}`
Values	`xx-small`, `x-small`, `small`, `medium`, `large`, `x-large`, `xx-large`, `larger`, `smaller` `<length>` `<percentage>`

continues on next page

font-size (continued)

Default	`medium`
Inherited?	Yes
Applies to	All elements
Cross-browser?	Yes

font-style

Description	Sets the style of the font of a text element
Example	`p {font-style: italic;}`

Values	`normal`
	`italic`
	`oblique`: Not available for all fonts, in which case `oblique` is computed by the browser, usually resulting in a slanted font

Default	`normal`
Inherited?	Yes (by text in descendent elements)
Applies to	All elements
Cross-browser?	Yes

font-variant

Description	Sets the variant for the font
Example	`h1 {font-variant: small-caps;}`
Values	`normal`: Maintains casing of original text `small-caps`: Changes text to all small-capital letters
Default	`normal`
Inherited?	Yes (by text in descendent elements)
Applies to	All elements
Cross-browser?	Yes

continues on next page

font-weight

Description	Sets the weight of the font
Example	`p {font-family: Arial; font-weight: bold;}`
Values	`normal`: Browser default
	`bold`, `bolder`, `lighter`
	`<100–900>`: Increments of 100, with 100 being lightest, 900 being "boldest"
Default	`normal`
Inherited?	Yes (by text in descendent elements)
Applies to	All elements
Cross-browser?	Yes

height

Description	Sets the height of an element
Example	`body {height: 200px;}`
Values	`<length>`: Negative values not permitted
	`auto`: Element expands to fit available area
Default	`auto`
Inherited?	No
Applies to	Block-level and replaced elements (excluding table columns and column groups)
Cross-browser?	Yes

letter-spacing

Description	Sets the amount of whitespace between characters in text. Negative values are not permitted.
Example	`p {letter-spacing: normal;}`
Values	`normal`: Browser default
	`<length>`

continues on next page

Properties (continued)

letter-spacing (continued)

Default	`normal`
Inherited?	Yes
Applies to	All elements
Cross-browser?	Yes

line-height

Description	Sets the height of a line of text (including, not in addition to, the font height). Negative values are not permitted.
Example	`p {line-height: 1.5;}`
Values	`normal`: Browser default `<number>`: Multiplier relative font size of the element `<length>` `<percentage>`: Relative to font size of the element
Default	`normal`
Inherited?	Yes
Applies to	All elements
Cross-browser?	Yes

list-style

Description	Shorthand property that combines `list-style-image`, `list-style-position`, and `list-style-type`
Example	`li {list-style: circle outside;}`
Values	See individual properties
Default	N/A
Inherited?	Yes
Applies to	Elements with display set as list item
Cross-browser?	Yes

continues on next page

list-style-image

Description	Sets an image to be a bullet in an ordered or unordered list
Example	`li {list-style-image: url(images/javaco.jpg);}`
Values	`<url>` `none`
Default	`none`
Inherited?	Yes
Applies to	Elements with display set as list item
Cross-browser?	Yes

list-style-position

Description	Sets the position of a bullet in an ordered or unordered list with respect to the contents of the list item itself
Example	`li {list-style-position: inside;}`
Values	`inside, outside`
Default	`outside`
Inherited?	Yes
Applies to	Elements with display set as list item
Cross-browser?	Yes

list-style-type

Description	Sets the type of bullets to be used in an ordered or unordered list
Example	`li {list-style-type: circle;}`
Values	`disc, circle, square, decimal, lower-roman, upper-roman, lower-alpha,` `upper-alpha, none`
Default	`disc`
Inherited?	Yes

continues on next page

list-style-type (continued)

Applies to	Elements with display set as list item
Cross-browser?	Yes

margin

Description	Sets the size of the margin(s) of an element
Example	`h3 (margin: 2em 1em .25em 1em;)`

Values	`<length>`
	`<percentage>`: Relative to the width of the immediate block-level parent element
	`auto`

Default	N/A
Inherited?	No
Applies to	All elements, excluding table display types other than caption, table and in-line table
Cross-browser?	Yes

margin-bottom, margin-left, margin-right, margin-top

Description	Sets the size of the bottom, left, right, or top margin of an element
Example	`#img content img.illus {margin-right: 2em;}`

Values	`<length>`
	`<percentage>`: Relative to the width of the immediate block-level parent element
	`auto`

Default	0
Inherited?	No
Applies to	All elements, excluding table display types other than caption, table, and in-line table
Cross-browser?	Yes

continues on next page

opacity, filter (CSS3)

Description	Sets the opacity of the foreground color for an element. `opacity` is recognized by most browsers, except for Internet Explorer, which uses the proprietary attribute filter (via the alpha channel) to achieve the same effect.

Example	`p {color: red; opacity: .5}`
	
	`p {color: red; filter: alpha(opacity=50);}`

Values	**opacity**: 0.0–1.0 (invisible–visible) **filter**: alpha: 0–100 (invisible–visible)
Default	1.0 or 100
Inherited?	No
Applies to	All elements
Cross-browser?	No; Internet Explorer uses filter

overflow

Description	Sets how browser treats content that exceeds (or "overflows") a defined content area/element box
Example	`p {overflow: scroll;}`
Values	**visible**: The content will overflow limits of the element box without altering the shape of the box. **hidden**: The content is clipped to fit element box. **scroll**: The content is clipped but overflow content can be accessed via a scroll mechanism, which browsers usually interpret as a scroll bar. **auto**: The browser determines what to do with overflow content.
Default	**visible**
Inherited?	No
Applies to	Block-level and replaced elements
Cross-browser?	Yes

continues on next page

padding

Description	Sets the size of the padding of an element. Padding is transparent and will inherit the color of the element's background. Negative values are not permitted.
Example	`p {padding: 1em 2em;}`
Values	`<length>` `<percentage>`: Relative to the width of the immediate block-level parent element
Default	N/A
Inherited?	No
Applies to	All elements
Cross-browser?	Yes

padding-bottom, padding-left, padding-right, padding-top

Description	Sets the size of the padding of an element on a particular side. Negative values are not permitted.
Example	`img {padding-right: 2em;}`
Values	`<length>` `<percentage>`: Relative to the width of the immediate block-level parent element
Default	N/A
Inherited?	No
Applies to	All elements
Cross-browser?	Yes

page-break-after, page-break-before, page-break-inside

Description	Sets whether page breaks happen after, before, or inside an element when the page is printed
Example	`p {page-break-before: always;}`
Values	`auto, always, avoid, left, right`
Default	`auto`

continues on next page

Properties (continued)

page-break-after, page-break-before, page-break-inside (continued)

Inherited?	Only `page-break-inside`
Applies to	Block-level elements
Cross-browser?	Yes

size (CSS3)

Description	Sets the size and orientation of the printed page. Must be used with the `@page` selector
Example	`@page {size: 8.5in 11in;}`
Values	`<length>` inches `auto`, `portrait`, `landscape`
Default	`auto`
Inherited?	N/A
Applies to	Page media (via `@page`)
Cross-browser?	Yes

text-align

Description	Sets the horizontal alignment of the text in an element
Example	`p {text-align: right;}`
Values	`left`, `right`, `center`, `justify`
Default	Browser-defined
Inherited?	Yes
Applies to	Block level and replaced elements
Cross-browser?	Yes

continues on next page

text-decoration

Description	Sets text effects. Values may be combined.
Example	`h3 {text-decoration: underline;}`
Values	`none`, `underline`, `overline`, `line-through`, `blink` (which is not supported)
Default	`none`
Inherited?	No
Applies to	All elements
Cross-browser?	Yes

text-indent

Description	Sets the indentation for the first line of an element. Negative values are permitted, causing "hanging indents."
Example	`h3 {text-indent: 1em;}`
Values	`<length>` `<percentage>`: Relative to the width of the immediate block-level parent element
Default	`0`
Inherited?	Yes
Applies to	Block level and replaced elements
Cross-browser?	Yes

text-transform

Description	Sets the case of the letters in an element. May apply differently depending on the browser's definition of "words"
Example	`p {text-transform: uppercase;}`
Values	`capitalize`, `uppercase`, `lowercase`, `none`
Default	`none`
Inherited?	Yes

continues on next page

Properties (continued)

text-transform (continued)

Applies to	All elements
Cross-browser?	Yes

vertical-align

Description	Sets the vertical alignment of an element's bottom with respect to its line height. Negative values are permitted.
Example	`h3 {vertical-align: sub;}`
Values	**baseline**: Aligns with baseline of parent element **sub**: Baseline is lowered (relative to parent element) **super**: Baseline is raised (relative to parent element) **text-top**, **text-bottom**: Aligns top/bottom of the element box with top or bottom of content area of element **<percentage>** Relative to the line height of the element
Default	`baseline`
Inherited?	No
Applies to	Inline elements
Cross-browser?	Yes

visibility

Description	Sets whether elements are visible. Similar to `display`
Example	`img {visibility: hidden;}`
Values	**visible**, **hidden** **collapsed**: Not recognized by most browsers
Default	`visible`
Inherited?	Yes

continues on next page

Properties (continued)

visibility (continued)

Applies to	All elements
Cross-browser?	Yes

white-space

Description	Sets how whitespace is displayed on the page (that is, whether carrier returns or line breaks are preserved)
Example	`p {white-space: nowrap;}`
Values	`normal`: Browser discards whitespace `pre`: Browser respects whitespace and carriage returns `nowrap`: Browser prevents text from wrapping
Default	`normal`
Inherited?	Yes
Applies to	All elements
Cross-browser?	Yes

width

Description	Sets the width of an element
Example	`#masthead {width: 50%}`

Values	`<length>`
	`<percentage>` (relative to the width of the parent element)
	`auto`

Default	`auto`
Inherited?	No
Applies to	Block-level and replaced elements
Cross-browser?	Yes

continues on next page

Properties (continued)

word-spacing

Description	Sets the amount of whitespace between words in text. A word is defined as any text string separated by nonbreaking spaces. Negative values are permitted and result in a crowding effect.
Example	`p {word-spacing: 3px;}`
Values	`normal`, `<length>`
Default	`normal`
Inherited?	Yes
Applies to	All elements
Cross-browser?	Yes

Pseudo-class Selectors

There is no cross-browser support for most pseudo-class selectors at the time of this writing. Where there is cross-browser support for a selector, it will be noted by an asterisk (*) in the following chart. Cross-browser support is defined here as recognition by the following browsers: Internet Explorer 6.0 (Windows), Internet Explorer 5.0 (Mac), Firefox 1.5, Safari 1.3, and Opera 9.

:active*

Description	Sets styles to be used at the moment a hyperlink is clicked on
Example	`#navlinks li:active {background: green;}`
Applies to	Hyperlinks or anchor elements with an **HREF** attribute

:empty (CSS3)

Description	Sets styles for elements that have no content, descendents, or whitespace
Example	`#content:empty {visibility: hidden;}`
Applies to	All elements

continues on next page

Pseudo-class Selectors (continued)

:first-child, :last-child

Description	Sets styles for the first or last child of a given element or elements
Example	`h1:first-child {font-style:italic;}`
Applies to	All elements

:focus

Description	Sets styles for the element a user is "focused" on, such as where their cursor is
Example	`p:focus {background: yellow;}`
Applies to	All elements

:hover*

Description	Sets styles on any hyperlink on which the user's cursor rests
Example	`a:hover {color: red;}`
Applies to	Anchor elements with an **HREF** attribute

:lang

Description	Sets styles for elements where the language is specified in the document markup
Example	`p:lang(en) {color: red;}`
Applies to	All elements

:link*

Description	Sets styles for any hyperlink that has not been visited
Example	`a:link {text-decoration: underline;}`
Applies to	Anchor elements with an **HREF** attribute

continues on next page

Pseudo-class Selectors (continued)

:not (CSS3)

Description	Sets the styles for elements that don't mention the attributes specified in the rule. This is not widely supported.
Example	`p:not(#sidebar) {font-style: italic;}`
Applies to	All elements

:root (CSS3)

Description	Sets the styles for a base element of a document. In XHTML, this is the `html` element.
Example	`:root {color: grey; margin: 1em 1em; background-color: green}`
Applies to	The base element of a document (in XHTML, `html`)

:target (CSS3)

Description	Sets styles for target elements in the document.
Example	`body:target {background-color: green;}`
Applies to	All elements

:visited*

Description	Sets styles for any hyperlink that has been visited
Example	`a:visited {color: red;}`
Applies to	Anchor elements with an `HREF` attribute

Pseudo-element Selectors

There is no cross-browser support for most pseudo-element selectors at the time of this writing. Where there is cross-browser support for a selector, it will be noted by an asterisk (*) in the following chart. Cross-browser support is defined as recognition by the following browsers: Internet Explorer 6.0 (Windows), Internet Explorer 5.0 (Mac), Firefox 1.5, Safari 1.3, and Opera 9.

:before, :after

Description	Can be used to insert generated content before or after an element. Used in conjunction with the **content** property to define what should be inserted.
Example	`body:after {content: "The End"}`
Applies to	All elements

:first-letter*

Description	Sets styles to be used on the first letter of any text element
Example	`p:first-letter {font-style: italic;}`
Applies to	Block-level elements

:first-line*

Description	Sets styles on the first line of an element (usually text)
Example	`p:first-line {font-style: bold;}`
Applies to	Block-level elements

:selection (CSS3)

Description	Sets styles to be used on the portion of a document that a user has selected. The only valid properties that can be used at this time with this selector are **color** and **background**.
Example	`p:selection {color: red;}`
Applies to	Block level and replaced elements

B

Troubleshooting FAQ and Technical Support Information

If you run into problems while following the exercises in this book, you might find the answer in the "Troubleshooting FAQ" section of this appendix. If you don't find the information you're looking for, use the contact information provided in the "Technical Support Information" section.

Troubleshooting FAQ

Q Are there any WYSIWYG (**W**hat **Y**ou **S**ee **I**s **W**hat **Y**ou **G**et) editors that support CSS (**C**ascading **S**tyle **S**heets)?

A A list of the latest editors (text and Web editors, as well as WYSIWYG editors) is available at **www.w3.org/Style/CSS/#editors**.

Q How do I change my link colors? I used the pseudo-class selectors, and my link colors aren't working.

A When using the pseudo-class selectors `:hover`, `:link`, `:visited`, and `:active` in any combination, you must list them in the correct order in your style sheet, or the link styles will not be recognized by the browser. The correct order (officially known as the **CSS anchor sequence**) is as follows:

1. `a:link`

2. `a:visited`

3. `a:hover`

4. `a:active`

The acronym is LVHA. It's not as easy to remember as TRBL, but try this mnemonic device on for size— (I) Love Very Hairy Apes. Or better yet, make up one of your own.

Q How do I get rid of scroll bars?

A A somewhat irritating feature of Microsoft Internet Explorer is that it adds vertical scroll bars to all pages, even when they're not required. To remove scroll bars, add the following code to your style sheet:

`body {overflow: hidden;}`

The **hidden** value means "ignore whatever content does not fit in this window and remove scrolling mechanisms."

Q I added classes to my table in order to style my table columns, but the browser isn't recognizing the styles. What's happening?

A Try checking your class names. Class and ID values cannot start with a number *or* a hyphen followed by a number.

Q When do I need to add quotation marks in my style sheet?

A Quotation marks are required when you have a single value that includes a nonbreaking space such as in the font Times New Roman or a single value that includes a comma in your CSS code. Quotation marks around URLs (**U**niform **R**esource **L**ocators) are optional, such as `body {background: url("images/javaco.jpg");}`. Single or double quotation marks are acceptable, provided they are consistent within the same rule.

Q What's the difference between **none**, **0**, and a measurement such as **0px**?

A **none** is commonly overused in CSS and won't always validate. For example, the rule `img {border-top: none;}` will not translate in any browser, because **none** is not a legitimate value for this property. You can omit units where 0 is used for any **<length>**, **<number>**, or **<percentage>** value. However, I recommend specifying units when you think you might need to make a quick change later.

Q I set the height of my content **div** to 100 percent, but it's not filling the entire window like I want. What's happening?

A When you use a percentage value with the **height** property, that means a height relative to the parent element. So, unless you've specified a height for the html and the body element (the parent elements of the content div) first, this declaration won't work. You could declare a 100 percent height for the html, body and then 100 percent for the content div, but chances are, you don't really want a 100 percent height- you want a *minimum* height of 100 percent. That way, if your content grows over the boundaries of the viewport (the area defined by the edges of the browser window), it won't be squashed.

The solution in this case is to set the height of your **html** and **body** elements to 100% and a min-height value of 100% for the element you want to take up the height of the page, as follows.

```
html, body {
    height: 100%;
}
#content {
    min-height: 100%;
}
```

Technical Support Information

The following are the technical support resources you can use if you need help.

lynda.com

If you run into any problems as you work through this book, check the companion Web site for updates:

www.lynda.com/books/HOT/css

If you don't find what you're looking for on the companion Web site, you can send Eric A. Meyer an e-mail:

csshot@lynda.com

We encourage and welcome your feedback, comments, and error reports.

Peachpit Press

If your book has a defective CD, please contact the customer service department at Peachpit Press:

customer_service@peachpit.com

CSS Resources

Many great resources are available to CSS (**C**ascading **S**tyle **S**heets) users. You can access a variety of newsgroups, conferences, and third-party Web sites to help you get the most from the new skills you've developed by reading this book. In this appendix, you'll find the best resources for further developing your skills with CSS.

lynda.com Training Resources

lynda.com is a leader in software books and video training for Web and graphics professionals. To help further develop your skills in CSS, check out the following training resources from lynda.com.

lynda.com Books

The HOT (**H**ands-**O**n **T**raining) series was originally developed by Lynda Weinman, author of the revolutionary book *Designing Web Graphics*, first released in 1996. Lynda believes people learn best from doing and has developed this series to teach users software programs and technologies through a progressive learning process.

Check out the following books from lynda.com:

Designing Web Graphics 4
by Lynda Weinman
New Riders
ISBN: 0735710791

After Effects 7 HOT
by Chad Fahs and Lynda Weinman
lynda.com/books and Peachpit Press
ISBN: 0321397754

Dreamweaver 8 Beyond the Basics HOT
by Joseph Lowery
lynda.com/books and Peachpit Press
ISBN: 0321228561

Flash 8 Beyond the Basics HOT
by Shane Rebenschied
lynda.com/books and Peachpit Press
ISBN: 0321293878

lynda.com Video-Based Training

lynda.com offers video training as stand-alone CD and DVD products and through a monthly or annual subscription to the lynda.com **Online Training Library**.

For a free, 24-hour trial pass to the lynda.com Online Training Library, register your copy of *CSS HOT* at the following location:

www.lynda.com/register/HOT/css

Note: This offer is available for new subscribers only and does not apply to current or past subscribers of the lynda.com Online Training Library.

CSS Video-Based Training

To help you build your skills with CSS, check out the following video-based training titles from lynda.com:

CSS for Designers
with Andy Clarke and Molly E. Holzschlag

Learning CSS 2
with Chris Deutsch

(X)HTML Video-Based Training

To help you build your skills with XHTML (e**X**tensible **HTML**) and HTML (**H**yper**T**ext **M**arkup **L**anguage), check out the following video-based training titles from lynda.com.

XHTML Essential Training
with William E. Weinman

HTML Essential Training
with William E. Weinman

Web Design Software Video-Based Training

To help you build your skills with Web design software, check out the following video-based training titles from lynda.com:

Dreamweaver 8 Essential Training
with Garrick Chow

GoLive CS2 Essential Training
with Garrick Chow

Photoshop CS2 for the Web Essential Training
with Tanya Staples

Flashforward Conference and Film Festival

The **Flashforward Conference and Film Festival** is an international educational conference dedicated to Macromedia Flash. Flashforward was first hosted by Lynda Weinman, founder of lynda.com, and Stewart McBride, founder of United Digital Artists. Flashforward is now owned exclusively by lynda.com and strives to provide the best conferences for designers and developers to present their technical and artistic work in an educational setting.

For more information about the Flashforward Conference and Film Festival, visit **www.flashforwardconference.com**.

Online Resources

css-discuss was established in 2002 with the help of John Allsopp, with server resources donated by Western Civilisation. After outgrowing the resources of its original home, the list migrated to **www.css-discuss.org** in early December 2002 and is supported by evolt.org. **css-discuss** is currently chaperoned by Eric A. Meyer, and the servers are tended to by John Handelaar. (Try the wiki!)

Web Sites

West Civ's Web Standards Software and Learning: Since 1998, Westciv has hosted one of the best places on the Web to learn CSS and Web standards (**www.westciv.com/style_master/ house/**). Dave Shea of CSS Zen Garden fame calls it *"the* place to learn CSS."

Max Design's Listutorial: This site (**www.css. maxdesign.com.au/listutorial/**) offers "simple tutorials on CSS-based lists."

CSS Zen Garden: This site (**www.csszengarden .com**) shows what you can accomplish visually through CSS-based design.

CSS Beauty: This site (**www.cssbeauty.com**) is focused on providing its audience with a database of well-designed CSS-based Web sites from around the world. Its purpose is to showcase designers' work and to act as a small portal to the CSS design community.

ILoveJackDaniels: ILoveJackDaniels.com (**www.ilovejackdaniels.com/cheat-sheets/ css-cheat-sheet/**) is the online playground of Dave Child, an e-commerce manager and Web developer from Brighton, on the south coast of the United Kingdom.

Veerle's Blog: The links listed on this page (**http://veerle.duoh.com/blog/links/**) are resources that Veerle Pieter (a.k.a. Duoh!) found over the years while learning the ropes of designing CSS-based Web sites.

Books

Cascading Style Sheets: The Definitive Guide
by Eric A. Meyer
O'Reilly
ISBN: 1565926226

Eric Meyer on CSS
by Eric A. Meyer
New Riders
ISBN: 073571245X

The Zen of CSS Design: Visual Enlightenment for the Web
by Dave Shea and Molly E. Holzschlag
New Riders
ISBN: 0321303474

Bulletproof Web Design: Improving Flexibility and Protecting Against Worst-Case Scenarios with XHTML and CSS
by Dan Cederholm
New Riders
ISBN: 0321346939

Index

I

i tags, 384
id attribute, 63–64, 71
ID selectors
    and capitalization, 65, 75
    vs. class selectors, 79
    defined, 15
    maintaining uniqueness of, 64
    use of spaces in, 74
    using, 63–64, 69–75
ID_selectors.mov, 64
Illustrator, Adobe, 188
ILoveJackDaniels.com, 427
images. *See also* background images
    adding borders to, 356
    adding color to, 161
    adding to background elements, 172–174
    applying margins to, 126–128
    flowing text around, 123–128, 151, 372–373
    linking to, 174
    positioning, 179–183
    repeating, 175–178
@import directive, 42, 50, 56, 57, 59
!important declaration, 99–103
importing
    external style sheets, 40–43
    vs. linking, 57
    multiple style sheets, 44–50
indentation, text, 82, 361, 413
InDesign, 188
inheritance, 104–107
    vs. cascade, 107
    defined, 104
    and document trees, 105
    and floating, 125
    of font size, 219
    of line height, 194, 195
    of text decoration, 246, 249
inline styles, 32, 97, 98
interaction design video-based training, ix
Internet Explorer. *See also* browsers
    Accessibility button, 113, 115
    applying user style sheets with, 113–115
    and attribute selector, 378

Internet Explorer *(continued)*
    and book's exercises, 11
    and case consistency, 75
    and class selectors, 378
    and empty-cells property, 403
    and imported style sheets, 57
    and margin auto values, 260
    and media descriptors, 50
    and pseudo-class selectors, 416
    and pseudo-element selectors, 419
    and table borders, 295, 348
    and text-align property, 260
    and vertical scroll bars, 421
italic font face, 211
italicized text, 384–385

J

JavaScript, 110, 111
joe program, 7
justified text, 230–232

K

kerning, 188
keywords
    for colors, 165
    for font-size values, 218
    for positioning images, 179, 181

L

landscape print orientation, 330
:lang pseudo-class selector, 417
larger value, 216
:last-child pseudo-class selector, 417
layouts. *See* page layout
leading, 188, 189
Learning CSS 2 video, 425
left keyword, 125, 179
letter-spacing property, 406–407
line feeds, 282
line-height property, 189–195, 225, 407

line-through property, 245

link colors, 421

link elements, 53, 55, 56, 57, 59

:link pseudo-class selector, 307, 417

linked style sheets, 31

linking
  to external style sheets, 51–57, 60
  to images, 174
  vs. importing, 57

list fonts, 221

list-style-image property, 408

list-style-position property, 408

list-style property, 157, 407

list-style-type property, 408–409

lists, 155–157, 220, 221, 287

Listutorial, Max Design's, 427

long hexadecimal colors, 30

lowercase text, 27, 240, 242

Lowery, Joseph, 425

LVHA mnemonic, 421

lynda.com, ix, 3, 316, 423, 425–426

M

Macintosh
  browsers, 11. *See also* browsers
  CSS-authoring programs, 7
  CSS system requirements, 1
  and hexadecimal colors, 165
  text editors, 7, 11

Macromedia
  Dreamweaver. *See* Dreamweaver
  Fireworks, 251
  Flash, 426

margin-bottom property, 409

margin-left property, 409

margin property, 409. *See also* margins

margin-right property, 409

margin-top property, 409

margin values, 255

margins, 251–260
  adding to text boxes, 117–122
  applying to images, 126–128
  assigning auto values to, 259, 260, 291
  browser considerations, 253

margins (*continued*)
  collapsing, 281–287, 357
  and CSS box model, 117
  default values for, 253
  em- *vs.* pixel-based, 120, 253
  establishing width of, 118
  inserting between cleared/floated elements, 147
  negative. *See* negative margins
  vs. padding, 270, 282
  removing, 253, 358
  transparency of, 117, 251
  TRBL acronym for assigning values for, 255
  ways of using, 251

markup, presentational *vs.* structural, 370

markup editors, 7

masthead
  adding bottom border to, 332–338
  applying styles to, 70–71
  italicizing text in, 90–92
  removing padding from, 285–286
  setting background color for, 16, 71, 168, 359–360
  setting margins for, 252–253
  using ID selector to label, 64
  using separate style sheet for, 59

Max Design's Listutorial, 427

McBride, Stewart, 426

media descriptors, 50

media-specific style sheets, 50, 311–318

Media Types table, 313

Meyer, Eric A., x, 423, 426, 427

Microsoft
  Internet Explorer. *See* Internet Explorer
  Office, 198
  Web fonts, 201
  Word, 7

mobile browsers, 316

modular style sheets, 59–60

monitors, 313

monospace fonts, 198, 199, 204

.mov files
  bgposition.mov, 183
  class_selectors.mov, 65
  colors.mov, 166
  css_essentials.mov, 11
  design_tour.mov, 11

X

Y

Z

Macromedia
Flash Professional 8
BEYOND THE BASICS

Includes Exercise Files + Training Videos

Shane Rebenschied

H·O·T
HANDS-ON TRAINING
lynda.com

Macromedia
Flash Professional 8

Includes Exercise Files + Training Videos

James Gonzalez

H·O·T
HANDS-ON TRAINING
lynda.com

Adobe
After Effects 7

Includes Exercise Files + Training Videos

Chad Fahs with Lynda Weinman

H·O·T
HANDS-ON TRAINING
lynda.com

Macromedia
Dreamweaver 8

Includes Exercise Files + Training Videos

Daniel Short and Garo Green

H·O·T
HANDS-ON TRAINING
lynda.com

Adobe
Premiere Pro 2

Includes Exercise Files + Training Videos

Jeff Schell

H·O·T
HANDS-ON TRAINING
lynda.com

Macromedia
Dreamweaver 8
BEYOND THE BASICS

Includes Exercise Files + Training Videos

Joseph Lowery

H·O·T
HANDS-ON TRAINING
lynda.com

H·O·T

HANDS-ON TRAINING

lynda.com™

www.lynda.com/books • www.peachpit.com